One Life Lost, Millions Gained

The Story of Joan Sullivan Garrett Flight Nurse turned MedAire CEO

By

Joan Sullivan Garrett

ADVANCE PRAISE

"Joan's journey is certainly worth reading and will inspire many. She had the courage to take a calculated leap of faith and the fortitude to persevere as a pioneer in a brand new industry. People believed in her vision and supported her quest because she exemplified transformational leadership — the ability to identify, influence, and implement." ~ **Michael Quiello, Vice President Avelo Airlines, Chair of the Board of Trustees National Aviation Hall of Fame, and former Vice President United Airlines**

"Were it not for this book, I would have never known how beautifully Joan writes, let alone the hardships she endured in her youth that might have steered her off course. Her huge heart kept her on track to quietly achieve a global safety net that most travelers don't know about until it saves their lives. Many thanks to this inventor and entrepreneur for doing the impossible." ~ **Michael Herman, pilot and board member of the San Diego Air and Space Museum**

"What a powerful story! We are all safer in the air, on land, and at sea because of Joan Sullivan Garrett, a pioneer in telemedicine." ~ **Don Short, Presidential Pilot to Lyndon B. Johnson and Director and Chief Pilot of Corporate Air Transportation, Northrop Corporation**

"I'm glad that Joan delved into the importance of remote medicine at sea in this book. She takes a close look at the hazards faced by crews aboard yachts and commercial vessels — a glimpse at life and death of which few are aware." ~ **Bill Mahaffy, Ship Captain and Vascular Surgery Physician Assistant**

"Like Joan, I encourage young people to pursue their dreams and consider lives of service. *One Life Lost, Millions Gained* inspires me and will surely inspire future generations of business and medical professionals." ~ **Barbara Barrett, 25th United States Secretary of the Air Force**

"Joan has written a historical and personal account of how she founded and built MedAire, which today is a subsidiary of International SOS. It's a rare story, quite gripping, and shares lessons that can benefit entrepreneurs, senior executives, and corporate leaders today." ~ **Laurent Sabourin, Group Managing Director, International SOS**

"I watched Joan pioneer a worldwide telemedicine service and experienced firsthand her remarkable role as a medical professional and visionary. She has it all — courage, personality, and the unique ability to inspire trust and confidence. What an inspiration for women everywhere, as well as business leaders, medical professionals, and those who serve within the aviation and maritime sectors." ~ **Robert Baron MD, MedLink Emergency Physician, Board Certified in Emergency and Internal Medicine**

"Joan is an absolute giant in the field of aviation. By celebrating her amazing story, we can inspire others to break through boundaries, chase their dreams, and change the world for the better." ~ **Ed Bolen, President and CEO of the National Business Aviation Association**

"Those of us in the industry who know Joan so well are thrilled that she is documenting her incredible career in aviation, in general, and her specific achievements in building MedAire into the successful world-class, global medical enterprise it is today. Joan is an entrepreneur extraordinaire who never looked back once she started on her mission of helping the medical profession save lives in the aviation world. It is a great story that needed to be told — I loved reading it." ~ **Wilson Leach, founding publisher of Aviation International News**

"Since 1985 MedAire's core mission has been to protect and save lives. Through MedLink, our "911 in the sky," on-demand medical assistance became available for airline passengers and crews, business and general aviation, and luxury yachts. This book is the story of Joan Sullivan Garrett's vision, hard work and leadership making MedAire the global provider of 24/7 medical assistance." ~ **S. Harry Robertson, Founder, Robertson Fuel Systems, LLC – HEICO and Enshrinee in the National Aviation Hall of Fame**

"Once in a while, you come across a story of personal success that is accompanied by ambition, hard work, and a measure of good luck along the way. Certainly, *One Life Lost, Millions Gained*, is such a story. However, there is so much more to the journey of Joan Sullivan Garrett and her creation of MedAire. The reader will be entertained by the dynamics of the transportation industry, learning how to save customer lives and how to reduce the risks of doing business internationally over land, sea, and the air. All of this from an intelligent woman who saw a need and then built a company to make this service work. This is a story that cases in entrepreneurship will be written about in our colleges and universities. Joan's life as a wife, a mother, and a breadwinner suggests that she mastered a way to warp time! Finally, a reader will be introduced to the sometimes vicious world of global competition as Joan's MedAire becomes a dominant force in Telemedicine." ~ **Roy Herberger, PhD, President Emeritus Thunderbird School of Global Management**

"You'll enjoy reading about Joan's visionary and entrepreneurial spirit, which lead to the creation of an extraordinary company — MedAire/MedLink. This company provides emergency care, equipment, and training to aviation, maritime, and remote clients worldwide. As a result, Joan has had many adventures all over the world, which are included in this delightful book." ~ **Patty Campbell RN MSN ANP ENP, Nurse Practitioner and former flight nurse**

DEDICATION

To Ralphie Lopez, the eight-year-old patient who died in 1984 after an accident on a remote road in the San Tan Mountains of Arizona. Your life and death had meaning and ultimately propelled me to found MedAire — a global company that saves lives on air, land, and sea.

TABLE OF CONTENTS

ACKNOWLEDGMENTS

It would take seven volumes (or more) to acknowledge every MedAire employee and contractor around the world. From our kit assemblers to our admins, communication specialists, IT professionals, software developers, nurses, doctors, and everyone in between, I'm so very thankful. Please know how valuable you are to the success of the company.

I'm also grateful for those who have personally contributed to this book, sharing recollections, participating in interviews, connecting me with significant people from my past, and helping make this a story that can be enjoyed by all — readers inside and outside the industries mentioned. I've listed these wonderful contributors below in alphabetical order:

Paolo Alves, Barbara Barrett, Robert Baron, Moneesh Bhow, Ed Bolen, Patty Campbell, Holly Chervnsik, Shelley Croyle, Bill Dolny, Ron Duncan, Mandy Eddington, Joanna Cicely Fennel, Frank Garrett, Richard Gomez, Aaron Hawkins, Josh Hawkins, Roy Herberger, Steve Holstein, Tore Laerdal, Wilson Leach, Connie Mableson, Bill Mahaffy, Karen Maier, Kurt Michelson, Jannicke Mellin-Olsen, Michael Quiello, Greg Principato, Harry Robertson, Steve Reinhart, Jeremy Rouille, Laurent Sabourin, Melanie Saxton, Don Short, Amy Spowart, Charlann Staab, David Streitwieser, Glenda Summers, Les Tukan

FOREWORD

Rarely in the 1980s did female entrepreneurs dare to found a global startup; rarer still, a complex aviation and medical technology firm. Joan Sullivan Garrett's courage is just one reason I find her story so compelling. Joan's bold vision and relentless resolve crushed any obstacles and forged a triumph of a business — MedAire, a trailblazing telemedicine company that spawned a lifesaving industry.

Along the way, her business day might include mundane office duties or training and outfitting the cabin crew aboard Air Force One.

In 2000, I was one of the judges for the Ernst & Young's Entrepreneur of the Year Award. Joan was a finalist for the award. What a contender — a self-made business leader and expert on inflight and onboard safety who founded and built a vital global service. Indeed, she won. Joan earned the Entrepreneur of the Year Award for her work as CEO of MedAire, where she revolutionized global aviation safety and more. By then, MedAire was already delivering remote medical, security, and operational support to clients on air, land, and sea. Anywhere in the world, when MedAire's clients face a medical crisis, they (or their pilot, driver, or ship captain) radio MedAire's emergency physician for immediate assistance and action.

Joan built upon her pedigree as a third-generation nurse by taking her training to the skies. Previous generations would look up to Joan for her service as a flight nurse, one of medicine's most harrowing careers. Comparable to war-zone medicine, Joan scrambled for search and rescue operations aboard planes and helicopters from remote deserts to rugged far-flung mountains. Saving lives under grueling conditions takes courage, training, and instinct. Joan implanted an emergency pacemaker to save one patient. She performed medical feats wherever necessary, undaunted even by ice storms or dust storms.

Joan wore her flight suit and worked as an emergency room nurse with the dual role as MedAire CEO before ever taking a MedAire salary. This book captures the sacrifices she made to launch her company and leadership lessons learned under fire. Imagine triaging urgent care patients while building a company with 30% annual growth! Meanwhile, she raised her family, squeezing soccer games amid her whirlwind of trauma centers, travel, presentations, and white papers.

I have followed Joan Garrett's career with abiding admiration for more than two decades. Recently, at the National Aeronautic Association awards ceremony in Washington, D.C., as 25th Secretary of the Air Force, I applauded the announcement that Joan Garrett would be inducted into the National Aviation Hall of Fame. An outstanding business leader, Joan saves lives by combining her skills as a nurse with the miracle of telemedicine and the reach of aviation.

Like Joan, I encourage young people to pursue their dreams and consider lives of service. *One Life Lost, Millions Gained* inspires me and will surely inspire future generations of business and medical professionals.

Barbara Barrett
25th Secretary of the Air Force

INTRODUCTION

What a trip it's been, this long, meandering stroll down memory lane. Every bit of it exemplifies the core of my passion and boils down to the five simple words in the book title: *One Life lost, Millions Gained.* That is the foundation of it all and the legacy that matters, as you'll see in the following chapters. The long and short of it is that my grandmother was a nurse, my mother was a nurse, and I became a nurse, then a flight nurse, the inspiration upon which my company was built.

It isn't easy to express the roller coaster moments and pure adrenaline required of this journey, although I do my best to give you a glimpse into the backstories. The first half of the book contains highly personal glimpses and takes a deep dive into the elements that shaped and molded me early on. The second half puts my fast-tracked nursing career and entrepreneurial drive under the microscope and examines how the MedAire,[1] "hypothesis" was proven. Yes, MedAire was a hypothesis in a successful and daring experiment, the first of its kind, an industry of its own, and a venture unlike any other.

Most of the public has no inkling that MedAire is their safety net. They are unaware that we provide the medical kits and defibrillators stowed in cabins aboard aircraft and ocean-going vessels. Perhaps this book will help inform travelers about radio or satellite links between crews and MedLink physicians who assist during emergencies. No matter where in the world a person roams, we are a call away.

---

[1] See www.MedAire.com, www.MedAire.com/business-general-aviation, and www.MedAire.com/products-services for an overview.

Thus, our slogan:

MedAire®
Expert care.
Everywhere.™

This book shares my true-life story — the twists and turns of a flight nurse turned entrepreneur. None of it would be possible without the ups and downs of a challenging childhood, my Irish heritage, a fast-tracked nursing career, the adrenaline involved in rescue and evacuation, the highs and lows of launching a startup, and my experiences in global business.

From flight nurse to MedAire CEO — and what a story that is!

Flight nursing, especially, prepared me to found MedAire, although I didn't know it at the time. Aboard fixed-wing aircraft and helicopters with my Air Evac flight crew — a paramedic and a pilot — most emergency dispatches took us to the most remote areas imaginable throughout Arizona. There was never a "good" call, for every scramble involved life, death, and the worst of the worst accidents, whether in the mountains or desert. MedAire was literally an idea inspired by the traumatic death of a little boy on a desert road, Ralphie, to whom this book is dedicated. His passing became a catalyst for much-needed change in remote medical care. I knew we could do better as an industry. We had to do better. And we did do better, as you'll see.

Mind you; my dream was never to be an entrepreneur or inventor. That's not what I set out to do. My purpose in life was to care for others. So how did I embark on this path?

It all started with a vision. In the mid-'80s, I realized that others who worked in remote environments, such as flight attendants and ship crews, had little medical training or resources. How could they react appropriately to a medical crisis when all they had were outdated first aid kits, two hours of first aid training, and a lack of personal protection equipment such as masks and gloves? Worse, they were stuck in the air or out at sea without access to an emergency physician. While they could make the familiar plea — "Is there a doctor on board?" — this was hit or miss. It would be exponentially better to talk directly with a doctor who was trained in all facets of emergency medicine. Whether crews were 36,000 feet in the air or in the middle of the ocean, I envisioned connecting them to medical professionals on the ground.

That was the epiphany. That's where I could help. And thus came my hypothesis, a "three-legged stool" that would provide top-grade medical kits, extensive environment-specific training, and telemedicine. Keep in mind; this was in the days when cell phones, the internet, and laptops didn't exist. Telemedicine was in its infancy. Remote medicine was limited to prehospital "Rampart 51" and satellite-related hospital systems, but not in a commercial application and certainly not worldwide in the clouds and at sea. Yes, this was a global pioneering opportunity that had never been attempted in the history of the world, a structuring of remote medical assistance in a way that caused a paradigm shift. That was the invention.

It never registered that my vision seemed impossible. All I knew was that my startup would benefit the traveling public, as well as flight and maritime crews, which was all the motivation required. People on commercial flights, business and private jet flights, and later on vessels would unknowingly count on a service that could potentially save their lives if the unexpected struck.

Since telemedicine was such an unknown quantity in the 1980s, especially on a global scale, it took copious research to develop technology that connected crews to an on-ground emergency physician no matter where a medical emergency took place. I'm still amazed that we pulled it off. It's one for the history books and really changed the travel industry forever — telemedicine as it had never been done before. Thus, MedAire became the world's first emergency response center, providing immediate real-time medical assistance and expert medical advice from emergency physicians and security specialists initially based in our Arizona headquarters and later from other continents.

Today, MedAire is a subsidiary of International SOS (ISOS), the world's leading health and security services company. As a privately held company initially, MedAire segued into a complicated international reverse merger with a public company owning a group of overseas medical clinics and went public on the Australian Stock Exchange. Later in the book, I expand on the many lessons learned during this transition, how ISOS came into the picture, our tug-of-war negotiations, and where we are today. The bottom line is, MedAire and ISOS struck a deal and enjoy a most excellent relationship and an unusually happy ending.

I'm gratified that MedAire remains the gold standard and continuously innovates its product line. Achieving this standing meant logging hundreds of thousands of travel miles around the globe — traveling to our customers and spreading the MedAire mission. We devoted resources to ongoing research and development, consistently meeting and exceeding international governmental standards with every product and service provided and seeking out our clients' needs in an ever-evolving and complex world of travel.

If that sounds like bragging, perhaps it is, but without

exaggeration. I'm proud of my startup and the global enterprise it has become. The essential aspects have remained the same — a culture of customer care and products and services that help safeguard millions of lives.

Outside of the industries mentioned above, my name may not ring a bell. How wonderful to introduce myself to aspiring entrepreneurs envisioning a business startup, inventors chasing the latest innovations, and nurses pondering careers in flight nursing and critical care. There's a lot to be said, as well, in sharing my rare role as a female who dipped her toe into business 40 years ago, especially in male-dominated industries. Perhaps readers will be inspired, just as I was inspired, by the people and books referenced in footnotes throughout each chapter, so meaningful in this trek through my personal and professional life.

I'm not suggesting that anyone found a business based on my methods or pursue a career based on my experiences. I do, however, encourage others to recognize the power of the word "yes" and consider serendipitous opportunities when they appear. Believe in yourself when no one else does and be persistent, especially when your dream is to benefit others. And if you happen to be in a position to help others dream, then mentoring and teaching is one of the most remarkable exercises to explore. That, too, is a part of this book — the "giving back" and "paying it forward" so crucial to younger generations.

I stepped down as CEO of MedAire in 2008 and am now semi-retired with the roles of chairman of the board and industry consultant. After such a fast-paced existence, it's quite nice to sit on my deck in the Arizona mountains and appreciate the little things that mean so much — good health, the freedoms we enjoy as Americans, and especially family. The sacrifices made by my husband and sons to support this monumental effort cannot be overstated.

It's wonderful to have reached this age of contentment and

fulfillment. I have time to enjoy the views of the forest, which are incredible. My Labrador retrievers Kady and Riley (both Irish names, and there's a reason for that) are always nearby.

Riley and his mother Kady enjoying a romp in the great outdoors

Being in the great outdoors includes spending time with Rosie, my 35-year-old Arabian quarter horse who looks half her age. She is a dear old soul, a confidante who listens to all of my complaints without talking back. Like the horses of my youth, she keeps my secrets, and there is no better friend. Babe the fox trotter is also a great distraction, as well as "Valiant Gazi," my Arabian thoroughbred (nicknamed Guzi), who has quite an attitude.

Meet my therapist!

Me bonding with Rosey

My goats, Daisy Mae and Billy Jack, are the horses' companions and not much of anything else (except destructive nuisances). Occasional turkeys, black bears, deer, elk, wolves, and mountain lions wander in the distance. Family and friends stop by. It is lovely — a world away from the hustle and bustle.

Decompression is a must for my health, and it's refreshing to spend time in my garden. Growing flowers and vegetables was nearly more than a hobby — it became a short-lived business after I stepped down as MedAire CEO. I was so geared toward entrepreneurialism and startups that "gardening as a business" made sense. But it occurred to me that not everything has to be an enterprise. Not everything is attached to a profit and loss statement. With semi-retirement came some "unlearning" and letting go of my corporate instincts, which has been enriching.

Sometimes it's just fine to stop and smell the roses, bask in nature and the rich soil, and give away what I don't need.

My friends and family are now recipients of non-GMO, organic, and pollutant-free fruits and vegetables that grow in abundance, including garlic and potatoes. There's a significance to those potatoes as well, considering I'm Irish. This endeavor continues today — cultivate, harvest and share.

Our winter garden in the greenhouse

I used to run the forest paths while listening to the music of Michael Flatley, Lord of the Dance. It was a great place to dream out loud, make business decisions, practice presentations, and rehearse speeches. There's that Irish reference again — Michael Flatley — an undeniable pull toward my heritage. I'm sure my DNA is responsible for my personality and persistence and requires a full chapter ahead just to explain the correlation.

Today it's all about hiking instead of running, with nothing in my ears but the sound of the birds in the trees. Or an elk, usually a female, on duty and guarding the rest of the herd. The elk cow chirps when a threat is seen or heard, and an elk bull bugles when he's rutting and raring to fight over "the harem." The horns smack and crack, sounding like a tree branch breaking. Witnessing it reminds me of a quote from John Muir: "In every walk with nature one receives far more than they seek."

In the midst of this serenity, my appointment calendar sounds an alarm, and I'm off again on a four-hour commute to Phoenix, leaving my mountain home for business in the city. There's still work to do and meetings to attend, and I'm able to visit my three grandchildren. Spending time with them and supporting their activities, experiences, and opportunities is a treasure. This was something I missed when my own two sons were growing up. The typical struggle that many single working mothers face was my struggle too although my situation was an extreme example — 12-hour days and then 18-hour days as I developed and expanded MedAire into a worldwide presence.

For years my friends and colleagues chorused, "Joan, you have to write a book!" MedAire celebrated its 35th anniversary in 2020, a remarkable experience with a fortieth anniversary in the not-too-distant future. There really is no better time than now to capture the twists and turns, poignant moments, and real life-and-death drama over the course of these decades. With less and less excuses and more and more time on my hands, I'm finally heeding their advice and chronicling decades of excitement and many lessons learned.

What an endeavor to capture this journey of good old-fashioned hard work, filled with many moving parts. How to sort it all became a whirlwind through the decades that seemed to sweep by in the snap of a finger. Ancestry searches, a treasure trove of media clippings, photo archives, and even filings at the Securities and Exchange Commission became memory joggers. Dear friends, colleagues, and former customers contributed insights and recollections stretching back across the decades as memory allowed. And then the writing began in earnest.

You'll see lots of personal photos, for my goal is to chronicle the family journey for my sons and grandchildren — a photo album of sorts — that preserves the history of MedAire as well. Some images are vintage, and others depict the present, and they all help tell the story from a sensory angle more meaningful than words alone.

Most of all, I share the importance of unwavering faith, a supportive family, and invaluable team members. I am so blessed that these elements were present and helped build such an essential company. Believe me, the people who stood behind MedAire, including our talented board members, deserve the utmost credit.

And there you have it. It took blood, sweat, and many tears, but MedAire grew wings, took off, and remains a giant in travel industries today — my most gratifying achievement aside from bringing two sons into the world.

There must be flowers along with veggies.

Chapter One: The Boy

He really was a special gift from God,
and it turned out that he had a special purpose.
~ Glenda Summers, mother of Ralphie

Many of my friends and colleagues already know the backstory that inspired the founding of MedAire — a heart-wrenching event that redefined the way I viewed remote emergency medicine and also my role in the medical community.

However, many reading this book may not know about the tragic loss of life that changed everything in my world. At that time, I was a flight nurse and veteran of critical care and emergencies, trained to compartmentalize the trauma of severe accidents and fatal injuries and focus solely on the crisis at hand. When every second counts and every decision can potentially save a life, there is no time for emotion.

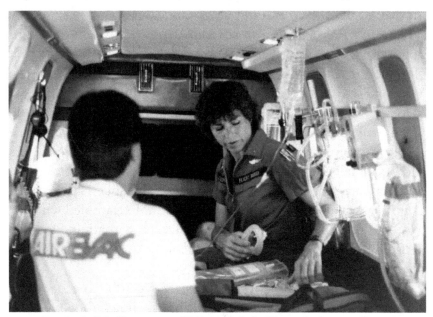

Prepping for flight. Photo courtesy of PHI Air Medical – Photo credit: Samaritan Hospital

1

But there was that one day, a summer day in 1984, when all the training in the world didn't help. An eight-year-old boy died after being injured in a rollover accident on a dirt road in the San Tan Mountains of Arizona. It still haunts me as I write these paragraphs, nearly four decades after the fact. I can still smell the helicopter's Jet A fuel. See the dust. Feel the sweltering hot Arizona sun and the adrenaline sweat in my flight suit. But most of all, I remember the enormous frustration that I was not able to save the little boy's life.

This is Ralphie's story as much as mine, a tribute to him and the family who still loves him. In fact, whenever I ever spoke about this event, I always referred to Ralphie as "Tommy" to protect his identity and out of respect for his family. But I can now reveal his name, Ralphie Lopez. I've reconnected with Ralphie's mother, Glenda Summers, after all these many years. It's such a great honor to feature her in this book, for this is her story too and the first time her perspective has been so publicly shared.

Together we detail the chain of events on that fateful day, me from a medical perspective (albeit emotional), and her as the mother of three who lost her eldest and only son, a very special son. I credit Ralphie as the posthumous hero whose life and death pointed me toward my visions. It was the jolt of lightning that ultimately sparked a vast improvement in global travel safety. Yes, one short life truly made an impact in the founding of MedAire.

Below is the event as I remember it. It was a hot August day. A station wagon lost control and rolled over, filled with teenagers and one small child who had been ejected from the vehicle. The boy, Ralphie, was in distress. The local ambulance EMTs called us in to assist at one-thirty in the afternoon. I scrambled with my pilot and paramedic from our base at Desert Samaritan Hospital in Mesa, Arizona. Our Air Evac helicopter was in the air in less than three minutes.

We knew the chances of survival narrowed due to geography, distance, and degree of injury. Response time, too, weighed heavily. If we could get to patients within the "Golden Hour," the chances of survival increased exponentially. This was a concern because we were 20 minutes away, and no one was sure of the precise moment the accident occurred or what time had elapsed before an ambulance was called.

Within five minutes of reaching our destination, the EMTs radioed that the youngster was no longer slipping toward death. They assumed he was okay because he was talking. In the confusion at the scene, the EMTs must have overlooked the mechanism of injury — ejection from the vehicle. When anyone is thrown from a vehicle, it's automatically a level 1 trauma. I wasn't aware at the time, but there was an on-scene fatality (one of the teenagers), adding to what must have been chaos.

In short, the EMTs were trained in basic life support. I was trained in advanced life support. As the chief medical officer aboard the helicopter, I argued with the EMTs' decision, knowing a child's body can at times compensate miraculously and hide internal injuries. But the EMTs were sure. As the first responders to the scene, they controlled the scene. Period. We were told that all was well and ordered back to base.

At just eight years old, Ralphie was strong. A real fighter. He demonstrated this by hanging on even though his injuries were ripping him apart. His body could no longer conceal the internal trauma, and sure enough, we were dispatched back to the scene the moment our skids settled on the helipad.

Back we flew, racing against time. After another twenty-minute flight, my paramedic, Kurt Michelson, and I hopped off the helicopter. One ambulance was at the scene. A sheriff's deputy was present. I directed Kurt to the teens (who appeared to be walking) and ran toward Ralphie. He was lying on a backboard on the front seat of a blue pick-up truck, all alone. This regular cab truck had two doors and not much room to maneuver. It must have belonged to a bystander.

It was imperative that we stabilized patients very quickly before loading them into the helicopter, always an initial ABC assessment — airway, breathing, circulation — and then further evaluation. I climbed in with little room to spare… and all I could see were my two boys. Just about the same age.

I introduced myself, and Ralphie responded. I explained we were going on a helicopter ride and that I needed to check him over. Before I started the IV, I mentioned it might pinch a bit.

"That's okay," he said. "I'm tough."

I noticed a very high pitch in his voice, not at all normal. It indicated a possible torn bronchus, a rupture in the airway path to the lungs. Almost like bubble wrap underneath the skin's surface, crepitus was working its way from his chest to his throat — air escaping from the airway into the tissue. I could see and feel it.

As I continued to work on Ralphie in the tight, cramped front seat, he looked into my eyes. He knew he was dying. "I'm not afraid," he said. "It doesn't hurt." Then out of the blue, he grabbed the collar of my flight suit and pulled me close to his face.

"I love you," he said. He didn't see a nurse. He wasn't seeing me. What he saw was his mother. Even while focused on his injuries, even while blocking out everything else, this touched me so profoundly. I knew it might be the very last "I love you" he ever shared.

And then Ralphie coded. He was in cardiac arrest and stopped breathing. I yelled for Kurt to help me get the backboard out of the truck and onto the ground so we'd have room to begin CPR. Initially, Kurt managed the airway. I managed compressions and pharmaceuticals. Chances were that he had more injuries than were apparent, any number of internal injuries. Thus every ounce of training I had ever received poured out of me — ingenuity, creativity, and care for one tough little boy who was not afraid. Not hurting.

I then attempted intubation. When I could not maneuver the tube into Ralphie's trachea, I prepared for a cricothyrotomy while Kurt made a second attempt at intubation. A cricothyrotomy is an extremely difficult procedure in which an incision is made through the thyroid cartilage in front of the larynx. Thankfully, it wasn't necessary because Kurt was able to intubate Ralphie successfully.

But it wasn't enough. We loaded him into the helicopter and continued ventilation and compressions, and landed at the Good Samaritan Hospital, a Level 1 trauma center in downtown Phoenix. The trauma team met us on the helipad. Ralphie was wheeled into the trauma room, where the team worked feverishly to address his injuries. Sadly, he could not survive the mortal insult to his body and was pronounced dead.

The loss of Ralphie stayed with me that day, the fate of this precious, courageous child. In the wee hours of the morning, just as I was about to sleep, I finally allowed myself to cry and process a swirl of emotions. It will remain with me forever, the thought: *What if it had been one of my boys in that front seat? Alone. No one understanding. With only one thing on his mind — 'Mom, I love you.'*

A couple of days later, I reached a heartbroken mother by telephone to relay some very important words that were intended just for her. She cried. And once again, I cried, just as I am now and have many times since.

And despite my hectic schedule and role-juggling and the pressures of life, all of a sudden, I seemed to have all of the time in the world to ponder such questions and the answers they might convey. Days. Weeks. Months. And they all pointed to one thing: I needed to bring emergency room level medical expertise to the scene of emergencies no matter where they took place — even on a remote dusty road along a desert mountain range.

Glenda's story

I was still in shock the day Joan called me, not too long after my son died. I can never thank her enough for that call. At that time, it was a struggle to go through each and every day, and even 37 years later, I still mourn the loss of Ralphie.

I'm so honored and proud that something wonderful came out of this tragedy. Ralphie would have loved that. He was special from the day he was born, Ralph Lavelle Lopez, my only son and oldest child.

5

Everyone loved him instantly. He was the purest form of love anyone could ever imagine, and I think Joan sensed that the day of the accident.

Ralph Lavelle Lopez was a very brave little boy.

Ralphie was eight going on sixteen — always a character. Such a personality! I remember how his kindergarten teacher loved him, even when he locked her in the supply closet. When he let her out, they laughed! That's Ralphie. He did well in school but went to have a good time, to enjoy each day with oodles and oodles of friends. He loved Transformers. He loved his little dog. He loved baby goats and other animals. He especially loved his younger sisters, seven years old and ten months old.

Ralphie was always on the go. He wasn't a groggy kid and was ready each morning for a new adventure. When I go back to the day of the accident, August 16, 1984, we had the very best morning. We played and laughed and told each other, "I love you." School was about to start, and we had just gone shopping for clothes. Ralphie asked me what to wear on the first day of class.

I had to get ready for work and take the kids to the babysitter. Ralphie didn't want to go. My 17-year-old nephew was with us that morning, and Ralphie wanted to stay with him. He loved hanging out with older kids. My nephew offered to take him to the babysitter, and I agreed. He had gone with my nephew lots of times before without any problems, but this time was different. Instead of taking Ralphie to the babysitter, my nephew, another nephew, and two of their friends took him on a joyride. One of the friends was the driver.

The accident happened in the desert area near a factory. Someone saw the accident and called it in. Then someone called my work and said there was a fatal accident. It turned out that the fatality was the teenage driver who was pinned under the car. One of my nephews was injured. My other nephew and the remaining friend walked away unharmed. Ralphie was taken by helicopter to the hospital.

There were no cell phones in those days. I called my husband from work (we were separated at the time), and we went to find Ralphie. It took an hour to get there. There were no freeways, just desert roads. We were frantic and cried and prayed the whole way, hoping Ralphie was alive. Finally, we got to the hospital and were told Ralphie didn't survive. They led us to the back to see him, and I held him one last time. There are no words to describe what that was like.

Joan told me she sensed Ralphie was with God and that he wasn't afraid and felt no pain. He knew that I would need the message he sent through Joan — that he loved me. That's exactly what you want to hear when your child is facing the final moments of his life.

On the day Ralphie was born, my husband knew we wouldn't keep him for long. I know that sounds strange, but it was true. It was like Ralphie also knew he would only be here for a short while. He lived life very large and got everything he could out of every single day. He really was a special gift from God, and it turned out that he had a special purpose.

Still, his passing was hard on the family. When people are grieving, there can be finger-pointing and blame. I was blamed for not taking him to the babysitter. I blamed myself for not taking him to the babysitter. Then time heals wounds, and people forgive. We learn to live with the memories. I'm sure other parents who have lost a child understand.

Today, I'm okay. I remarried, and my daughters are grown. I have three wonderful grandchildren. You learn a whole lot when you're a grandma about what's important and what's not — things you didn't realize when you were raising your own kids. You appreciate life in a whole new way.

I'm so glad Joan reached out after all these years and told me that Ralphie inspired her to build MedAire. She explained that hundreds of thousands of lives have been saved, and millions of sick passengers on planes and ships have gotten the help they need — all because she and my son crossed paths that day. Ralphie would have wanted it that way.

Ralphie is alive through Joan and me; he's still with us. That's what's amazing.

On March 6, 2017, I was interviewed by KTAR[2] and mentioned "Tommy," the name I used in lieu of Ralphie whenever I spoke publicly about his impact on my life. It just so happened that Glenda's nephew heard the interview and reached out to the MedAire office. I returned his call and kept in touch. Thanks to him, I was able to contact Glenda about this book and Ralphie's place of honor within these pages.

Reconnecting after all these many years, mother to mother and heart to heart, led to the meaningful conversation above. I thank Glenda for taking the time to speak with me. I thank her for providing Ralphie's story for this chapter.

I'm glad I got to know more about Ralphie through her eyes. She filled many gaps in the story, many nuances that escaped me on that fateful day. It's gratifying that she knows how Ralphie touched many lives and that I think of him often. Most of all, I'm glad she knows his death wasn't in vain.

---

[2] This article includes a video. Corbin Carson. "Off Central: Arizona nurse pioneers treatment for in-air medical emergencies," *KTAR News*, March 6, 2017.

See https://ktar.com/story/1479478/off-central-arizona-nurse-pioneers-in-air-medical-emergency-treatment/ (accessed May 4, 2021).

Chapter Two: My Bold Irish Roots

We have always found the Irish a bit odd.
They refuse to be English.
~Winston Churchill.

I've alluded to my Irish heritage in the names of my dogs and references to Michael Flatley, my DNA, and potatoes. There is something special, something unique about the *Na hÉireannaigh*, the people of Ireland, and my big, bold Irish roots. It seems so fundamental to who I am and how I'm wired. Thus, this chapter begins with a poem that hangs in my hallway.

He Wishes for the Cloths of Heaven

Had I the heavens' embroidered cloths,
Enwrought with golden and silver light,
The blue and the dim and the dark cloths
Of night and light and the half light,
I would spread the cloths under your feet:
But I, being poor, have only my dreams;
I have spread my dreams under your feet;
Tread softly because you tread on my dreams.[3]

~ W. B. Yeats

As a third-generation Irish American, the words of Irish poet William Butler Yeats resonate. His poem, however, has a deeper meaning tied to my role as an entrepreneur. Entrepreneurs are dreamers. I was a dreamer. I still dream, for there are visions to

---

[3] Interestingly, W.B. Yeats was Protestant as contrasted to my Catholic great-grandfather featured in this chapter. For further reading see *The Collected Poems of W.B. Yeats* (Wordsworth Poetry Library) by W.B. Yeats. (Wordsworth Editions; New edition (2000-09-05) (January 1, 1800).

chase and catch even in semi-retirement. And with dreams come responsibility. Yes, responsibility. In my experience, dreams are gifts meant to propel us forward — not to be ignored but acted upon.

My rationale is that if the vision appears, it's an opportunity to ponder, chew on it, and go for it. That is, if intuition and instinct point in that direction. If so, then someway, somehow, an entrepreneur becomes equipped to carry it through. That really is the bottom line of how MedAire came to be. It took a lot of faith and a strong sense that this startup had to be founded, regardless of how impossible it seemed. Perhaps being Irish was part of the equipping, for stubbornness and determination helped facilitate my dreams as well.

There's another backstory regarding Yeat's poem. The government of Ireland purchased a Gulfstream jet, and MedAire's services were included in the sale. I detail this Gulfstream contract in a further chapter but suffice it to say, it was quite an experience to fly to Ireland once a year and train the Irish Air Corps in the management of inflight illness and injury. They were responsible for the defense minister and the President of Ireland, Mary McAleese, who served from 1997 to 2011. I was responsible for ensuring they had the medical training needed to perform emergency duties.

MedAire contracted through the defense minister's office and the colonel who headed the Irish Air Corps. During these training sessions, I became great friends with the officers and other flight crew. After training classes, we'd go to the officer's mess hall in Baldonnel for a "pint of Guinness." One year they gave me a paperweight from the hall that still sits on my desk today, a treasured keepsake.

Speaking of keepsakes, I caught sight of a unique tapestry that hung in the flight department foyer. On that tapestry was Yeat's poem. How eye-catching, this beautiful piece of art, and I looked closer to see who had created it. The artist, Bernadette Madden,[4] was (and is) renowned for her wax-resist dying technique. I decided I could not leave Ireland in 1998 without commissioning her to replicate the tapestry. It wasn't easy to arrange an appointment, considering she didn't have fax, email, or social media at the time. But once at her home... how enchanting!

The aroma of wax wafted through her downstairs studio, where she designed her batik on linen masterpieces. We had tea upstairs in her living quarters and talked of our mutual fancy of silver spoons, each having a collection. She had quite an amazing assortment to admire, and we enjoyed discussing our shared hobby. The Yeat's poem had to be handcrafted and mailed, and with payment and shipping details provided, it was a matter of waiting for the gorgeous batik linen mural to arrive via DHL.

And that's how Yeat's poem came to hang in my hallway. Every morning as I prepared for the day ahead, it became a habit to stop and read the words. Whether headed to work or out for a sunrise jog, it reminded me to keep dreaming (and still does) and became another fond memento of my time spent in Ireland. There was a sense of belonging among the people and landscapes — hard to describe, but nevertheless a connection.

In 2001, I became one of Bernadette's repeat customers and commissioned a gorgeous batik of begonias titled "Fuchsia" — seven feet wide and ten feet tall. The tapestry hung in my dining room for years, just lovely, a reminder of time spent in my ancestral homeland.

After personally training the Irish Air Corps all those years, we handed it off to the MedAire office in London, very much a decision of good business over sentiment. As much as I loved spending time in Ireland, working with the officers, and visiting sites such as Bunratty Castle, it made better financial sense to save my travel fare and have our European staff take over the training. So I had to settle for the memories, mementos, and the

---

4 See Bernadette Madden's website. https://bernadettemadden.ie/biography/full-biography/

wonderful sense of belonging, which is a pretty good trade-off overall.

Bernadette Madden's tapestry hangs in my hallway and reminds me to dream.

One of my Labradors, Guinness, named in honor of the beer I shared with the Irish Air Corps. I called him "the foam on top of the draft."

My time in Ireland also nudged me to explore my Irish roots, feeling somewhat guilty that my ancestry was not yet traced or shared with my sons. My only justification was that there was little time to spare and only a few breadcrumbs to follow, and I hit a brick wall. *The Atlas of the Great Irish Famine*[5] became available in 2012, an enormous tome weighing more than eight pounds and quite a good investment. The artwork, graphics, and maps pulled me further into this distant homeland, the words and stories leading straight into the heart of my people — a highly recommended book.

---

[5] J John Crowley, William I. Smyth, Mike Murphy. *The Atlas of the Great Irish Famine* (Cork, Ireland, Cork University Press, 2012).

With Aaron, visiting a Dublin bookstore (and later Shannon Heritage, Bunratty Castle)

My son Aaron and I were in Dublin, visited a bookstore, and found this piece of artwork from The Atlas of the Great Irish Famine. It spoke to me, and I've cherished it ever since.

My eldest son, Aaron, attended Arizona State University, finished his degree in England, and occasionally met up with me on these trips (my younger son, Josh, attended the University of Arizona at Tucson and finished his degree in Spain). Aaron and

I once visited a quaint little bookstore in Dublin, and a framed photo straight out of *The Atlas of the Great Irish Famine* sat on a table. We bought it, and I cherish it today as both a reminder of Ireland and the time spent with my son. Our centuries-old roots in Ireland had laid the foundation of our family business today. We stood on hallowed ground in that bookstore, as far as I'm concerned.

By this time, I had managed to establish what had been passed down word of mouth from my grandmother Mary and her father's citizenship records, along with a few other documents. Ireland, the second-largest island of the British Isles, was Timothy Sullivan's native home. He and my great-grandmother Kate Burke were Catholic. Somehow, they worked their way across the country and arrived in Contra Costa County, California, and brought with them a deep faith in God, a patriotic love for America, a respect for elders, an incredible work ethic, and heaps of moxie — all evident within these pages.

I felt so close to my great-grandparents, these perfect strangers who shared my lineage, my heritage. I wanted them to be more than strangers. I wanted to give them a voice and honor every step, every mile they traversed to reach America. This chapter remedies my lack of progress. Perhaps readers of Celtic descent share my passion for Ireland, the Emerald Isle, and the land of a thousand welcomes — and limericks and leprechauns and lilting brogues.

What isn't there to love about St. Patrick, four-leaf clovers, rainbows, pots of gold, and the Guinness beer my grandparents almost certainly drank? The Guinness brewery was established in Dublin in 1759. No wonder I enjoyed drinking this authentic Irish delight more than two and a half centuries later with the Irish Air Corps.

Timothy and Kate exemplified the "immigrant story" so iconic to the fabric of our nation. They left everything behind, everything familiar, and crossed the ocean in a voyage that lasted at least three months. What challenges had they endured, and what did their lives entail? How did they get here? What were their stories?

Recently, genealogist Joanna Cicely Fennel came to my aid to help piece together the puzzle. If you've heard of the television shows *Who Do You Think You Are?* and *My Family Secrets Revealed,* her name might be familiar. But the real draw was her credentials — an Irish-born member of the Council of the Irish Genealogical Research Society. Her preliminary sleuthing commenced, and still many mysteries remain, but so far, we've learned that my great-grandfather Timothy was born in 1857, just five years after the end of the Great Potato Famine.

Ah, the potato famine. It's why I grow Irish potatoes in my garden today, a tribute to the struggles of my ancestors. Pre-famine, they survived on a particular type of white potato. You may wonder how potatoes alone could keep them alive, but apparently this tuber was highly digestible, lower in starch, and rich in vitamin C, protein, thiamin, and niacin. Then came the potato blight of 1845 and subsequent crop failures across the nation.

With large broods and many mouths to feed, the famine undoubtedly impacted every Irish branch on my family tree, Timothy and Kate's most certainly. The aftereffects were still evident as they grew up, and this horrible, heartbreaking period is also known as "The Great Hunger," a phrase almost too unbearable to process. It claimed one million Irish lives due to starvation and disease, with another million fleeing the country to North America, the UK, and Scotland. We are still trying to decipher how and why Timothy and Kate's family managed to dodge annihilation when so many perished — but survive, they did.

In a highly Catholic nation, it appears the population endured religious persecution as well, threatened by the Protestant monarchy of Great Britain. I wonder if any of my distant relatives were coerced into giving up their beliefs, the very Catholicism that helped them cope with the famine. Timothy was obviously a highly stubborn Irishman because he refused to renounce his faith. I know this because he arrived in America with his beliefs intact and passed them down to my grandmother and mother.

I was raised in the faith as well. While not a practicing Catholic today (for reasons detailed later), I am a nondenominational Christian with traditional values and conservative views — the same values and views that Timothy shared with my grandmother, Mary. If only he could have lived to see the day when John F. Kennedy became president in 1961, a fellow Irishman and Catholic — a first for the nation and somewhat controversial.

With a flood of pride, I watched his inauguration on television with my siblings. It validated that our nation was becoming more tolerant and appreciative of Irish Catholics and our many contributions to society.

In 1879 around the age of 22, Timothy boarded a ship most likely anchored in Queenstown (now Cobh) in County Cork and voyaged to New York. I doubt he was completely impoverished in Ireland simply because he could afford the passage across the pond. But based on American standards, he was probably considered very poor and fell into a demographic of immigrants all vying for jobs.

He almost certainly faced discrimination here and an anti-Irish sentiment based on decades of refugees, and an anti-Catholic sentiment as well. Since the Irish were faithful to what they considered "the one true faith" led by the Pope, their allegiance to the United States was questioned (as was the case with President Kennedy even decades later).

Ellis Island didn't open until 1892, so Timothy's arrival was likely an unceremonious landing at the Port of New York, with only his wits and luggage as company. He arrived a subject of the Queen of Great Britain and Ireland, a foreigner in a foreign land,

and made his way across the country to settle in Contra Costa County, California. There he would eventually meet and marry my great-grandmother Kate, born in Ireland in 1860.

I'm not yet sure if my great-grandfather voyaged aboard the Abyssinia (ca 1870), although many Irish immigrants arrived via the Liverpool–New York route.

Kate emigrated in 1880, a year after Timothy. At just 20 years old, she also made the perilous journey overseas and settled in Contra Costa County. I do not know if Kate and Timothy knew each other in Ireland — probably not. But, somehow, they connected (San Francisco was a magnet for the Irish) and eventually tied the knot in 1891, more than a decade after they immigrated. Kate was a 31-year-old bride, and Timothy was a 33-year-old groom, unusually advanced in age for a wedding in those times. We're still digging to see what that backstory entails.

By then, Timothy was a citizen. He followed a formal process by pledging his intent to become a U.S. citizen on June 14, 1886. Unfortunately, he had to wait another two years as required by law to renounce the Crown and officially become an American citizen. Both original documents are stored securely in my home — such a nostalgic tie to a long-ago past.

Timothy and Kate's marriage certificate

August 6, 1888 must have been a very happy day for Timothy as he received his citizenship decree. I suspect 1888 might have been a happy year for Kate too, due to unconfirmed information that she also became a naturalized citizen that year, and only time and research will tell. She and Timothy became later-in-life parents to my grandmother Mary Elizabeth, their only child born August 2, 1899. Kate was 39, and Timothy was 41 when they ushered my grandmother Mary into the world, and I'm sure they considered her a miracle and a blessing — and probably a surprise!

To make matters even more heartfelt, I was born on my grandmother Mary's 50th birthday, making her a very special grandmother indeed. It cemented an exceptional closeness to her for this and many other reasons.

21

In the Superior Court of the County of Contra Costa,

STATE OF CALIFORNIA.

Monday August 6th A. D. 188*8*.

Present, Hon. *Joseph P. Jones*, Judge.

In the Matter of the Application of

Timothy Sullivan

to be admitted a Citizen of the United
States of America.

Decree Admitting to Citizenship.

Timothy Sullivan
a subject of *the Queen of Great Britain & Ireland,*
appeared this day in open Court and made application to be admitted a citizen of the United
States of America. And it having appeared to the satisfaction of the Court, upon due proof
and the production of a certified copy of the record, that the said applicant has heretofore, and
more than two years previous to this date, declared on oath, before the Clerk of a Court of record
having common law jurisdiction, that it was bona fide his intention to become a citizen of the
United States of America, and to renounce forever all allegiance and fidelity to any foreign
prince, potentate, state or sovereignty whatever, and particularly to *the Queen of
Great Britain & Ireland* whereof he was a subject. And further proof having been
made to the satisfaction of the Court by the testimony of *Daniel Casey*
and *John Burke* two witnesses—citizens of
the United States—who were sworn and examined in open Court: that said applicant has re-
sided in the United States five years, and in this State one year, and that during that time he
has behaved as a man of good moral character, attached to the principles of the Constitution of
the United States, and well disposed to the good order and happiness of the same.

Thereupon said applicant declared on oath that he will support the Constitution of the
United States, and that he doth absolutely and entirely renounce and abjure all allegiance and
fidelity to every foreign prince, potentate, state or sovereignty whatever, and particularly to
Victoria Queen of Great Britain and Ireland
whereof he was before a subject.

Now, Therefore, it appearing to the satisfaction of the Court from the foregoing proofs
that the Naturalization Laws of the United States have in all respects been complied with in the
matter of this application; the Court doth hereby ORDER, ADJUDGE AND DECREE that
the said *Timothy Sullivan* be, and he is
hereby admitted and declared to be a CITIZEN OF THE UNITED STATES OF AMERICA.

Decree entered *August 6th* 188*8*

L. C. Wittenmyer Clerk.

By Deputy Clerk.

My great-grandfather's citizenship record

The Federal Census shows that in 1900 the family was living in Port Costa Precinct No. 2. Timothy was a 42-year-old stevedore. I know that at some point, he was employed by the Southern Pacific Railroad because I have his gold retirement watch. Thanks to the Contra Costa County Historical Society, I'm sharing one of many photos donated by Les Zuerner, retired photographer for Standard Oil Company in 1979, to the El Cerrito Historical Society. The image shows the railroad yard where my grandfather labored.

El Cerrito Historical Society Secretary, George C. Collier, provided the following caption:

> *Port Costa was built on the shores of Carquinez Straits in 1879 by George W. McNear as a wheat shipping port. At its greatest development, the wharves and warehouses extended from west of Crockett to Martinez. McNear's concrete warehouse, built about 1887 or 1888, is shown in lower left foreground. The Southern Pacific RR shops are shown just above the wooden tank and the ferry slips are to the far right.*

Kate and baby Mary are mentioned in the 1900 census as well, and interestingly the census also shows that two "roomers" lived in their home. What fascinating news because ten years later, those "roomers" had multiplied. My great-grandmother Kate ran a full-blown boarding house, an entrepreneurial enterprise that closely mirrored my own. In the chapter ahead, you'll see that I became a landlord as well, way back in the day before I earned my nursing license.

I was curious about my roots as a Californian. When my great-grandfather became a U.S. citizen in 1888, California had officially been a state for only 38 years (since 1850). He landed in an area originally populated by Native Americans, Spanish colonials, and Mexican nationals amid an influx of White settlers and immigrants. I can't help but wonder if the "No Irish Need Apply" signs were as prevalent in Contra Costa County as they were across the nation back in his day.

Westerly view of Southern Pacific Railroad yard & town, about 1910 – Photo courtesy of the Contra Costa County Historical Society

Contra Costa was one of the original counties formed when the California Republic gained statehood, located north of the East Bay region of the San Francisco Bay and home to my great-grandfather's employer, the Southern Pacific Railroad. And that's how and why my beloved grandmother Mary experienced the great San Francisco earthquake of 1906 as a seven-year-old first-generation Irish American. I'll never forget her storytelling as she shared the tense moments when she thought she might die.

She was just a little girl but old enough to remember that the floor shimmied and the roof swayed, and her world seemed to tumble. During this estimated 7.9 magnitude earthquake, fires broke out — great billowing fires that swept San Francisco and decimated the city over the course of several days.

My grandmother Mary and her parents survived unscathed, which seems miraculous. She was raised in the long, warm California summers and short cold winters so reminiscent of my childhood. She married and gave birth to my mother named Catherine Ellen — Catherine, after my great-grandmother Kate.

The ruins of San Francisco in the aftermath of the 1906 earthquake, taken from the tower of the Union Ferry Building and looking southwest down Market Street – Photo credit: National Archives and Records

Interestingly, both my grandmother and mother were singletons without siblings. So my mother was the only child of an only child. That changed in my generation with the birth of my sister and brother. Then along I came, also born in San Francisco, and was given the middle name Ellen after my mother.

Chapter Three: A Sad Little Clan

Be kind. Everyone you meet is carrying a heavy burden.
~ Ian McLaren.

Carl Wittke, an ethnic historian born in 1892, wrote an interesting observation about the attributes of my ancestors:

> *The so-called Irish temperament is a mixture of flaming ego, hot temper, stubbornness, great personal charm and warmth, and a wit that shines through adversity. An irrepressible buoyancy, a vivacious spirit, a kindliness and tolerance for the common frailties of man and a feeling that 'it is time enough to bid the devil good morning when you meet him' are character traits which North Americans have associated with their Irish neighbors for more than a century.*[6]

Is this sweeping generalization just blarney... or spot on? Maybe a mixture of both. The words of Irish writer Edna O'Brien reflect a darker interpretation, probably much closer to reality:

> *When anyone asks me about the Irish character, I say look at the trees. Maimed, stark and misshapen, but ferociously tenacious.*[7]

These words remind me of my mother and grandmother. Although my great-grandparents Timothy and Kate appeared to have a happy union, this was not an inheritance they passed down. The marriages of my mother and grandmother were indeed maimed, stark, and misshapen — and filled with abuse.

And thus begins this chapter, probably the most difficult to write. I'm not a fan of exposés or tell-alls or confessionals, but I

---

[6] Carl Frederick Wittke. *The Irish in America* (Louisiana State University Press, 1956).

[7] Dermot McEvoy. The Little Green Book of Irish Wisdom (Skyhorse Publishing, 2014).

do think people can and should share their truth — especially if that truth can help someone else overcome traumatic events and not feel so alone in their circumstances. So while this is not a pretty story, it's one mirrored by millions of women worldwide, and certainly many Irish women in California and elsewhere.

It certainly affected me that our so-called patriarchs married into our family, much to the detriment of our matriarchs. With all the wonderful, responsible, and caring men in the world, I'm not sure why my mother and grandmother attracted the worst — other than opposites attract. Unfortunately, I had an awful excuse of a grandfather, not to mention my father and especially my stepfather. They cast dark shadows on us all. I don't say this lightly, and it's painful to express, yet part and parcel of who I am and the raw truth of an imperfect upbringing.

It's also very much a survivor story.

A dark and frightening element lurked in my childhood, a convoluted story, as you'll see. It may sound somewhat choppy, a bit out of sync, and that's because the dysfunction colors the memories. So, bear with me as I do my best to share these recollections, some still suppressed (I'm sure), of a family that faced many trials and tribulations.

I have no memory of my biological father. I only know the stories of his alcoholic behavior as told by my mother. He hocked her wedding ring when she was eight months pregnant with me. When she protested, he kicked her down the outside stairs, and that was the end of that marriage.

My mother was born in 1925, and Catholic women, especially Irish Catholic women, didn't divorce their husbands despite broken bones or, worse, broken spirits. In those days, regardless of abuse, the vows "Till death do us part" were sacrosanct and literally describe my mother's near brush with death at the hands of a raging alcoholic. Not willing to risk her life or mine, nor the lives of my older siblings, my mother bucked convention, divorced, and was excommunicated by the Catholic Church.

My beautiful mother

How unfair that she was made a pariah for leaving a man who almost murdered her and me both. Perhaps this explains why, as an adult, I chose not to be a practicing Catholic and found a different spiritual path — the one thing about my Irish heritage that I rejected. After all, my mother's whole life, from baptism to catechism classes, first confession, first communion, into high school, her wedding, and throughout her nursing program, revolved around this deeply held belief system. That was her strength, the Catholic worldview from which her existence flowed... now disintegrated.

The embarrassment of the divorce compounded the shame of the excommunication — a cycle of humiliation. I'm sure my mother felt ruined. My grandmother Mary was mortified at the stigma. She was also very much a product of her generation and didn't approve of divorce under any circumstances. However, she did recognize that my mother needed to escape. She took us in, and one of my earliest memories is of climbing into grandmother Mary's bed, always at 3 a.m. on the dot for some reason, and her arms encircling me. I felt safe and loved, so important during those days of upheaval.

My mother as a student (holding a basketball)

Grandmother Mary had grounds for divorce herself. She felt duty-bound to endure her marriage to my grandfather James Dunn (not that I ever met him), even though he ran off to Mexico with another woman. Worse, he tied the knot. Thus he was a bigamist, married to two women simultaneously and choosing to support only one… and it wasn't my grandmother. Thank heavens she had a nursing license and a career, for she remained married to this cad until her dying day.

My siblings, my mother, and me on her lap

My mother remarried after a short courtship. While nursing at a hospital in San Francisco, she met a patient, Curtis Carpenter, from Texas. He worked in the ranching business and had broken his back during an accident of some kind. They hit it off. It didn't matter that he was controlling. It didn't matter that he forced my mother to quit her nursing job because she earned a larger salary than his. When she met this suitor, what mattered was the chance at a new life for herself and her children, ages six, four, and me at two and a half. She married him when I was three.

Life in Taft, California

My stepfather legally adopted us, and you'll soon see why I cannot refer to him as "dad," "father," or even "parent." He will always be "the stepfather." While things didn't start badly, the situation evolved into a nightmare no child should have to endure. It still occasionally haunts me despite the fact that I survived and overcame it.

This stepfather moved us to Taft, California, a hot and dry desert-like community on oil-rich land. I remember living in a housing track with a small and dirty yard. Later, I learned it was public housing and that we were struggling financially. My stepfather landed a job in neighboring New Cuyama, 30 minutes away, as a foreman for the Russell Brothers Ranch. It came with a house and many horses — a dream setting for growing up in the country. And so, we moved to what became a perfect job for him and a wonderful area for us to grow, play and learn all about country life.

In our Sunday best and ready for church

Speaking of playing, some of my best friends were our horses, especially Papoose. We'd stack four or five kids on the back of this faithful steed and head up a hill to see who could stay on without a saddle. With nothing but a rope around his neck, Papoose seemed to understand that this was his lot in life and went along with our antics. What a good horse, and I absolutely adored him.

We also raised pet deer. When poaching hunters orphaned these fawns, we took them in and bottle-fed them until they could fend for themselves. They were allowed in the house and sat on the couch and watched TV with us. It was hilarious! Then one day, we found half of our oil tablecloth in one of the fawn's mouths. After a tug-of-war with "Bucky," we retrieved the shredded fabric, and from then on, our fawns became outdoor pets.

Me and my trusty Papoose

Then things started to change. During this marriage, my younger half-sister was born, and suddenly I was no longer the baby. In hindsight, I think my mother may have suffered from postpartum depression because she would not come out of her room. I also think she still suffered (and always would) from her status as a divorced, remarried, and excommunicated Catholic. Whatever the case, I heard noises one night for hours on end, and then suddenly, we were all loaded into my stepfather's '56 Chevy.

After the long ride into town, we stopped at a hospital. My stepfather escorted my mother inside with us in tow, and we did not understand what was happening. All we knew is that our mother stayed behind, and we were taken home. Then we found out she was admitted to the mental ward after suffering a complete breakdown. Weeks passed, and we visited her when school was out, but the distance was far, and those visits became less frequent.

Elementary school days

It's a struggle to articulate the experience of visiting my mother in the mental ward. It wasn't a scary place filled with crazed inmates, not at all. But it was a stark reminder that something was wrong with our mother, something that separated her from us. One time I cried because she did not know who we were. There was only a blank stare. Later I understood she had ECT — electroshock therapy. As a young child, I didn't know how to process this. I loved my mother. I remember that she sang so beautifully (a gift I don't share). I remember that once upon a time, she smiled and laughed and hugged me. That ended abruptly.

Unfortunately, all was not good at home while she was away. My stepfather hired a cruel housekeeper who locked us out of the house while he was at work. We could only come in for meals until he returned at the end of the day. My stepfather, himself, was heavy-handed with the belt, and the nights were even worse. This is something I hesitate even to mention — the unspeakable sins of my stepfather. Suffice it to say that my big sister wanted to protect me from his abuse and her own but was not always successful. We were threatened into silence and cried and prayed for our mother to come home.

My sister and I decided to run away. She had recently been diagnosed with juvenile diabetes, needed insulin shots twice daily, and had to follow a restricted diet. She resented this due to her sweet tooth. We'd catch her sneaking candy and other things she shouldn't eat, and ultimately she'd pass out and have to be treated for diabetic coma. The doctors couldn't understand why her urine tests were perfect, and yet she was so unstable. It finally came out that she was giving my brother and me a nickel to urinate into a jar for her.

My sister and I packed our small suitcases with books, trinkets, no food or water, and zero insulin as runaways-to-be. But our plan to escape was foiled. Instead of staying up as we planned and crawling out of our bedroom window, we fell asleep. Later, once I was old enough to understand what this adventure could have entailed, it's a good thing we didn't run away. My sister could have become very ill without food, water, or medicine. Plus, I'm sure we would have attempted to hitchhike with strangers, and that was also risky for young girls even in those days.

Still, I can't help but wonder if perhaps some kind stranger would have picked us up and turned us over to the authorities. In turn, we would have been placed in foster care. Sad to say, what a relief that would have been in our circumstances. Thankfully, my mother gradually improved and came home. This meant our lives improved too, yet things were never the same. A photo of our sad little clan perfectly captures our feelings. There we were, all lined up on the couch, my older sister, brother, and mother, solemn. Unable to smile. It hurts my heart even today to see my older sister looking so unhappy. I can barely gaze at this photo without a swell of melancholy.

This image epitomizes our sad little clan.

Yet in the foreground, my younger half-sister, barely out of toddlerhood, was mugging for the camera without a worry in the world. I was smiling in the photo at her antics, glad that she was carefree because the rest of us were not — at least not without our mother's presence to shield us from our stepfather.

Soon I turned 11, and life threw us another curveball. My stepfather had a dream to own his own property and bought 100 acres near Guy, Arkansas, 45 miles north of Little Rock. I'm not sure how he came up with the money to buy this land, but buy it he did. It was determined that my mother would stay behind with my sister and brother so they could finish school, with the caveat that they all would join us in the summer.

This meant I had to leave the ranch with my seven-year-old half-sister and stepfather, who had bought a big truck and fully loaded it with furniture, belongings, and Dusty, our dog. The back was outfitted to haul Papoose. What a traumatic drive, almost 2,000 miles, and we lost poor Dusty in Winslow, Arizona. I was distraught, even more so when Papoose almost died from the heat and jolting bumps he endured during the cross-country trek. Somehow, he managed to hang in there all the way to Arkansas.

Our new home came with a one-bedroom house, no running water, an old shed, a dilapidated barn, and an outhouse where big, scary spiders lurked. Worse, we had to drop a bucket 80 feet into a well and haul it back up in order to retrieve water. After living in California with all the modern conveniences, this was disillusioning and depressing. At least I got to ride Papoose to school. The best thing about that year was earning an A in English (and the rest, not so much). The moving, the drama, the trauma, and constant disruptions did affect my grades, so this A was a huge accomplishment, at least to me.

The second-best thing was the awesome cafeteria lunches. Hot meals were served with homemade bread and meat and potatoes.

For my half-sister and me, that was the main meal of the day, for there wasn't much else to eat. As kids who were considered poor by any standard, we fit in with our classmates, most of whom were in the same boat.

My stepfather, however, did not fit in — at least not in this Baptist region of the country. The neighbors warned him not to repair our barn on a Sunday, the Sabbath, or it would bring hell and damnation to us. Indeed, they were right. Three weeks later, a dark cloud appeared in the sky. I was riding Papoose in the tall grass about 100 yards from the house when a clap of thunder gave warning of what was to come. The wind blew wildly, and the rain poured down. I raced old Papoose to the house and pulled him into the small shed where I was raising a calf. A loud noise, sounding like a freight train, hammered down on us. The roof on the barn was ripped off with an unworldly screech, and the whole shed lifted off the ground, barely missing me and my horse's head.

I'll never forget Papoose's wild eyes and his utter panic. Unfortunately, he stomped square on the poor calf, killing it. We had experienced a horrific tornado that devastated several homes and barns beyond us. Today it's easier to be philosophical. I was spared for a reason, and everything I experienced and survived in childhood prepared me for my future. But back then, I was anything but philosophical. I was a kid who went into shock and broke out in a rash, bedridden for days and fretting under the weight of the "Sabbath curse."

Indeed, life did get worse. It was the beginning of the extra heaps of bad luck that would befall our household. How I hated this place and everything in it and was relieved to hear that my mother and siblings would soon join us. They arrived, and the weeks turned into midsummer. My stepfather went to look for work as a carpenter or any job to bring money in the door. Each day he came home empty-handed. Thanks to my mother and siblings, we had a prolific garden, but that couldn't sustain a family of six for long. Eventually, my older siblings and I were put to work chopping cotton. There was no complaining because we knew the money we earned was for food.

Our mother made us each a lunch, and we hopped into the bed of an old truck and were transported approximately 30 minutes away to a cotton field. We nearly broke our backs for 50 cents an hour and were the youngest field hands among many other laborers, mostly White and Black. It was unbelievably difficult work and sweltering hot, and the humidity undoubtedly exceeded the temperature.

We had to chop the weeds in between the rows and rows of cotton plants. Sweat bees and horse flies stung us straight through our clothing. We drank from a communal bucket with a dipper and were just thankful to have water, any water, even warm, dirty water. Already a rail-thin girl, I dropped several pounds I couldn't afford to lose.

Finally, we were done, physically and emotionally, and what a surprise to learn that our cotton-chopping wages bought linoleum for the kitchen floor. I privately questioned why we chopped cotton for a linoleum floor — not within earshot of my stepfather, mind you. True, our wood floors were nearly worn clean through, but it seemed to me that food was a more significant issue. I had long since given up trying to make head or tails of my mother and stepfather's decisions.

Then my mother got sick again. This time we understood that the stress of the move and the circumstances of our new living conditions were more than she could take. She was admitted to the Arkansas State Hospital in Little Rock, nothing like the one in California. It looked like something out of the Dark Ages, and the treatment was equally barbaric in the eyes of us children. We were scared for her.

After more shock treatments, she was sent home again, and my stepfather finally admitted defeat. We packed up and moved back to California, to a town called Shandon. He landed a great job at the Sinton Ranch, about 45 minutes from town. Ah, running water and a beautiful yard! And I was starting high school, truly a new chapter. A fresh start.

Life seemed to be turning around. My mother was singing again. She had a lovely voice, and it made us happy. This life on the Sinton Ranch would become my salvation.

Our home in Cuyama, California

My mother and brother posing with a car of that time period

Two cowgirls and a cowboy

Another shot of my siblings and me in Taft, California

Chapter Four: High School and a Turning Point

After moving around from place to place, I was now entrenched as a teenager in Shandon, California, and relished the great outdoors. Always a tomboy with a lifelong love of animals, it was a slice of heaven to live out in the country with cows, horses, goats, chickens, dogs, and cats to keep us company.

After a long and noble life, my beloved Papoose crossed the Rainbow Bridge, and my new horse, Patches, entered the scene. She was an Appaloosa and my very best friend. Oh, those long rides along the fence line and through the pasture. I poured out my heart to an animal who couldn't talk back.

Dear Patches – Photo credit: Steve Sinton

But Patches was an excellent listener, rotating her ears at the inflection in my voice and keeping all my secrets (just as my horse Rosie does today). Those soulful excursions meant the world to me as I struggled with my past and dreamed about my future. Patches, too, was an excellent therapist, as most horses tend to be.

And yes, chores awaited before and after school — mucking the barn, feeding the horses, collecting eggs, helping with the gardening, and soaking up every minute of it. The livestock needed to be fed on weekends and holidays as well, so I was on the hook 24/7/365. The sun, the fresh air, the dirt, the fields of grass, the animals — what kid wouldn't want all of that in a backyard, spreading across acres and acres.

Showing my little neighbor how the milking is done – Photo credit: Steve Sinton

My most important responsibility was milking our Guernsey cow, located about a 15-minute walk from the house. There was no returning home unless I had a gallon of milk. To get the cow to "let down" her milk, her calf had to latch onto her teats. Then I had to break the suction, wipe off the saliva, and push the calf out of the pen. It wasn't easy, as the calf wanted his breakfast too and was about half the size of the cow.

Many times, the cow let loose a stream of urine which splashed into my pail! How dreadful when this happened because I had to toss out the milk. This created a dilemma in meeting my quota, for there was only so much milk a cow could give. Luckily, a water faucet was located nearby and hence the reason there was less "cream" on the top of the milk. Sometimes the contents seemed suspiciously close to skim milk, and that's when my stepfather caught on. Therefore, twice a day, that cow had to be milked by me personally. *Voila!* The skill of "expert milkmaid" could now be added to my list of accomplishments.

The Sinton Ranch milking barn and the pond we swam in during the long, hot summer – Photo credit: Steve Sinton

These chores fell to me because my brother left early and arrived home late due to his sports. My sister kept busy indoors, cleaning the house, doing the laundry, and cooking. She helped in the garden too. All in all, my chore-heavy outdoor experience taught me responsibility — living creatures depended on me — and thus, an important work ethic was instilled.

It took about an hour each way to get to school, which meant waking up early to get my chores done and have breakfast. My high school campus was small and included 7th and 8th grade, and still, the headcount was only 57 students. In my senior year, a grand total of 13 students were in my class. Yet, I was shy and embarrassed to be at school. We still didn't have much money, and clothes were expensive. Every year my grandmother sent outfits, but more often, my sister's hand-me-downs swallowed my frame. She was about two sizes larger, and I wore my coat to hide the oversized garments.

My small high school in Shandon, California – Photo credit: Steve Sinton

My grades were still nothing close to stellar, and my mother and stepfather promised my milking duties would be lifted if I became an Honor Roll student. That was highly motivating, and soon my grades were mostly all A's. I joined the Student Nurses Association and miraculously became an outstanding senior student. I discovered tennis as well, and lucky for me, the ranch had a tennis court. My mother and the ranch owner's wife were good tennis players and made our matches fun and challenging. The high school tennis team welcomed me on board, another great extracurricular outlet.

Grandmother Mary remained a huge influence in my life, the calm in a storm. She lived in San Francisco, and we lived in central California, yet even from a distance, I could feel her love and sense her encouragement. So, it was a treat when my mother took all of us to San Francisco on a summer break visit. My mother's best friend from her high school days was also present, Jane, who was somewhat of a surrogate aunt to us.

My sister told Jane about the abuse we experienced, and while it was largely behind us, Jane went ballistic. All hell broke loose. Jane told my mother and called the sheriff in the county where we lived. My stepfather was arrested, and we had to go back to Shandon and be interviewed by the sheriff department investigators. My sister and I were separated and questioned in graphic detail. It was humiliating, as if they were trying to convince us we were lying. Not so.

It ended with my stepfather being released a couple of weeks later, and the stress of this event put my mother over the edge again. She had another mental breakdown and was admitted to the state hospital psych ward. My sister and I stayed at the ranch boss's house for a couple of days and were treated like royalty, but eventually had to return home to our brother, half-sister, and stepfather, who were waiting.

Our home on the Sinton Ranch – Photo credit: Steve Sinton

It was an extremely emotional and challenging environment, to say the least. My stepfather managed to hang on to his job. I couldn't forgive him and refused to speak to him for many months. My older sister graduated that year from high school and left for San Francisco. She soon married a great guy named Ron. I was happy for her but feared retaliation from my stepfather and slept with a knife under my pillow at night for my own sense of security. I'm not sure how many other teenagers have ever felt compelled to sleep with a knife, but if you are one of them, I completely understand the terror and adrenaline of never knowing what could happen next. The instinct to survive is strong.

I know that sounds horrible, and it was. It all seemed like a bad dream. Finally, my mother returned home, and we wondered what the fallout would be. Would she confront my stepfather? Divorce him? None of that occurred in her fragile state of mind, and no one spoke of my stepfather's transgressions. *At least he served time in jail*, I thought and had to settle my soul with that tiny sliver of justice.

It seemed that things might calm down for a while. I reengaged in high school, came out of my shell, was popular, and could see the light at the end of the tunnel. My teachers seemed to recognize I might need some extra support. My home economics teacher and tennis coach, Mrs. "Scotty" Kester, was a wonderful person who introduced us to baked Alaska and cherry jubilee — dishes we would not normally taste, let alone create. Once a week this special teacher took me home with her to clean her house so I could earn some extra money. Mrs. Kester was so kind. She always cooked me dinner and offered me counseling for my future. Then she drove me all the way home, more than an hour, and encouraged me to think about leaving this small-town environment to "make something of myself." I credit her for broadening my horizon.

Believe me, most of the money I earned was hoarded away, a tiny nest egg for my future. Girls were deemed old maids if they weren't married or at least engaged by their senior year. While I was crowned Queen at the junior-senior prom and Harry Miller was King, that didn't seem to be my destiny. Thus, my secret stash of savings. To all the girls in the world, I promise you it doesn't have to be your destiny either. No matter the circumstances, no matter the trials, if you have a dream, you can chase it. I am living proof.

I was one of the younger students in my class going into my junior year at the age of sixteen. The Vietnam War was still raging overseas, and our televisions broadcast it constantly. Most children of this era were worried (if not terrified) as images flashed in newspapers too, and we prayed for our military loved ones who were serving and our friends who would soon be drafted. The war was very much on my mind when I became a recipient of the California League's Outstanding Student Award and a $100 check.

My favorite teacher, Mrs. Kester – Photo credit: Steve Sinton

My lengthy essay below, I'm sure, played a part in landing this honor, and I've kept it all these years as a portal into those uneasy times. Also, it's something I shared with my sons when they were around that age and will also share with my grandchildren one day. Perhaps you will find it interesting as well, a historical snapshot told from the lens of the Sixties. My missive wasn't perfectly written but was heartfelt and showed some critical thinking mixed with the hope of a girl who abhorred death and wanted the world to heal — naive, perhaps, but nonetheless a constant prayer.

Peace is Attainable

A sharp knock on the door awoke Kim Lai around two in the morning. When he opened the door, he was brutally stabbed, and he and his wife were dragged into the street and shot. Since conspirators had a price on their heads by the government, it was easy money for the communist soldiers. Even though Kim Lai and his family were only farmers, he could not prove otherwise now.

Is there any possible way to free these people from such brutalities? How do you change this way of life? How can we bring harmony from discord? Is the answer peace?

What is peace? How can it be defined? Peace to me is a wonderful possession. One rarely knows of its presence until it is destroyed. Peace is the freedom from conflict, disturbance, and most of all, war. It is a feeling of knowing you are secure from the troubles of the world. For how long depends upon you and how much you treasure your beliefs. I believe that peace can be obtained by knowledge and understanding. I believe that if all the countries began working together instead of against one another, we would not have half the amount of trouble we have today. If an alliance is set up among several countries, then the allied countries should abide by all the rules upon which they agreed through peaceful negotiations.

Yet in the Vietnam conflict, Hanoi refuses to accept our offer for peace. All that was necessary to stop the war, as Secretary of State Dean Rusk has said, was for North Vietnam to stop its assistance to the Vietcong and to 'let its neighbors alone.' President Johnson said that the United States was prepared to negotiate unconditionally to end hostilities with North Vietnam but would not negotiate directly with the Vietcong because the guerrillas were only an arm of the North Vietnamese government.

In Vietnam there is much torment, and many lives are lost every day. These people are fighting for a cause they believe will soon lead to peace. They, like you and I, have families fighting and dying for existence in the world. These people want peace and they want their children to grow up in better surrounding. To sleep at night now knowing whether you may wake up the next morning for fear of being killed. To plow your fields in hope to raise enough food to keep your family alive just to have it destroyed as evidence of war. Such antagonizes is a way of life and the course of human nature is affection again and again. Many of the Vietnamese are farmers by day and Vietcong by night. This is a way of living and supporting a family. Many are not fighting for a cause, but for a meal now and then. By aiding the people of Vietnam, we can hope to obtain their interests instead of resentments. It is up to us to win their trust which we are slowly but surely gaining.

Some people in their world have never known peace either in mind spirit and the only way for them to learn is through knowledge and understanding. In order to have an understanding among different countries, it is necessary to educate the people about world situations because if there was a better conception of the conflicting interests, there would be less opportunity for crises. To educate these people ignorant from political, traditional, or financial blocks would mean eliminating one of the most important harassing problems preventing peace. That is just a steppingstone toward the right direction. We also must be educated to understand the need for peaceful effort in Vietnam. If we knew more about the people and controversial situations, we could have a better idea about their problems.

Education alone cannot cure the world's troubles. In order to bring peace throughout the world, every country must want peace. One has to believe in the fight for peace because without belief there is little hope. In our Constitution, we are assured of our many freedoms, but unless we want the freedom, the words have little meaning. We are promised the pursuit of happiness, but it is up to us to find happiness.

We also are promised liberty but not peace. Peace is attainable if the people of the world are united and sincere in their feelings toward this goal.

To our adversaries, we should present the advantages of peace as well as the disadvantages of conflicts. The nuclear war is a potential threat whereas smaller wars are assumed to be controllable. How and when will our destiny be? Will it be in peace? There is so much competition for world power today that each country is trying to out do the other. To think of the weapons created today is a total nightmare. Their power of destruction is so great, that if there should ever be a nuclear war, chance for survival would be very slim. How can the leaders of the world speak of peace when the threat of nuclear power is at their fingertips?

We speak of peace conferences today but all along we are far apart. Woodrow Wilson said in his address to Congress in June 1915 — "There must be, not a balance of power, but a comment of power; not organized rivalries, but an organized common peace."

We live in peace in America today and approximately 11,000 miles away, a cruel war is taking place. Why is it that we are the country bestowed with wealth, power, and happiness, and the others are overpopulated, hungry and uneducated? Where is our turmoil to begin? Who is to determine who lives in peace and who will not? Who has this right? Does it belong to the individual, the country, or to some unknown power in the world today? Time is the determine factor. In the past, people have prophesied what would occur in the future as Alfred Lord Tennyson did when he wrote "Locksley Hall" in 1842.

I believe that if the greatest minds of the world and leaders of the countries have not found a solution for peace, it is up to us and the generation of tomorrow to eventually do so. This time has come, and we go on looking for peace; how and when will depend upon the people of the world.

Behind wisdom, understanding, and patience lies the answer to peace. When all diplomacy fails, we seek to find spiritual guidance. Could we unite all the nations of the world with faith and trust in the Divine power? If we reach a point when we can no longer turn to this help, we will no longer need to seek peace.

God willing and the people of this world willing, we will never reach this point but rather enter into that time when — "The common sense of the most shall hold a fretful realm in awe, and the kindly earth shall slumber, lapped in universal law."

The essay took quite a bit of effort, and it was a thrill to be invited to Morro Bay for the awards banquet, closing out a successful high school experience. However, I felt sorry for one of my classmates who didn't graduate, knowing students might or might not be able to repeat the school year. In those days, if you didn't meet the grade, you were held back, period, regardless of your lot in life or the pressure to graduate, earn a living, and support a family. The other 12 of us received our diplomas, and it just so happened that I was voted the "most outstanding senior student" — another accomplishment for a kid who had been dealt some bad hands.

During my final year in high school, ranch work was a primary focus, especially during cattle roundups and branding. I went with the ranch hands into a canyon at five in the morning, bareback on Patches. My only saddle was a McClellan, an old calvary type of saddle that was very uncomfortable, and bareback was much preferable. We brought the cattle to a central point where we separated the cows and calves. I could ride like the best of them and hold my own, putting in my share of the work. The best part of the brandings was the food at the end. The women cooked all day, and I sat with the guys and enjoyed the rewards of my labor.

Who treated all the sick calves? Me — another indication that I was meant to be a nurse. It enabled me to lock away my past and focus instead on a future that was beginning to form in my mind. I would leave the ranch like my sister and find a way to support myself until I could go to college. That was my secret plan and the reason for saving every nickel, every dime. Heeding Mrs. Kester's advice as a 17-year-old with an understandable urge to get off the ranch, I thought about what I wanted in life. What did I want to become? Since my mother and grandmother were nurses, that legacy was huge. My high school membership in the Student Nurses' Association also made an impact. Deep down, I knew nursing was my true calling since never wanted to do anything but help people (and animals too).

But one day I picked up a travel magazine and momentarily flirted with the idea of becoming a Pan Am flight attendant — referred to as "stewardess" back in the day. The thought of being up in the air and traveling the world while still taking care of people had a certain ring to it. Plus, I was skinny and met the weight requirements.

This element of travel and adventure appealed to me at that young age and resurfaced many decades later in ways I couldn't imagine. In fact, you'll see throughout this book that many serendipitous events shaped my journey, overlapping and intertwining and guiding me on an astounding, peculiar path. It was as if God dropped seeds right onto my lap and allowed my experiences to water them, and I'm so grateful for that.

By the way, I was curious if this particular Pan Am ad still existed. Amazingly, I found it on eBay as I wrote this chapter, as mesmerizing now as it was then. I recall looking into the role of a stewardess in the school library and learned the earliest were exclusively male and referred to as stewards, cabin boys, or pursers with duties similar to those on trains and ships. And then came the females, all nurses at the time and referred to as hostesses and stewardesses. That perked up my ears — nurses in the sky — and the first was Ellen Church, a 25-year-old registered nurse employed by United Airlines in 1930.

Stewardess wanted.
Must want the world.

This is a real want ad.

And the gal we want has to be someone special. Because she'll be living in the special world of the Pan Am® stewardess.

With a home base in San Francisco, Los Angeles, New York, Chicago, Washington, Miami or Seattle. And a second home all over the world. Europe, the South Pacific, the Caribbean, the Far East, the Middle East, Africa, South America.

She'll make as much as $550 a month after three years.

With food, housing and transportation paid for by Pan Am while she's away from home base.

Thirty days paid vacation a year.

Pan Am discounts after her first year. Up to 90% off on vacation travel for her and her eligible relatives.

And a great opportunity to see things, do things, learn things all over the world. It's a second education in itself.

But, back to our gal. How does she qualify for our Pan Am Stewardess training?

Well, if she's single, healthy, over 21, between 5'3" and 5'9", at least a high school grad with a knowledge of a foreign language, that's a good start.

There are more qualifications, but they'll require an interview. So, if you'd like to arrange one, just fill out our coupon. Or call a Pan Am ticket office.

Do it soon. The world is waiting.

Pan Am makes the going great.

Lynn Mechler, Hangar 14,
John F. Kennedy Airport,
Jamaica, N. Y.

I have the qualifications outlined above and would like to find out more about becoming a Pan Am stewardess.

Name_____

Address_____

City_____ State_____

Zip Code_____ Phone_____

TIME, NOVEMBER 17, 1967

The Pan Am ad that had me thinking about flying

My grandmother Mary was familiar with Ellen Church, an original "Sky Girl" as this group of nurse-stewardesses was sometimes called. She mentioned Ellen Church to me on several occasions, and I discuss this in an upcoming chapter. Even in high school, I found this unique blend of nursing and aviation fascinating. Subconsciously, a seed was planted.

I was also interested in everything pilot-related and looked up some of the female "aviatrixes" of my grandmother's era — Amelia Earhart the explorer and Louise McPhetridge Thaden the daredevil, both inducted into the National Aviation Hall of Fame. I would never have dreamed back then that I would join these two remarkable pilots as an enshrinee in the National Aviation Hall of Fame myself. Seriously, it's rather mind-blowing. Fast forward more than half a century, and I met Louise Thaden's daughter-in-law on a cruise in Maine. What an interesting set of coincidences!

Chapter Five: A Mind of My Own

If you're brave enough to say goodbye,
life will reward you with a new hello.
~ Paulo Coelho

I relinquished the fleeting notion of becoming a stewardess as high school graduation approached, fully embracing that I was meant to be a nurse, a third-generation nurse, and continue the family tradition of working in the medical field. I applied and was offered a scholarship to a private medical assisting school in San Francisco. Classes were scheduled to start in the fall, and I was determined to attend! My mother and stepfather were aware of none of this, not my scholarship nor my intent to skedaddle to San Francisco. They were asleep in bed when I walked in and announced I was leaving.

A 17-year-old high school honor graduate

Since I was a minor, my stepfather threatened to call the sheriff. Why would he even bother? I told him, "Do what you need to do." I could not bear to live in this awful, dysfunctional environment one second longer, and he knew it. I didn't have a driver's license and had already arranged for a close girlfriend to drive out and pick me up. I hopped in with one suitcase and no regrets, and away we drove to the bus station. With the money I had managed to squirrel away, I bought a ticket to San Francisco — a ticket to freedom and a chance to reinvent myself far away from the past.

I had also already made arrangements to move in with my grandmother Mary, who had just retired that year in 1967. My grandmother and her colleagues never went to the ocean, three miles away by streetcar. World circled around work, home, work, home. They came from the depression and were sensible, rarely such survival instincts never went beyond day to day.

I had to find a job. I had very little money, and it was up to me to carve out a life for myself. My goal was to get my own apartment. So, I went to the Southern Pacific Hospital at 1400 Fell Street in San Francisco to seek employment, an older facility for people who had worked for the railroad. Most were elderly male patients.

I'm not sure what pulled me to that location. At that time, I didn't know my great-grandfather Timothy had been an employee of Southern Pacific Railroad — quite a coincidence in hindsight. The hospital was built in 1908, two years after my grandmother Mary was born, and ceased operations in 1967 (the year I became employed there). However, the building continued to be used as the Harkness Hospital until 1974.

I walked in and told Mrs. Green, the head nurse, that I wanted a job but had no training. I also fibbed about my age and said I was 18. Perhaps the spirit of my great-grandfather was with me, for I was offered a job as a nurse's aide! It was the hardest work I could ever imagine. The shifts were long, and I was on my feet, which was expected. What I didn't expect was the manual labor involved — lifting patients, cleaning messes, and giving baths.

The elevators were too small to hold gurneys, and we pushed patients up and down the ramps installed in the center of the hospital. I was stationed on the fourth floor, so you can imagine the exertion it took! Yet it was steady income, and I didn't complain, for it enabled me to save enough money to rent a studio apartment not too far away in the Sunset District.

The wind beneath my wings, grandmother Mary

61

The thought of living near Haight-Ashbury sounded rather posh. But it was actually rather "pot," meaning I wafted through the heavy smell of marijuana during my mile-long walks to work and back. I was scared to death, trudging along that route at six in the morning for my seven to three shift. I even managed to take a few karate classes for self-defense, not that it was ever much help — what a relief when I could finally afford to take the bus or streetcar. But the funny thing was, the part of Haight-Ashbury I traversed was probably the safest of all places because everyone was either stoned or passed out in their tents!

I made an acquaintance with a pharmacist at the hospital, Mr. Spinelli, who knew I had grown up with horses. He asked if I'd be interested in exercising his horse on the beach. The stable was located in the Sunset District on the beach, and I answered, "Heck yeah!"

One weekend, I saw a guy whipping a horse. Actually, he was riding behind a little girl who was trying not to fall out of the saddle as he whipped her horse's hindquarters. Was he training her to be a jockey? A barrel racer? What he was doing to this poor child was ridiculous, let alone her horse. I cannot stand to see a child or animal abused (it brings out the Irish in me), and so I trotted up on horseback and screamed at him to stop. In the commotion, his horse spun around and kicked at my horse. Unfortunately, its hoof caught my lower left leg. The pain was intense, and I knew I was injured, so I hightailed it back to the barn.

And who came charging up? The man with the whip. This was my chance to use my self-defense skills, except it wasn't karate that saved the day. It was tears! I was scared and cried my way out of that confrontation, and the pain in my leg added to the sobbing.

The next day my leg was still sore, and I told my nurse supervisor. "Let me take a look," she offered. The wound was swollen and hot to the touch. She insisted I get a leg scan, and it turned out I had a blood clot and subsequently a pulmonary embolism. I was prescribed high molecular weight dextran and heparin, which drew the clot from my lungs.

I was now barely 18 and the epitome of health, aside from my injury. I had blossomed into a happy-go-lucky young lady who had escaped a troubled home life and embraced the future. With this positive attitude, I quickly recovered, counted my blessings, and attended medical assisting school during the mornings and worked at the hospital during the 3-11 shift. I was determined to demonstrate my commitment and work ethic.

Perhaps my attitude paid off, for Dr. Price, a general practice physician, noticed me in the hallway one day. He smiled, and I smiled back. Then he asked about me, and I filled him in. Apparently, whatever I said impressed him, for he made an offer: "Come work for me." He needed a medical assistant for another practice he had just purchased. I was a month short of graduation and thought, *Great! I have a job! Goodbye, nurse's aide. Hello, medical assistant!*

I met his Danish wife, Lena, a nurse, and learned that Dr. Price had kept a pet raccoon in medical school. This was my heads up that he was a bit eccentric. I was stationed in his office on Post Street by St. Francis Hospital and grew to love my new job over the course of time. It was great to report directly to a doctor instead of a hospital system. The work was still intense but in a different way. I was using my mind for a change instead of my muscles. One of my biggest tasks was billing.

Dr. Price and I had a running joke. He accused me of billing only enough to pay for my own salary. Perhaps this jinxed things, for the practice didn't do well and was closed. So, I became Dr. Price's medical assistant in his role as director of the outpatient department at Harkness Hospital. It was great! I made rounds with him in the morning and during the afternoons had my own little office from which I billed patients. Once again, I was teased that I billed just enough to pay my salary.

He and his wife liked me, and the feeling was mutual. I was

invited to go on trips with them, feeling like a bumpkin who, for the very first time, was exposed to the finer things in life. They picked me up from my apartment in a big, black LeBaron sedan and took me to their property at Sea Ranch. I took care of their two children, ages two and four.

Dr. Price's wife had a husky voice, blue eyes, and beautiful blond hair. She managed their real estate, much of it in Potrero Hill. They accumulated a lot of wealth in rental properties, and one of their homes was just dazzling, complete with a large pool. They also owned a convalescent hospital — the only one I ever walked into that didn't smell. Dr. Price's wife imported Danish nurses to work in this hospital, and they committed to two years in which to learn drugs, protocol, the English language, and sit their boards.

It was interesting to be exposed to Danish culture, something completely new. I wonder now if the odorless environment in Dr. Price's convalescent homehad something to do with Denmark itself. As I wrote this chapter, I stumbled across the term "hygge" (pronounced "hooga" or "heega"), a concept that has been around since the 1800s. Today it's a lifestyle movement that seems to evoke happiness. Year after year, Denmark and the Nordic countries rank high in the World Happiness Report. I'm sure it has something to do with this notion of hygge — cozy atmospheres among those you love, sharing meals, the wellbeing of all, feeling sheltered and safe, simple pleasures, and a sense of comfort. This was the feeling I had in Dr. Price's convalescent hospital, and it was apparent that his patients felt the same.

The constant stream of Danish nurses provided an opportunity for me to make new friends, and I became besties with a few. I was quite shocked when their less-than-modest uniform included black bras and panties, completely visible under their white dresses. The elderly male patients enjoyed this immensely, nearly falling out of their wheelchairs. I guess this further compounded Dr. Price's reputation for eccentricity, at least in my mind, for he allowed this deviation in the dress code based on the positive feedback from his geriatric patients.

In short, Dr. Price had a lighthearted sense of humor, and on one occasion, I was very glad he did. In his role as director of the outpatient patient department, he oversaw orthopedics, ENT, gastrointestinal, orthopedics, etc., all run by different specialists. Once when I was present in an exam room, an ENT patient with severe symptoms was cultured in a chair. Dr. Price, the specialist, his nurse, and I all waited impatiently for the results.

Finally, Dr. Price said, "Joanie, call pathology!" and I ran to my small office to use the phone. I was told that no organisms were present, and in my haste, rushed back to Dr. Price and announced: "No orgasms present."

I had no idea why heads turned as laughter rippled throughout the room. Then it dawned on me that I had mispronounced the word organisms and turned scarlet red. I had no idea what that mispronunciation meant but clearly understood I had made a blunder. I was so embarrassed and so young.

It just so happened that Dr. and Mrs. Price owned a nearby apartment complex as well and paid me to manage it. That's how I met my first husband and the father of my children. He was straight out of the military, had served as an alternate in the 1960 Rome Olympics as a hunter jumper equestrian, lived with two roommates, and was employed by Golden Gate University in the registration department. I thought he was dashing, and we dated almost a year before getting married.

By then, I no longer worked for Dr. Price. I was employed by a group of OB/GYNs and was about to find out what it meant to be a wife and mother, both brand new roles in which I hoped to excel and experience the deepest happiness.

Chapter Six: Baptism by Fire

Management is doing things right; leadership is doing the right things.

~ Peter Drucker

There I was, a 19-year-old bride and pregnant with a honeymoon baby. I remained confident that I would somehow, someway, become a licensed nurse and was excited to learn I could attend Golden Gate University, one of California's oldest private universities. The tuition was free, thanks to my husband's employment — a great perk! Located near the Bay Bridge, it wasn't necessarily a scenic campus but provided my one and only experience of being a student at a traditional four-year university.

The university didn't offer a nursing program and was geared toward law, business, taxation, and accounting, so I opted for courses in pre-law and ancient history. I worked days at the OB/GYN practice and took evening classes. Without a driver's license, I took the bus to work. I hopped off more times than I care to remember due to bouts of horrible morning sickness and then caught the next bus. What a hassle!

When I was around seven months along, I decided to scratch a pending item off my to-do list. I wanted to learn to drive! It irked me that I had to depend on others to get me to work, school, and the grocery store. I certainly didn't want to catch rides to the pediatrician after my baby was born. So, I tackled the driving coursework and took the road test in my husband's 1965 Ford Mustang, four on the floor, on the hills of San Francisco. My driving evaluator maintained a white-knuckle grip on his clipboard the entire time.

Once I pulled back into the parking lot of the Department of Motor Vehicles, he asked, "Do you really think I should pass you?"

"Yes!" I answered immediately, puzzled at such a stupid

question.

"Well, I'll pass you, but you aren't allowed to drive alone for six months."

I guess he thought I was dangerous! How silly! I happily drove away with my laminated license, quite a trophy, and headed home to incubate my unborn son, work, and continue my university courses as long as possible. Soon I'd have to drop out of the university as my due date approached but I made the most of it before focusing on motherhood and caring for my newborn.

It was my good fortune to work for an OB/GYN practice, for it prepared me for what childbirth entailed. Yet, there is no way to fully appreciate the miracle of birth until you experience it yourself. It was the most epic and gratifying moment in my life, and I felt as if I had given the world a gift in the form of a tiny fourth-generation Irish lad, Aaron.

Soon I was pregnant again with lad #2, Josh, so excited at the prospect of being a mother times two. Unfortunately, I had placenta previa and delivered Josh six weeks early. In those days, and even today, early births could be problematic, but Josh was a healthy and beautiful baby. He was so easy, mellow, and not at all fussy. This became a true blessing when I experienced postpartum depression shortly after his birth. I'm not sure how I would have managed to tend to him and his brother otherwise.

It also helped that I was familiar with postpartum depression and postpartum anxiety, which was gaining recognition in the 1970s. Many mothers suffered through this malady and I recognized my own symptoms. It just so happened that the Son of Sam murders were in the news (terrible timing), which didn't help one bit. I was freaked out by the unrelenting media coverage, to the point that we sold our home in San Francisco and moved to Marin County.

Grandmother Mary and my boys

As we settled into our new home, I admit to missing my grandmother Mary. She didn't want us to move, of course, and I felt bad. Aaron and Josh were so cute and endearing, and I knew she pined for her great-grandsons. Still, I felt safer in Marin County and was soon back to my normal self. I found a babysitter and enrolled in Indian Valley Community College to get some of my nursing prerequisites out of the way (microbiology was one of the courses). Yet, I faced a three-year wait to formally enroll in the nursing program.

My husband was a man of ideas, a risk-taker who was willing to jump on opportunities. Perhaps he was too young and inexperienced to fully think these ideas through (which was sometimes the case). At this point, we were not a happy couple for several reasons, including a difference in the socio-economic circumstances of our upbringings. I was a kid straight off the cattle ranch with very little formal education while he aspired to get his Ph.D. I married into academia and wasn't at all familiar with this type of polite society. His mother didn't approve of our marriage. Honestly, I was miserable.

We had a realtor friend who found an opportunity in Scottsdale, Arizona. Unbeknownst to me, my grandmother loaned my husband $30,000 to purchase this apartment complex, referred to as a "winter resort" in the description. The problem was, he had no firm idea of how he would pay back the loan. And he had no real estate experience. I'm sure my grandmother was trying to help smooth the wrinkles in my marriage. She adored my husband and didn't want to hear that I was unhappy. She certainly didn't want me to divorce and become forever ruined like my mother.

Once the apartments were in escrow, and with my grandmother's money on the line, I decided to pack up my two sons, now six months and two and a half years old, and move to "the resort." After all, I had a bit of experience under my belt managing apartments for Dr. Price, and it made sense that I would take the reins. Oh, and my teenaged babysitter came along. She had gained permission from her mother to make the trip, and I wholeheartedly agreed. I needed the help.

Another sweetener in this move was the nursing program at Mesa Community College in Arizona. It had a one-year waiting list for enrollment versus the three-year wait at Indian Valley Community College in California. I had researched nursing programs at several colleges and found that Mesa Community

College had the highest pass rates on the boards.

Also alluring was the fact that about 760 miles would separate me from my circumstances. My husband stayed behind in San Francisco, and in the back of my mind, I secretly wondered if this might be my "out" — a graceful exit and another fresh start.

We made the long road trip in my overstuffed Volvo containing my two sons, the nanny, and copious amounts of boxes, suitcases, and two diaper bags. Mind you, I was around 23 ½ years old at the time. Finally, we pulled up to the property on April 15, not knowing what to expect. I liked what I saw as we walked the premises. The building was in good shape externally and structured around a nice pool in the center. An unfenced pool. This meant my babies could fall in. In short order, I had an important conversation with my babysitter about supervision in general and poolside vigilance specifically.

The interiors were also nice but strangely bare. That raised an alarm bell because they were supposed to be fully furnished, and they were not! The former owner had taken his tenants and much of the furnishings up the street to his other complex, and I was left with the massive and expensive task of replacing lamps, linens, towels, lightbulbs, flatware, dishes, toasters, and more!

Worse, some of the former occupants had left their units in a state of disrepair. This required buckets and buckets of paint and a thorough cleaning of stovetops, floors, and every nook and cranny. Fortunately, my babysitter's father was a house painter, and she was quite handy with a brush. She was upbeat and positive as well and saved me during this transition. Oh, and I learned about defrosting compressors and replacing broken windows, not to mention the glories of plumbing.

This was far more property management responsibility than I had ever faced previously. Purchasing agent, electrician, housekeeper — I did it all and went from skinny to skin and bones. At five foot seven and weighing a whopping 105 pounds,

I now knew how Atlas felt with the weight of the world on his shoulders. But it was an opportunity to learn many trades, wear many hats, and discover a lot about running a business from the ground up, no doubt about it. I was more determined than discouraged and motored on.

The complex came with a four-bedroom house that would have been nice to live in but was already leased. Thus, my small tribe of dependents and I lived in a one-bedroom apartment, the headquarters from which I managed the apartments and tried to figure out how to cover the $3,500 monthly mortgage.

Of course, life couldn't consist of all work and no play, especially for my two baby boys. Fortunately, the complex included an enormous lawn, about a half-acre and very well-manicured, on which they could romp. The grass was soft and green, and that's because the previous owner put a lot of care into the landscaping. I didn't realize it at the time, but I would have to do the same. It took me five hours to water it twice a week, and what a chore that was. Keeping up appearances became part of my marketing plan.

As for marketing, this was brand new territory too, another skill set to master. The bottom line was that I needed summer tenants — and fast. The business model was to lease to snowbirds from Nebraska, New York, Illinois, and Canada during the winter from October to April at three times the summer rental rate. Since this was April, only two tenants remained out of 21 units. What I needed immediately were short-term occupants to fill the vacancies until my winter visitors arrived in October. But that was six months away, and no one was flocking to my oasis. I had to fix that.

The apartment complex was named "The Orioles" after the Baltimore Orioles. At one time, the team used to stay at the complex during training season. That was then and this was now, and I changed the name to the Sun Valley Garden Apartments.

It sounded much more appealing, in my opinion, and it felt pretty darn good that I had the power to make such decisions. I placed a metal vacancy sign near the street. With the help of flyers and newspaper ads, I was soon promoting the Sun Valley Garden Apartments near and far.

And then a miracle happened. It's actually a funny story, almost unbelievable. A couple of polite gentlemen in expensive suits arrived at my doorstep and explained they wanted to set up businesses in the Phoenix area. Somehow, they heard about my multiple empty units and not only signed leases but paid upfront in cash. This included the deposit, the first month's rent, and the last month's rent. I couldn't believe my good fortune and was at 100% occupancy within three months.

These new tenants appeared to be responsible, well mannered, and well off. They drove Cadillac El Dorados, Coupe de Villes, and other expensive cars. What a bonus that seemed, having my parking lot filled with fancy vehicles. It was great advertising for the complex and demonstrated that the Sun Valley Garden Apartments had the highest caliber of tenants.

Then the FBI called.

Yes, the FBI. I was informed that I was leasing to the Mafia. What?! How could that be? I couldn't believe my ears, but it did seem suspicious when the Boss, his wife, his mistress, her daughter, his bodyguard, his brother, and several associates moved in. What did the FBI want me to do about it? It turned out they didn't want me to do anything and were simply informing me about the background of my tenants. And that they'd be monitoring the situation.

Good Lord, I would have rather not known any of this at all because *The Godfather* movie came out in 1972, and its sequel, *The Godfather Part II*, debuted in 1974 — the same year when all of this took place. The FBI had freaked me out, and now thoughts of Al Pacino rattled around in my brain. I called my husband. It seemed the only thing we could do was wait out the short-term lease and pray that no nefarious activities occurred at the complex.

What a relief that my Italian tenants were actually great neighbors. They cooked every Sunday and invited everyone to the pool for authentic cuisine. Otherwise, they kept to themselves. I must give them credit for ensuring my complex was the most secure place to live in the city and perhaps the entire state. My boys could play in front or back in complete safety. No one, and I mean no one, ever caused a ruckus. The Boss was involved in charities and outreach and purchased bicycles at the police auction for all the kids at the complex. He appeared to be the most upstanding resident in the city.

Me and my boys

The only issue I ever had with these generous Italians was toward the end of their lease. The snowbirds started arriving and were shocked and concerned at the scantily clad females who were now coming and going at the complex. What businesses were the Italians establishing? Nude clubs. Actually, they were nude clubs minus the alcohol, which wasn't allowed at that time in these clubs, at least in Phoenix.

I'm not sure why the Italians thought it was appropriate to interview strippers right there at a complex filled with kids and vacationing snowbirds. I was at my wit's end and finally decided to level with them, explaining my dilemma and politely requesting they interview their candidates elsewhere.

Problem solved! They did as I asked, and soon their leases expired. And so, what did I discover about myself as the manager of an apartment complex? The epiphany was that I really was capable of doing anything and pretty darn smart. I could market, negotiate, persuade, and get things done. This realization was the boost I would need to get my nursing license, and years later become the founder of MedAire.

Yet as the Mafia left, a new dynamic entered. My husband decided to leave California and join us in Scottsdale, and so I had another dicey situation on my hands. I wasn't sure what the outcome would be.

Chapter Seven: More Milestones

Dear Optimist, Pessimist, and Realist,
While you guys were busy arguing over the glass of water,
I drank it.
Sincerely, the Opportunist
~ Unknown

My husband had been out of our lives for months, and my babysitter and I were handling things just fine. Yet in that era, just like the eras my mother and grandmother lived through, men were the boss. The king of their castles. The "Grand Poobahs" — a term Fred and Barney used in *The Flintstones* cartoons. I only knew this because my boys and their babysitter liked to watch those shows.

So when my husband arrived, he wanted to take charge of his castle — the apartments, that is. After all, they were newly refurbished. The marketing was working like a charm, and we maintained a decent occupancy rate, at least enough to break even. However, the tenants were used to coming to me with apartment-related issues, which created more trouble in a marriage that was already on life support. That, and the fact that our sons were so young. They had to reacquaint and re-bond with their father. I would call us an awkward little family, but a family nonetheless.

We hung in there and discussed what to do with the property. There weren't a lot of options — either we could set down permanent roots in Scottsdale or sell the complex. I didn't want the apartments in the first place, so the decision was easy from my end. Fortunately for me, my husband agreed to sell so that he could open a business school and I could enroll in the nursing program at Mesa Community College.

That's what I wanted. My heart ached for a career in nursing, and it very privately dawned on me that with a formal education and nursing license, I could be self-sufficient and support my sons in the event of a divorce.

My marriage wasn't working out, I wasn't getting any younger, and most of all, I wasn't beholden to the edicts of my grandmother's Catholicism. I needed to be prepared for any contingency, including divorce, and if I didn't make the leap into nursing now, then when?

We packed up the boys and relocated to Mesa near my campus, a great place to live and work. I was in pre-nursing and had an evening job as a unit secretary at Scottsdale Memorial Hospital. My babysitter quit to attend school herself, and I hired someone new to help me balance the needs of the boys, my morning coursework, and my 3-11 shift.

Due to this arrangement (and to my eternal embarrassment), my grandmother's loan payments were set aside. She never received full repayment, and I felt torn and helpless in that regard. We were in the red as much as we were in the black, barely making it, and it was distressing. I knew how hard she worked for her money. It came from her life savings, and a $30,000 loan in those days is the equivalent of $125,000 in today's economy — an astronomical amount from that perspective.

I was raised to avoid debt. If I didn't have cash, I didn't make a purchase. If a rare, unavoidable type of debt had to be incurred, such as a mortgage, I was taught to pay it off as quickly as possible. I was taught to be financially responsible and frugal. And I was taught to keep my word. And yet, my grandmother encouraged me to focus on my education. I was able to become a nurse because she believed in me.

"Go to nursing school," she said. "You won't be sorry." That was more important to her than any loan.

Transferring whatever credits I could from Golden Gate University and Indian Valley Community College, I got started, diving first into the remaining prerequisites and coursework, and then into the hands-on environment of labs and hospital settings. The curriculum at Mesa Community College was thrilling. I recall taking courses in biology, microbiology, chemistry, human

Grandmother Mary

anatomy, physiology, critical thinking, science, mathematics, nursing theory, psychology, and modern dance as an elective—and that was back in the '70s. Today's curriculum is likely more exacting and challenging, and there are specialties to pursue as well.

By the way, I scored highest in psychology, although I had an aversion to the coursework. My mother's mental challenges, her suffering, and my childhood had exposed me to these topics early on, which I believe helped my grades. Yet, the class reminded me of a very painful past. I would have skipped psychology altogether if it had been allowed.

I was entering a profession with a growing number of

opportunities in many fields — cardiac nurses, nurse anesthetists, ER nurses, family nurse practitioners, geriatric nurses, O/R nurses, oncology nurses, flight nurses, and mental health nurses just to name a few. It's remarkable, this wide-open and ever-evolving vocation. And yes, I had (and have) a special level of respect for nurses who work in the realm of mental health, knowing they help not just patients, but also affected families. I wish we knew more about the treatment of mental illness when my family was caught in the throes of my mother's ordeal. Unfortunately, all I witnessed was the fallout when the pharmaceuticals and therapies didn't work.

My job as a unit secretary helped me soak up terminology, medical systems, diagnoses, etc. Around this time, my kids were starting elementary school. There was a definite sacrifice of family time, but I had to work to earn an income. Otherwise, we wouldn't have a roof over our heads or food on the table.

I moved forward in my nursing training, in awe of the flexibility and adaptability of nurses in general, and the variety of roles they filled. I was about to fill several of those roles myself. After the first year of nursing school, I could "sit the boards" to become a licensed practical nurse (LPN) and was able to earn more money while employing my nursing skills at the same time. I worked as a student nurse as part of my clinical rotation in my second year. Two aspects of hospital nursing appealed to me as a student nurse. I felt the maternity floor was a happy place where babies were born and the moms were thrilled with their new arrivals. The emergency room was also a draw — the fast pace and adrenaline rush fit my skillsets and personality. After taking various trauma and cardiac courses, I was the sole student among my classmates who knew, without a doubt, that this line of work was right for me.

Graduating with an associate's degree in nursing and becoming a registered nurse was a huge milestone, something I had chased for years! My grandmother graduated from the Mary Help Hospital training school for nurses on September 16, 1920. I proudly keep her certificate in my family archives today, a reminder of the noble nursing tradition in my family. My mother graduated as a diploma-registered nurse. And at long last, I graduated with honors from Mesa Community College in 1978 as a registered nurse, just shy of my thirtieth birthday and 58 years after my grandmother's graduation.

My grandmother's nursing certificate, earned after three years of study

It was a proud moment for me, my grandmother, my sons, and also my soon-to-be ex-husband. They had all witnessed me tackle this difficult goal. The boys have always been proud of me, but more importantly, they could count on me despite my grueling schedule. And there was more of that ahead. Since my heart was set on emergency medicine, there were qualifications to pursue to become a critical care nurse. During my last year of nursing school, I became a basic life support provider, an advanced cardiac life support provider, and an instructor in advanced cardiac life support (ACLS).

Normally, in order to work in an acute care setting, it required three years of "floor" experience. This was not something I wanted to wait for. After scheduling an appointment with Viola Cochran, head of the emergency department, I postulated that I was going to get the job — positive thinking, no doubt. I walked in and presented all of my certifications and then begged her to take a chance on me.

"You will not regret it," I promised. I was hired and overjoyed at this news. It confirmed that being an over-achiever had its rewards. This position became an excellent steppingstone into further learning and career opportunities.

My temporary license was in effect for three months before I received my official license after passing the nursing boards. I donned my hat, white uniform, and white shoes, and it was off to an exciting new start in the emergency department of Desert Samaritan Hospital (DHS) in Mesa, Arizona. I was in my element and loved the fast pace, never knowing what would come through the door next. After a few months, I decided to apply for a charge nurse position in the emergency department. I was offered the job and said "YES" to that opportunity as well — a real fast-tracking of my career.

As an ER nurse with some educational background in teaching advanced life support, I still had no clue about pre-hospital care in receiving patients from ambulances. Yet, I was promoted to Paramedic Base Hospital Coordinator — another example of saying yes and learning by doing. I was responsible for continuing education for paramedic units in fire departments for the cities of Chandler, Tempe, and Mesa, Arizona, 11 rescue units in all. I knew I could master and lead the paramedic training and add valuable insights into the program. I then co-developed curricula in a unique paramedic training program that enabled students to obtain an associate degree, as well as their paramedic certification, a first in Arizona or anywhere west of the Mississippi. Yes, another milestone. Once again, this career trajectory is an excellent example of the power of "yes" — a remarkable word that opens up possibilities in numerous, life-changing ways.

I should backtrack a bit and explain what was percolating under the surface as I passed my boards. My marriage hadn't improved. I moved out of the house to stay with a fellow nurse who lived nearby. During this trial separation, I left the boys with their father, not wanting to uproot them from their familiar surroundings. He and I made several attempts to make an irreconcilable marriage work. Yet after a lot of prayer and soul searching, the divorce commenced, not a decision I made lightly. It was extremely hard on my sons, in particular, my oldest son. He begged me not to go through with it and was just devastated.

I think that's the most difficult thing as a parent, making life decisions that impact your children. Perhaps other divorced women can attest to this feeling of being between a rock and a hard place. No matter the decision, someone would be hurt. Yet, I sensed that I could not do what I was meant to do if I was trapped in this marriage and listened to a deep internal ping that told me that an impending but undefined mission was in my future. It's rather difficult to explain because it was a feeling, a sense of knowing, or perhaps a fuzzy premonition. I had no clue what that mission would be, but if I was to undertake it, the end result could not be achieved within this marriage. That much was certain.

It turned out that MedAire would be the mission, although I didn't realize any of this at the time. I had to focus on my present circumstances and get stabilized in a new reality of single motherhood and a demanding career. Work was a must, as there was no other source of income. It was up to me to support my boys on a nursing salary and provide insurance.

I scrimped and saved to enroll my boys in a private Christian school, the best education I could possibly give them. I wanted them to have a foundation in faith from which to grow, learn, and heal from the disruption in our family and the pain of the divorce, not to mention a platform from which they would become young scholars. I didn't want them indoctrinated by a public school system that seemed to be veering away from the values instilled and passed down by my great-grandfather — a love of God, a sense of patriotism, and respect for parents and the elderly. My prayers were always that my children would find comfort in their faith and courage in their journeys.

Me and Josh spending rare quality time together

Aside from the divorce, I was feeling more confident and competent than I ever thought possible, both personally and professionally. I was meant for nursing, and nursing was meant for me. I could feel it. My grandmother assured me that this career path would improve every paradigm in my professional life, and she was absolutely correct. What an extraordinary feeling to be following in her footsteps and my mother's footsteps too, as if I was fulfilling my destiny.

Chapter Eight: My Calling

Save one life, you're a hero. Save a hundred lives, you're a nurse.

~ Unknown

For any aspiring nurses out there, you might enjoy hearing about the history and background of our profession through the eyes of my grandmother Mary and why I found it so compelling. I always appreciated her great gift as a storyteller. I mentioned she lived through the infamous San Francisco earthquake of 1906, but also the industrial revolution that thrust her into a "modern world" of gas-driven cars and talking motion pictures. World War I and II followed, and then the Korean and Vietnam Wars.

What an interesting perspective my grandmother had regarding the roles of nurses on and off the battlefield. She was not a war nurse, for she graduated from nursing school in 1920, two years after World War I ended on Armistice Day in 1918. To coin a phrase, she "dodged a flu bullet" because the infamous Spanish flu outbreak was so common among the enlisted and also the general population.

Grandmother Mary recalled the winter of 1918 as the coldest ever, with 100 million dying — more in 24 weeks than from AIDS in 24 years. She compared it to the Black Death of the 1300s and the Great Plague of London (bubonic) in the 1600s when horse-drawn carts and drivers picked up bodies in the street and hauled corpses.

So little was known about this illness, or viral transmission in general. Influenza attached to the respiratory system and spliced the blood cells, causing horrific bleeding on the skin, face, and eyes. Epidemiology was still in its infancy, penicillin hadn't yet been discovered, gloves weren't in use (at least not much), masks were in short supply, and basic first aid kits weren't offered until 1924 (six years too late). Farmers were required to send their sons and field workers to the battlefields, and young, single nurses, most in their late teens and early twenties, were shipped overseas to military bases to care for the troops. These nurses were exposed to highly unsanitary conditions. Hand washing was next to impossible in battlefield arenas. They died along with service members overseas, and those who survived were shipped back home. Some nurses carried the disease with them.

Emergency hospital at Brookline, Massachusetts to care for influenza cases – Photo credit: National Archives, The Unwritten Record

Military personnel in American training camps also spread the disease, all young, strapping soldiers. This was a frightening time in world history and somewhat parallels the COVID-19 pandemic of the years 2020 and 2021. My grandmother and her parents, all San Franciscans, were encouraged by the Board of Health to wear masks — a trend across the U.S. and mandated in some areas. She told me about how food and fuel were rationed. They took cable cars and trains — no cars were on the road.

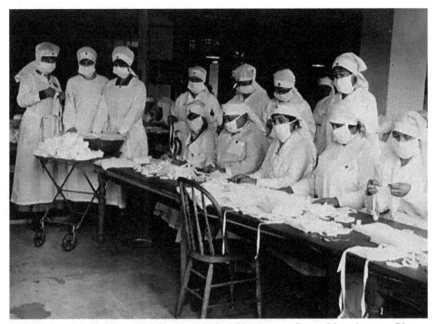

Red Cross workers making anti-influenza masks for soldiers in camp. Boston, Massachusetts. – Photo credit: National Archives, The Unwritten Record

President Woodrow Wilson focused like a laser on the war effort and controlled every aspect of life. Censorship of free speech and the press was rampant (as was propaganda for the war movement) while the president strove to "make the world safe for democracy." But oddly, the president didn't publicly address the Spanish Flu, despite escalating deaths in Europe and stateside in training camps.

This contrasts with those in higher office here in America who have spoken out about COVID-19 and the various new drugs that could save lives. These prophylactics were labeled as "misinformation" and discounted until this book neared publication during the summer of 2021. Practicing physicians who knew better attempted to speak out and were dismissed, and the suppression of medical knowledge was dismaying and very likely cost lives. In my opinion, there must be a "right to try" various drug regimens, especially when it appears as a last ditch effort. History will tell the story as it did in 1918.

Police court officials of San Francisco holding a session in the open, as a precaution against the spreading influenza epidemic – Photo credit: National Archives, The Unwritten Record

For historical context, I highly recommend *The Great Influenza* by John Barry[8] for its eye-opening account of what young, healthy nurses endured without the ability to protect themselves with readily available gloves or masks and therefore dying like flies. The book also showcased the forced recruitment of anyone with any type of medical skills to help the military and the restrictions placed on the public. Several good articles exist online that describe this overwhelming period in time as well.[9]

---

[8] For further reading, I suggest John Barry's book for its vivid detailing of the Spanish flu pandemic.

John M. Barry. *The great influenza: The story of the deadliest pandemic in history* (Penguin UK, 2020).

[9]Shirley Williams. "World War One: The many battles faced by WW1's nurses," *BBC,* April 2, 2014, https://www.bbc.com/news/magazine-26838077 (accessed May 4, 2021).

Speaking of today's pandemic from a business perspective, the pre-COVID travel industry was booming. But according to the International Air Transport Association (IATA), travel decreased 65% in 2021 with a $370 billion decline in revenue. Travel restrictions and public fear have been distinguishing factors in the drop in flights. Businesses have had to make difficult decisions and get very creative in order to survive. That has been apparent across the board in various sectors, and MedAire, like other companies, has adapted.

My grandmother could never have envisioned the test runs experienced by MedAire that led up to this current challenge in the travel sector. The 9/11 attack in New York City, the Severe Acute Respiratory Syndrome (SARS) of 2002, the H1N1 swine flu of 2009, and the more recent avian (bird) flu — all had an impact of some sort on our customers. In fact, most outbreaks, epidemics, or pandemics can affect travel regionally, nationally, or internationally.

The differences are noteworthy. SARS was a small but unusual outbreak with an abnormally escalating number of cases. An epidemic, technically, is an outbreak over a larger area and spreading. Oddly, HIV/AIDs is referred to as an epidemic by the World Health Organization, although it's a global disease.

Centers for Disease Control. "1918 Pandemic Influenza Historic Timeline," https://www.cdc.gov/flu/pandemic-resources/1918-commemoration/pandemic-timeline-1918.htm (accessed May 31, 2021).

Christopher B. Daly. "How Woodrow Wilson's Propaganda Machine Changed American Journalism," *Smithsonian Magazine,* April 28, 2017, https://www.smithsonianmag.com/history/how-woodrow-wilsons-propaganda-machine-changed-american-journalism-180963082/ (accessed April 31, 2021).

"American Hospital of Paris Ambulance," *American Nursing History,* https://www.americannursinghistory.org/military-nurses-in-wwi (accessed June 19, 2021).

Carol R. Byerly, "The U.S. Military and the Influenza Pandemic of 1918–1919," 2010, *Public Health Report,* https://www.ncbi.nlm.nih.gov/pmc/articles/PMC2862337/citedby/ (accessed June 1, 2021).

Generally, any global and pervasive disease or illness is referred to as a pandemic, for example, the COVID pandemic we are currently experiencing worldwide.

American Red Cross activities in Middletown, Connecticut. Emergency Hospital equipment being inspected by the committee of the Middlesex Chapter. This equipment was sent to Wesleyan University at the outbreak of the Influenza epidemic – Photo credit: National Archives, The Unwritten Record

Grandmother Mary shared other stories and was particularly interested in the history of the nursing profession. She was fascinated with "bucket brigades" in which nurses stepped up in supportive roles outside of their regular duties. This often involved manual labor during any number of escapades.

She spoke of the bucket brigades of the Civil War that involved nurses who formed human chains to bring water and supplies to the battlefield. They trekked through the horrors of musket fire and puddles of blood and assisted in tents and cabins — bathing, bandaging and holding down the wounded during amputations.

Variations of these bucket brigades exist in nursing history, and my grandmother knew of nurses who assisted fire departments in passing pails of water toward burning buildings. Her favorite example was the "Sky Girls" of Ellen Church's era, the same Ellen Church who became the first nurse stewardess aboard a United Flight. In white shoes and stockings and dressed to the 9's in their jackets and skirts, these nurses-stewardesses also formed bucket brigades to pass fuel to the airplanes.

Can you imagine how carefully they must have handled those containers of fuel to avoid sloshing it on their uniforms? Few things could be worse than having flammable liquid seep into the fabric of their clothing. The safety aspects alone are mind-boggling, but also the thought of what fumes from the fuel would do to the eyes and throats of passengers and the flight crew. The planes had no air conditioning and thus poor ventilation in those days.

According to the book *From Sky Girl to Flight Attendant: Women and the Making of a Union*, these "Sky Girls" also carried baggage on board, sat on the mail sacks in flight, and sometimes helped pilots push planes into hangars. I highly recommend this book for those interested in a historical account and snapped it up after it was published in 1982, eager to learn more about the legendary nurse stewardesses my grandmother spoke of. I read the book in her memory just after she passed away in 1983.

Unfortunately, grandmother Mary did not live to see the day in 2003 when the military expanded the roles of nurses in Brigade Combat Teams. Today, brigade nurses work within the Army and NATO and assist surgeons and physician assistants, oversee medic training and immunizations, and more. She would be so proud of the military brigade nurses and all of the specializations available today.

The world of nursing was extremely different when my grandmother answered the call. In 1920, the nursing colleges were overflowing with students. Nursing candidates were required to be single and of the highest moral caliber. Amidst a lot of competition, she was accepted and found that student nurses were often used as "cheap labor" — the cleaning crews, so to speak — and also substitutes for licensed nurses. Nursing students were paid pennies on the dollar. Still, my grandmother gained valuable experience and entered the workforce when tuberculosis and polio were issues, front and center of a worried public with a focus on eradication.

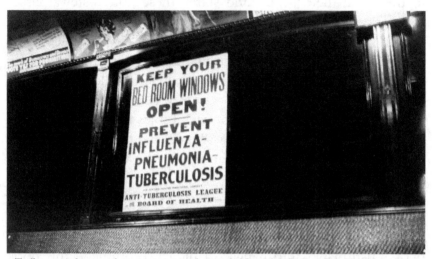

Trolley car windows were kept open to prevent the spread of Spanish Influenza which did much to slow up war progress in this country. This photo was taken in Cincinnati. The practice of keeping windows open was nationwide." Photo credit: National Archives, The Unwritten Record

Grandmother Mary was tasked with sputum collection, treatment monitoring, and updating patient charts — a high-risk exposure to latent TB infection and TB-positive patients. She was truly on the front line, for TB was a dreaded disease and a leading cause of death in the United States. Not all nurses left their shifts unscathed, and some died in the line of duty. My grandmother was spared and eventually gravitated toward surgical and post-surgical care.

And then Great Depression hit. Grandmother Mary shared her views on how this era affected the nursing profession, stating that many nurses lost their jobs. This was devastating as most were living paycheck to paycheck with little, if any, savings. Some went on "relief" or government assistance, but my grandmother managed to stay employed and keep food on the table, considering she was basically a single mother with an absent husband and a daughter to raise. However, she told me that during the Great Depression, she sometimes stole milk from doorsteps to feed my mother. Still, she must have been good at her profession and truly called to be a nurse because she worked in hospitals for more than 30 years.

Her training seemed so basic compared to mine. As she told it, even licensed nurses were the "handmaidens of the physician." She was completely subservient to the doctors she worked for. They were omnipotent and rarely, if ever, interested in the opinions and intuitions of their underlings, at least in her experience. While my grandmother was allowed to apply a mustard plaster or collect saliva and urine samples, she could not take a blood pressure reading. She could apply bandages but in no way was allowed to make decisions on behalf of her patients. Nor could she advocate for her patients, which seemed so strange to me since advocacy is part of nursing coursework today. Imagine her shock when I shared my dream of becoming a flight nurse and all the inherent dangers and emergency procedures this career path entailed — chest tubes, intubations, and even burring holes in skulls to relieve pressure in the brain. She was aghast. .

As a matter of fact, she would say, "Oh, go to grass!" in disbelief, one of her old expressions. But despite her encroaching dementia, she was quite proud of my role as a flight nurse. Sadly, we buried my beloved grandmother before she could appreciate my flight nursing career. I was sad that she wasn't there to witness this enormous milestone, for she was so instrumental in helping me achieve it. I sense that up in heaven she knows how her special stories of Ellen Church and the "Sky Girls" influenced my decision to become a "flying nurse."

Rarely is any fame attached to being a nurse. A sense of altruism, a call to duty, a life saved — that's the reward with few exceptions. Florence Nightingale and Clara Barton of the American Red Cross — and perhaps Ellen Church — did achieve acclaim. But most nurses labor behind the scenes with little recognition.

The spotlight seemed to shine on athletes and celebrities instead, that is, until COVID-19 hit. Suddenly, the importance of what medical professionals do was front, center, and in the news. In my opinion, our dependence on nurses had been sorely understated up to this point. A nurse's calling is to serve humanity — and I do mean serve — and that is what ultimately matters. Yet, it took a pandemic for the invisible staff in hospitals to share some portion of the limelight. It dawned on the public that unnamed caregivers in nursing homes were incredibly brave, and a new appreciation surfaced. And who could get testing and vaccinations without the background support of clinic staff? These brave nurses often stood in parking lots to dispense swabs or shots to drive-through recipients or stood in temporary tents to do the same.

I'm such a strong advocate for nurses and promote the vocation every chance I get. When I die, the nicest thing a person could possibly say in remembering me is: "She was the greatest nurse." That would be the ultimate compliment and the very best eulogy I can imagine because I believe nurses and first responders are heroes — superheroes. They often care for multiple patients in teams or individually and must constantly keep up with new treatments and cutting-edge technologies. They compassionately interact with families during the most trying of times and run toward danger while everyone else scatters. The instinct is to help, and that's admirable.

So absolutely, nursing is a calling, a high calling, and I'm proud that my mother and grandmother answered the call and influenced me to do the same. Some families become political dynasties. Some become Hollywood dynasties. My family was barely middle-class and had no name recognition or notability, but I believe we managed to forge a dynasty anyway — a humble three-generation dynasty of nurses.

Chapter Nine: Taking Flight

Modesty? Please! I'm a nurse. I've seen more privates than an
Army General.
~ Unknown

I served as the Desert Samaritan Hospital paramedic coordinator and paramedic trainer for three years, beginning in 1978. During one of the student practicals onboard a ground ambulance, a helicopter landed at an accident scene. I saw firsthand how the flight nurse jumped out and quickly assessed the situation. The patient was intubated — load and go — and I liked all of the action. It seemed I had the temperament, skill set, and personality needed in this unique frontline environment. Flight nursing in the U.S. began in the late 1960s for both fixed-wing and rotary-wing aircraft, and prior to that in the 1940s Air Force, a proud tradition.

I applied and was accepted into the Flight Nurse Training Program, which entailed 13 weeks of physician-led instruction on all aspects of emergency medicine and aviation-related safety, including altitude physiology as it related to every disease process. Coursework included neurologic and spinal cord injuries, obstetrical emergencies, care and transport of the neonate, pediatrics, extrication and scene management, flight physiology and triage, communications, aircraft safety, survival principles, risk management, quality assurance, and toxicology— to name a few.

There is no way to overemphasize the value of this training — the highest level I could receive without being a doctor, exceeding even most military and other programs. Specialty physicians and emergency room doctors equipped us to deliver excellent high-level trauma and critical care.

I graduated and accepted a position with Samaritan Air Evac in 1981, the largest air medical program in the country. Thus, I entered a dangerous field, knowing I could make a difference. The decision would change everything, I later discovered.

The Air Evac team (I'm on the bottom left.) – Photo courtesy of PHI Air Medical – Photo credit: Samaritan Hospital

This "adrenaline chapter" is filled with the feats and stories of rescue and evacuation. As a flight nurse on board helicopters of every make and model, I was designated chief medical officer and flew with a pilot and paramedic. For fixed-wing flights, most of our calls were hospital-to-hospital transports, all critical care cases. These particular flight teams included a single pilot, respiratory therapist, and flight nurse. Other specialty flights were staffed for maternal and neonatal transports with specialty nurses.

By the way, there was no hazardous duty pay in most of the aeromedical programs. For instance, in Chicago, flight nurses flew with resident doctors, whereby the resident was the chief medical officer (versus the flight nurse). I asked why we didn't fly with resident doctors too, and was told, "You are easier to replace," or "It's too expensive."

We never knew what awaited with each scramble. Our mission was to care for severely injured and ill patients, treating them and keeping them as stable as possible during transport out of the most remote areas imaginable. If you are familiar with Arizona, by "remote" I mean desolate areas such as mountains, deserts, state land, reservations, unpopulated landscapes, and "no man's land."

There was no end to the life and death emergencies, and there was never a "good" call. It was always a race against death, with one foot in the grave and the other slipping. Although the role of a flight nurse is certainly not for everyone, I was drawn to the specialized critical care level of training, medical skillsets, decision-making, and ingenuity involved in each scenario.

We flew patients to whichever hospital was equipped to handle a specific emergency in closest proximity. This was often a level I trauma center or tertiary care center, depending on the severity of injury or illness. My team might respond to a gunshot victim, a heart attack, an animal attack, a car crash, near drowning, or third-degree burns — and the next day respond to a gangland execution, a suicide, or a pediatric drowning (the worst). Fridays were paydays, and it never failed that the "knife and gun club" was out in full force. We picked up the pieces.

Our pilots usually had military backgrounds (Vietnam, especially), which explained why they were so comfortable dodging high power lines, flying at night, and landing in dubious conditions while avoiding "cumulous granite" mountains.

During summer monsoons, we dealt with dust storms and occasional severe thunderstorms that dimmed visibility and were downright scary. Imagine hovering over a cliff, one skid on an embankment and the other midair, blades whirling and debris kicking up. I would climb out with my paramedic, and we backboarded and stabilized the patient to the best of our ability. Then we loaded the patient and the pilot flew us to the appropriate trauma center. Our patients' lives depended on this type of impromptu innovation and teamwork.

A rescue helicopter against the backdrop of a cumulous granite mountain – Photo credit: Patty Campbell

The pilots themselves were not supposed to be physically or emotionally involved in-patient treatment. In other words, if they knew a mother and infant were in distress or knew a mountain climber was fending off a mountain lion, their natural compulsion might be to "push the envelope" so to speak, to make the mission. That would not bode well for the accident rate. Helicopters and fixed-wing planes were already involved in crashes far too often (one out of every thirteen helicopter programs at that time). Instead, they were to focus on flight safety, deploying, landing, and moving patients from point A to point B. These flights were either hospital-to-hospital transports or scene calls interfacing with police and firefighters.

Fatigue contributed to the accident rate. Pilots worked long hours for $17,000 a year in those days. Sometimes after our shifts ended, I took the pilots to my home and served them breakfast.

Air Evac boasts a group of pilots with a combined total of 91 years of helicopter experience (Thank you, Uncle Sam!) – L-R: Gary Loban (U.S. Army), Larry Brice, Lynn DeVries, Joe Waters, Neil Finch Photo courtesy of PHI Air Medical. Photo credit: Samaritan Hospital

In safety meetings, we pinpointed another reason for the increase in helicopter crashes. Some of our experienced military pilots were retiring, and civilian pilots took their place. Many of the new civilian entrants didn't have raw war experience to rely on, which definitely honed skills and prepared pilots for the rigors of the Arizona terrain. Our flight paramedics were also highly-trained and very savvy about how on-scene calls were handled. They often worked part-time in their flight roles and full time at fire departments where they saw much of the same type of trauma.

Sometimes I'm asked how emergency flight teams handle the human suffering on an emotional level. Every case, every patient, took a toll. You never get used to it, yet our excellent training prepared us to compartmentalize and react appropriately. For me personally, this was my calling, something quite natural and what I was meant to do. I was good at my job and proud to be a flight nurse.

I was taught to focus like a laser on the situation at hand, in the heat of the moment when seconds mattered and minutes could mean life or death. My mental checklist was deeply ingrained, and I triaged these emergencies with the support of street-savvy Air Evac paramedics who knew how to manage a scene. We instinctively worked as a team and divided responsibilities, interfacing with local paramedics as well. Sometimes we could load, go, and treat patients in the helicopter. In other cases, we responded to a sheriff's call with very little care given prior to our arrival and treated patients on the ground before transport.

There wasn't much we could do other times except fly the patient directly to the hospital. For instance, once a rock climber was envenomated by a Gila monster (named for Arizona's Gila River basin). This large lizard's gnawing teeth and rotating jaw injected poison into the victim's hand. It would not release its vise-like grip, and we had no choice but to transport the Gila monster with the patient aboard the helicopter.

Helicopters lined up on the helipad – Photo courtesy of PHI Air Medical – Photo credit: Samaritan Hospital

Often, the blood, guts, and gore were the very clues that helped us assess what was wrong and take action. As always, there was no room for emotion. I had the tools needed to take care of my patients and kept all of my equipment organized and color-coded. I knew what type of pouch to open, what to unwrap, and automatically reached for the right apparatus. In hindsight, this organized approach would prove invaluable when I launched MedAire and supplied medical kits to the aviation and maritime industries — sort of a foreshadowing of the innovations that would drastically improve safety in the travel industry.

At the same time, I was a representative of the profession and interacted with the public during extremely anxious events. I was clearly in my element and interfaced with other medical colleagues such as nurses, doctors, and sometimes the medical examiner and police officers and sheriff's deputies as an emissary for the medical community.

We were prepared for anything, although at times, that wasn't enough for my patients. In some instances, I exhausted my repertoire of knowledge and needed assistance while transporting a critical patient. I got on the radio and consulted with ground-based emergency room doctors who provided real-time guidance. They gave advice about procedures, drugs, and medical decisions, which saved untold lives. Thank God for these supervising physicians who listened as I explained what I had done and asked what else I could do to help with the outcome. The ability to reach out for medical advice was so crucial that it also planted a subconscious seed regarding the need for global telemedicine (more on this later as well).

How interesting to see the best and worst of human nature during these emergencies. Once a man tied a rope around his ankle and the other end to a tree at the bank of a river. This was so he could find his way back to shore while swimming upstream after drinking a fifth of vodka. We rescued him and performed a nasotracheal intubation in the middle of the river, inserting an endotracheal tube through his nose and into the trachea and inflating a balloon to keep it in place, providing him oxygen. This patient sued us because one of his shoes had been lost during the rescue (the case was thrown out, of course).

My paramedic, Lisa Cardareli, and I transported a prisoner from Casa Grande to the hospital in Phoenix, a 30-minute flight following the highway. We loaded the prisoner and assumed he had been thoroughly searched according to protocol. Wrong! Once we were airborne, Lisa reached over the prisoner to tighten his safety belt (she was at his head and I was at his side). Suddenly, we saw the knife in his hand, and he nearly stabbed her. We managed to wrangle the knife out of harm's way, then calmed him with morphine. I made a call following the flight and demanded that the prisoners be weapon-free the next time we made a transport.

Lisa and I also flew into Young, Arizona, at night. There are a lot of mountains between Phoenix and the outskirts, and that's when experienced pilots really show their skills. We were called to a home in this very rural setting during snowy winter conditions without enough lights to safely land. Neighbors drove in and pointed their headlights to an area where we could set down. I remember the snow being so cold, but the house was hotter than Hades the minute we walked through the door, thanks to a large pot-belly stove.

Then, bizarrely, family members on the right told us, "Let him die." The people on the left said, "Save him." Lisa and I looked at each other and then at the elderly man who laid on the sofa, barely breathing and unconscious.

I turned to the people who wanted him to die and responded, "We're here to save this patient, and the ability to hear is the last sense to go." This let them know that the poor elderly patient was likely aware of the debate over his fate, and also discouraged them from discussing it further. We intubated the patient and flew him to Phoenix.

I married again, this time to a talented cardiothoracic surgeon who happened to have his pilot's license. We met in the emergency room during a trauma situation. He had sole custody of four sons. Combined with my boys, six children depended on me and an absent husband who was always on call or in surgery.

On occasion, I had to scrub in to talk to him! On the upside, we lived on an amazing estate with a stunning pool and lots of room in which a band of boys could play. Never before had my sons lived in the lap of luxury or been exposed to affluence, so this was an intriguing experience for them.

On the downside, my sons never got to know their stepfather because he simply wasn't present. I felt lonely, even surrounded by six energy bundles, several household pets, and a demanding job. We were like two ships passing in the night, and a lingering sense of disappointment prevailed. I do believe he loved me, but really just needed a mother for his children. It felt overwhelming to be raising six boys on my own while holding down a much-cherished job and dreaming of future advancement. I felt that I was drowning without a life jacket in sight.

The union was short-lived for obvious reasons. I talked it over with my sons, who had no real objections to the divorce. I kicked myself for ever agreeing to the marriage in the first place and left with nothing, not that I expected anything. I had willingly signed a premarital agreement that made sure of it — no ifs, ands, or buts — and walked away from a fleetingly lavish lifestyle, relieved to do so. Perhaps wedlock wasn't meant for me after all. I had my hands full with a demanding career and my own little family.

This second marriage was why the news media referred to me as Joan McCorkle when reporting on Air Evac rescues. Charles Thornton, an *Arizona Republic* medical writer, described my encounter with Lucy Evans, a 63-year-old Oregonian who was visiting Arizona with her husband and experienced a cardiac event:[10]

> *'Without her, I wouldn't be here,' Evans said from her home at Hood River, Ore. 'She just wouldn't give up on me.' The 'she' is Joan McCorkle, 35, an athletic-looking flight nurse for Air Evac who didn't quail when it came to performing an operation normally*

---

[10] Charles Thornton." Wouldn't Give Up: Flight Nurse Operates, Saves Lives," *Arizona Republic*, September 7, 1984.
https://www.newspapers.com/newspage/120156510/ (accessed April 5, 2021).

done only by a physician in a hospital.

When pain ran through her arm and exploded in her chest, Lucy's husband, Paul, called for help, and she was taken by ambulance to the nearest hospital in Parker, Arizona. We were dispatched to fly her to a trauma center in Phoenix.

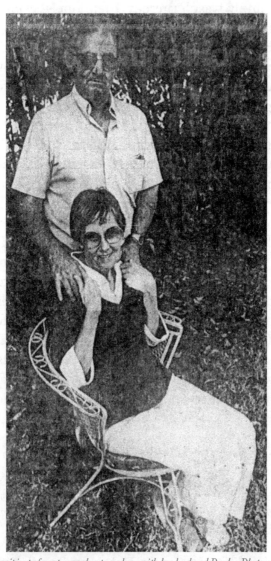

Lucy Evans, recipient of my pacemaker procedure, with her husband Paul – Photo credit: Arizona Republic

When I arrived in Parker at a very small medical facility, Lucy seemed relatively stable in an intensive care area. Yet as my paramedic and I loaded her into the helicopter, she went into a third-degree heart block and then ventricular fibrillation. It was pretty obvious that she had blockage in the electrical system of her heart. Of the heart's four chambers, the right anatomical chamber contains the sinoatrial node (also known as the SA node) that controls electrical impulses to the lower chambers. This causes contractions (the pumping of the ventricles). When blockage interrupts the electrical signal, a patient can experience all kinds of chaotic rhythms due to a lack of oxygen to the heart.

I checked Lucy's rhythms on a mobile electrocardiogram (EKG) machine and watched the cardiac monitors, which indicated a right ventricular infarct or heart attack. In essence, the only way to convert fibrillation is through defibrillation — a transfer of energy conducted between two areas on chest. We shocked her, and she remained unstable. We continued to shock her as we unloaded her and headed back to the emergency room.

The ER doctor took over and continued to shock Lucy, and then realized he had used all the batteries in his small emergency department. So he began to use my batteries.

Then he said, "What she needs is a pacemaker. I don't have one."

I said, "I do."

"I've never placed a pacemaker," he responded.

"I have," I assured him and instructed my paramedic to retrieve the pacemaker kit from the helicopter.

I should pause here and explain how I was able to perform pacemaker procedures. In continuing education classes, we practiced on cadavers and inserted chest tubes and pacemakers into anesthetized elderly dogs doomed to be euthanized, as well as other life-saving procedures. My God, I love dogs. I love all animals and am aware of the noxious reaction this training may evoke. I had to remind myself that these types of teaching interventions saved untold human lives and that the "death row" dogs ultimately played an enormous and noble role.

Newspaper image from Lucy Evan's article – Photo credit: Arizona Republic

If not for that experience, Lucy Evans may not have survived a cardiac arrest. In short, I inserted a sterile needle about ten inches long below the diaphragm. I looked down, envisioned a dog's chest, and had my landmarks. All the training kicked in, and I took the needle through the diaphragm, through heart muscle, and then threaded my wires through the needle into the heart chamber. I attached other end of the wires into the pulse generator that transmitted an electrical signal and caused the ventricles to pump.

How did I know it worked? I felt a carotid pulse. And then my cardiac monitor batteries died. We immediately re-loaded Lucy into the helicopter and high tailed it to Phoenix to the tertiary care center. She was unconscious and I constantly checked her pulse, which told me she was getting blood to her brain, heart, and vital organs.

Once we arrived at the trauma center, I was met with exclamations from the emergency staff and cardiologist — "You actually put in a pacemaker?" and "This is amazing!" and "I think this is the first, if not the only, transthoracic pacemaker procedure that has ever been successful!"

My response was, "I was just doing my job." That may sound corny, but honestly, it was the simple truth and all in a day's work.

They took Lucy to surgery put in a real pacemaker. I went back the next day to check on her. She raised her fist above her sternum and indicated it hurt. She wasn't real happy with me (I had probably separated her ribs from her sternum during CPR), and thus was sore for more reasons than one!

"Hey, it saved your life," I told her, "and you'll feel better soon." What a relief that she was well enough to communicate. In fact, she recovered fully and lived another 11 years. I kept in touch with her son Roger in Washington state who kindly sent me apples quite a few years thereafter.

In 1984, Samaritan Air Evac promoted me to Director of Flight Personnel for Air Evac. In the course of my new duties, I was asked to be an American Hospital Association Representative for Arizonans to protect quality health care. This involved representing the health care professions in an active campaign to defeat propositions on the ballot, which would have devastating effects on health care in the state.

My stance against Proposition 200, in particular, was published in the Yuma Sun.[11] I believed the proposition threatened the emergency care of Arizonans who might experience accidents, injuries, or critical illnesses and need transportation by airplane

---

[11] My op-ed was published in various media. I'm citing the *Yuma Sun* here. Quality Care Editor. "Letter to the Editor from Joan E. Mccorkle, RN, DDG.RN, Director of Flight Personnel Air Evac," *Yuma Sun*, October 16, 1984. https://newspaperarchive.com/yuma-sun-oct-16-1984-p-4/ (accessed May 1, 2021).

or helicopter. It made it far more difficult for air ambulances to operate 24 hours a day, every day of the year, and I delivered an impassioned opposition piece to quite a few newspapers:

I'm a flight nurse and director of flight personnel for Air Evac, one of the two major private air ambulance firms in Arizona. I believe that Proposition 200 threatens my patients and all those Arizonans who through accident, injury or critical illness have need of transportation by airplane or helicopter. Proposition 200 would make a subsidy of vital community services such as air ambulances far more difficult if not impossible. This, in turn, could put the continued high standards of air ambulances in jeopardy.

As some health care experts have said, Proposition 200 even could mean the end of such private services. There is no doubt that air ambulances are expensive. They must be available 24 hours a day, every day of the year. The flight crews must have superior training and sophisticated, expensive medical and communication equipment.

A large percentage of our patients are trauma patients. Time is critical to their survival. The human body, even with serious damage, continues to function during the "golden hour." Often, it is a matter of life or death whether my colleagues and I can get victims to a specialized treatment center in a very short time. For example, victims of near drownings must be transported quickly if they are to survive and resume normal lives. Patients are transported by air regardless of their ability to pay. We do not perform "wallet biopsies" to guarantee payment.

After reading Proposition 200 in its entirely (18 pages), I feel the sponsor's concern is simply money, not what is best for the patient. As an advocate for my patients and as a member of Arizonans to Protect Quality Health Service, I am concerned, as are most Arizonans, about the costs of health care and the availability of technological advances. There must be an answer that will control costs and yet allow access for quality health care to all Arizonans.

I wrote and delivered speeches, spoke in radio spots, participated in statewide televised debates, and was determined to crush this measure. Proposition 200 was defeated along with the other problematic propositions — my first taste of politics.

I also organized a course with the help of Central Arizona College to provide flight nurse and paramedic lecturers for EMT courses in Maricopa and Pinal Counties. The goal was to generate more calls from these areas and provide continuity and a higher level of care to patients. Then I organized Air Evac's first educational fund for the American Society of Hospital-Based Emergency Medical Service (ASHBEAMS), soliciting for raffle prizes and sponsorship of the inaugural MASH BASH — at a profit. All the while, I maintained clinical proficiency as a flight nurse and remained cognitive of changes within the profession.

Professionalism, adrenaline, concentration, skill, organization… I'd say these are the attributes of an emergency flight nurse then and now.

Unfortunately, we were not always successful in staving off death, as Ralphie's story entails in the first chapter of this book. This accident spurred me to envision a way to help non-medical crews such as pilots, flight attendants, and those aboard sea vessels to appropriately respond during emergencies with the proper supplies, tools, training, and support.

Chapter Ten: What If?

This chapter captures the "what if's" as I pondered personal choices and professional possibilities for my startup. Without these thought processes, I'm not sure there would be a MedAire today. A lot of thinking was done in a quaint cabin, a favorite getaway to spend time with my sons.

I shared custody with their father and made the most of my time with them. Due to my innate frugality, I rented a room from a fellow flight nurse. She had white carpeting — you can imagine the havoc wreaked with two boys underfoot — and we made it a habit to remove our shoes once we stepped through the front door. Interestingly, I still remove my shoes to this day and must admit it's made a huge difference in the amount of housekeeping and floor maintenance required.

What if I can find a way to alleviate our cramped quarters? I wondered, already owning a plot of land at the idyllic setting of Ojo Bonito, Arizona, a little private development outside the small town of Vernon with one way in and out. The lot was bordered by the national forest, just beautiful, but the cost of building a house from the ground up just wasn't in my budget.

Lo and behold, I managed to purchase a cabin where Aaron (in junior high) and Josh (still in grade school) could roam the forest and experience adventures in the great outdoors on weekends and holidays. What an interesting saga that became! It just so happened that the tribal lands of the White Mountain Apache Tribe had been leased out for decades. People leased plots and built houses, but these long-term 50-year leases were coming to an end. The owners of these homes weren't allowed to tear them down, and they either had to abandon or move the structures. Some even burned them down. I learned about one of these homes, a cabin at Hawley Lake, in the newspaper want ads — for $8,000. I can afford that! I thought and put $500 down. Better yet, the cabin (and a "sister" cabin in Lake Tahoe) had been designed by a famous architect from San Francisco, Henrik Bull, reminding me of my roots in California. It was 1000 square feet and two stories, with glass walls on two sides.

So now, I had to build a foundation and find a house mover. I contacted a moving company that could maneuver the structure through the forest to my lot. In the meantime, it started to snow. Hawley Lake is one of the coldest places in winter in the country, and everything was delayed due to deteriorating weather. The house movers now wanted $8,000 to move the cabin — way out of my price range.

A vintage view of the cabin on tribal land – Photo credit: Patty Campbell

Another view of the cabin before we moved it to our property – Photo credit: Patty Campbell

The cabin during the refurbishing phase – Photo credit: Patty Campbell

I called the owners of the cabin and explained my dilemma. I simply could not afford the price of the movers, which was the same price as the cabin itself. They said not to worry and agreed to let it go for the $500 down payment I had already paid. What a stroke of good fortune!

However, the movers were still delayed, and Chief Ronnie Lupe was impatient. He was adamant that the houses on the reservation be cleared by the end of the lease, no exceptions. Fortunately, I used to transport high-risk pregnant tribal women to critical care hospitals in Phoenix for maternal complications. What if I called Chief Lupe personally and reminded him of this relationship? Then I could plead for an extension.

Apparently, the Chief appreciated my service. You cannot imagine my relief when he gave me an additional six weeks.

"I'll take it," I said. "Can you put it in writing?"

This must have insulted the Chief because he retorted, "If I have to do that, the deal is off!"

"That's okay, your word is golden," I quickly replied and thanked him profusely. By the way, I will always feel indebted to Chief Lupe for this personal favor and mourned his passing in 2019.

The weather finally broke, and I was able to proceed with this odyssey of cabin-moving. Then it began to rain. The bridge into the development washed out, and my cabin sat in the forest for six weeks until the Army Corps of Engineers could repair the bridge. Finally, after what felt like forever, the cabin was in place. However, the homeowner's association required that I replace roof and deck, and add another 200 square feet to meet their deed restrictions. Ultimately, the entire project cost $50,000 with an interest rate of 17%. Yikes! I crossed my fingers and hoped to cover the interest (forget the principal).

Yet there was a bit of a rainbow when all was said and done. I acquired additional contracting experience (more than I encountered at the resort apartments in a previous chapter) which definitely came in handy later as I formed my startup. Most importantly, my boys loved the cabin, our go-to place most weekends. Their friends were welcome, all going through puberty, which created an interesting dilemma when the water system went down. If any reader happens to be the mother of boys this age, you know how important showers are. Suffice it to say, our abode temporarily smelled like a locker room.

My boys were generally covered in dirt from head to toe, thanks to their mountainside revelry. They smudged everything they touched, of course, and ground dirt into the cushions on my indoor wicker swivel chairs. I'm talking the permanent kind of dirt on the two nice pieces of furniture I had managed to acquire. But I wouldn't have it any other way. The lack of creature comforts forced us to improvise. We melted snow to flush the toilets. We melted more snow to cook meals. I loved to cook, which was a good thing because my boys and their friends had the appetite of three men each. I'm not exaggerating when I call it the "hollow leg syndrome."

How we loved our home away from home – Photo credit: Patty Campbell

Would I do it all over again? Was it worth the financial worry of buying, moving, installing, and maintaining the cabin? Yes, absolutely yes. We had such fun. These bonding periods did a lot to make up for the time I spent at work, and I loved, loved, loved every weekend during these precious formative years. The memories we built are priceless.

Speaking of memories, during this timeframe I envisioned what would become MedAire, and credit the cabin as a serene place that seemed, somehow, to encourage introspection and open creative channels. I also credit back-to-back convergences that caused me to think hard about my career path as a flight nurse. I share more "what if's" below.

First, a fellow flight nurse who specialized in maternal emergencies had been involved in a fixed-wing fatal crash, along with the pilot. I'm sure every single one of my co-workers privately wondered, *What if that had been me?* Yes, what if? The possibility was always there.

During this tragedy, it was all hands on deck. The program director, myself, and 135 operators (pilots were employed by a contractor) interfaced with the media, the FAA, the National Transportation Safety Board (NTSB), and the Department of Transportation (DOT). It was determined that pilot error (fatigue) was the cause of the accident. Thankfully, the Flight Safety Foundation was in the process of formulating working groups which ultimately resulted in the FAA mandating rest times and changing duty times. Airplane accident rates decreased.

A non-flight accident took the life of a special emergency physician, the father of one of my flight nurses. This amazing clinician was at the top of his game throughout the U.S., and was involved in a head-on collision with a gravel truck. His daughter was dispatched to the scene — no one knew this accident involved her father. She realized the victim was her father by his red socks. He always wore red socks. She treated him but could not save his life. Can you imagine? I took her off duty right away so she could process this horrific event.

Channel 5 Interview. Photo courtesy of PHI Air Medical – Photo credit: Samaritan Hospital

It was always hardest to interact with the members of my staff and their families who were so profoundly touched by these fatalities. Mind you, the medical personnel we lost were more than co-workers. They were more than direct reports. They were friends, and their deaths were excruciating on a personal level. I was still flying and having nightmares of being trapped in a burning helicopter due to the number of accidents experienced by the air medical industry in this line of work.

What if something happened to me and my boys were left motherless? This was on the heels of the loss of Ralphie in 1984 on a desert road, the little boy who was the main inspiration behind my startup. His death was constantly on my mind, and I simply listened to my inner voice and brainstormed concepts that might, somehow, improve the odds of saving lives in these types of remote regions.

I paid attention to the news. Medical kits were definitely in the news.[12] Airlines were using first aid kits designed by Johnson & Johnson in 1924, updated in 1950s and nothing since! And now, legislators and the Federal Aviation Administration (FAA), albeit reluctantly, were looking at upgrading these kits. *What if this is my opportunity to start a business?* I thought, rather excited by the prospect. Having my own medical kit and flight experience, who better to design medical kits for the commercial airlines?

Yet every major U.S. airline was opposed to upgrading the kits, citing expense, potential misuse, etc. The American Medical Association's Commission on Emergency Medical Service opposed the upgrade too, as did the Air Transport Association. However, powerful proponents supported medical kit upgrades, for which I'm thankful. The Association of Flight Attendants and its National Air Safety Committee was in favor of the initiative and very vocal. The Aerospace Medical Association was supportive. Notably, Ralph Nader, his Public Citizen Health Research Group, and his Aviation Consumer Action Project strongly advocated for the improvement of medical kits for the traveling public.

Arizona's Republican Senator Barry Goldwater (a former Air Force officer and pilot who had co-sponsored legislation creating the Federal Aviation Administration in the 1950s) introduced a

---

[12] Peter S. Greenberg. "Controversy Over Airborne First Aid," *Los Angeles Times*, October 13, 1985. https://www.latimes.com/archives/la-xpm-1985-10-13-tr-15669-story.html (accessed April 29, 2021).

bill titled the "In-Flight Medical Emergencies Act of 1985."[13] Its intent was to force U.S. airlines to carry medical kits that could help treat cardiac emergencies, allergic reactions, seizures, diabetic comas, choking, bleeding, and more.

Senator Barry Goldwater, Republican-Arizona, speaks at a ceremony dedicating the Strategic Air

[13] Sen. Barry Goldwater (R-AZ). "S.63 — In-Flight Medical Emergencies Act. 99th Congress (1985-1986)," Introduced January 3, 1985. https://www.congress.gov/bill/99th-congress/senate-bill/63?s=1&r=11 (accessed May 3, 2021).

Command's Air Command's first B-1B aircraft at Offutt Air Force Base, Nebraska.
Photo credits: Scene Camera Operator, A1C Blade H. Smithee; Creators, Department of Defense

Senator Goldwater's proposed legislation was intriguing, especially when I considered how it could benefit travel safety and my potential startup at the same time. I anticipated that the FAA would ultimately rule (albeit reluctantly) to upgrade the kit requirements. This was my cue to jump into the medical kit business sooner rather than later and develop a product that met and exceeded FAA standards, and just as importantly, my own personal standards.

I had to really think it through. The complexities of designing, manufacturing and supplying organized, high-end medical kits — complete with appropriate supplies and pharmaceuticals for the commercial aviation mandates — was not an endeavor to be taken lightly, as you'll soon see.

As these ideas bubbled up, the name of my company materialized — MedAire. It stood for "medical" and "flight" and made perfect sense to me. It was imperative that I roll out my company while the opportunity existed — again, first in the commercial aviation medical kit market, and the rest to follow.

Before I officially launched my company in 1985, I wanted to know what the medical community had to say about medical kits aboard the airlines. Like any government agency, the FAA issued a notice of proposed rulemaking (an NPRM) and invited comments about kit standardization. Three massive binders were filled with feedback, and I made a trip to Washington D.C. to plow through each binder and study what MDs, DOs, nurses, and paramedics were recommending — easier said than done. I had to really press for this information and was finally granted permission. The suggestions were all over the map — some appropriate and some not, for instance, outlandish drugs that should only be prescribed and never dispensed by untrained people. It appeared that 99% of the input was wrong, probably because most doctors were unfamiliar with the aviation environment and air travel emergencies.

The orthopedic community weighed in with helpful information regarding splinting for broken bones that might occur during hard landings and turbulence. By the way, the rules at the time required one first aid kit for every 50 passengers. If you think about turbulence affecting a large plane filled with 300 passengers, then six first aid kits might or might not be appropriate — certainly not with such woefully outdated kits in place.

It was interesting to see the areas of specialization respond, and that's where I assumed my background as a flight nurse would be valuable. I believed gloves and masks should be included as a minimum, considering that HIV was prevalent, and crews lacked personal protection equipment (PPEs). I also felt that medical kits should include enough medications, assessments tools, and resources to cover contingencies most often related to altitude-specific illness (above and beyond gastrointestinal complaints and fainting episodes). A passenger's medical history is unknown when they board, and the flight crew has no clue about what may trigger an illness. Yet passengers are exposed to artificial altitudes when aircraft cabins are pressurized to between 6,000 and 8,000 feet. This may or may not affect their health. For instance, passengers with lung or heart conditions are the most vulnerable to altitude changes. Barometric pressure fluctuations related to altitude, especially with preexisting conditions, could cause these passengers to become symptomatic.

But one of the larger concerns was — and is — cardiac arrests. Passengers could decompensate, meaning they might experience chest pain and, in some cases, have a heart attack. There could be aggravated factors like drinking alcohol or smoking prior to boarding. Therefore, I strongly advocated for onboard automated external defibrillators even in those early days. It seemed medically negligent that these devices were not mandated (a battle that I would ultimately wage for years).

Yes, I provided the medical perspective of someone who knew

about medicine and flight. But did anyone listen?

No. No one took me seriously.

I left Washington (it felt more like I was kicked out of Washington) without making an impact. A sense of tone-deaf bureaucracy was precisely why I felt more change was needed. The altitude issues I expressed should have been part of the driving force behind the proposal for rulemaking, or at least acknowledged, considering I shared valid reasons for the occurrence of so many inflight medical emergencies. However, the rejection did not stop me then or later from continuing to advocate for passenger safety in the public square and Congress itself, especially regarding defibrillators — as you'll see in the following chapters. In other words, there was no way I would be silenced when I knew lives could potentially be saved with the appropriate equipment and training.

For an overview of these controversial times, with numerous opinions floating in the media, I recommend a *Chicago Tribune* article, "FAA Reviews Decade-old Rules for Medical Kits."[14] You can also read a thorough retrospective of the proposal for rulemaking and the robust research I gathered throughout the following decade in a paper I co-authored titled "The Evaluation Of In-Flight Medical Care Aboard Selected U.S.Air Carriers: 1996 To 1997."[15] It was published by the FAA Civil Aerospace Medical Institute (CAMI), Department of Transportation, and the Office of Aviation Medicine in the year 2000, clearly detailing the outcomes of more than 1,000 inflight emergency cases (a historical perspective of inflight medical events). Believe me, after my company became a data tracking source, the government certainly did listen, along with the travel industries.

---

[14] John Crewdson. "FAA Reviews Decade-old Rules for Medical Kits," *Chicago Tribune,* November 10, 1996. See https://www.chicagotribune.com/news/ct-xpm-1996-11-10-9611100259-story.html

[15] Charles A. DeJohn, Stephen J. H. Veronneau, Alex M. Wolbrink , et al. "The Evaluation Of In-Flight Medical Care Aboard Selected U.S.Air Carriers: 1996 To 1997," (DOT/FAA/AM-00/13), Office of Aviation Medicine, Washington, D.C., May 2000. See https://apps.dtic.mil/sti/pdfs/ADA377878.pdf

However, back in the mid-1980s, I was considered nothing more than a nurse with an opinion. I assumed my suggestions would not appear in the final regulations (and they didn't), but this didn't dissuade me. My goal was to address the issue of replacing the outdated first aid kits on commercial airlines with MedAire medical kits — according to my own high standards.

As this idea percolated in my head, I delved into Federal Aviation Regulations and how they impacted commercial pilots and flight attendants as well. FAR Part 121 was designated for commercial flights. Although commercial was my immediate focus, I kept up with FAR Part 91 for business travel, FAR Part 25 for transport category airplanes, and FAR Part 135 for charter flights or regional carriers as well. After all, my plan was to ultimately service every segment in the industry, which meant keeping up with the regulatory end.

Oh, boy, did I ever have a ton of work ahead of me. Suddenly, I was wearing many hats. I incorporated MedAire in 1985 in anticipation of the FAA kit mandates and spent the year planning and strategizing. I now carried triple titles as Air Evac's director of flight personnel, flight nurse, and MedAire CEO. Thankfully, all of these positions overlapped and complimented each other, keeping me on the cutting edge of medicine and aviation and encouraging me to think boldly and daringly outside the box.

Chapter Eleven: Vision to Reality

I'm convinced that about half of what separates
the successful entrepreneurs from the non-successful
is pure perseverance.
~ Steve Jobs, Co-founder, CEO, Chairman Apple
Inc..

If we look back to the introduction of this book, I mentioned that MedAire was initially a hypothesis built on the foundation of a "three-legged stool" — medical kits, training, and telemedicine. Well, let me tell you, each "leg" was built individually. The plan didn't materialize all at once. And so, commercial kits came first, thanks to the FAA mandates, which created a definitive and immediate need.

Kit manufacturing sounded like a great business opportunity, but how in the world would I fund my startup, considering I was a single mom living on a modest salary? Well, I refused to take out a bank loan and didn't think a financial institution would approve a loan anyway since my company was a hypothesis — still unproven. I did speak with venture capitalists who liked the idea but didn't want to put money on the table. Or, if they made an offer, they wanted to own the company. No, thank you.

So I relied on my sparse savings and a personal credit card to get "Leg One" of my startup off the ground and, hopefully, bring business through the door. I did not take a MedAire salary because there was no income at the time. In fact, I took no MedAire salary for nearly a decade because I plowed everything back into R&D, marketing, and later, payroll for employees and contractors.

I'm often asked why I "worked for free." Well, I didn't know what I didn't know about a business startup, especially a startup up that would ultimately offer services that were totally new to the travel industry. I anticipated that MedAire would face a lot of obstacles and expend a lot capital in developing the three-legged stool (and it did). As we grew, salaries for my staff came first so they could support their own families. I was able to work multiple jobs in the nursing field to support myself and my sons, and this spared MedAire the expense of my salary until a steady profit was realized. That took about ten years.

In my Air Evac uniform

Fast forward to 2008 when I read the book *Outliers* by Malcolm

Gladwell.[16] I wish it had been available when my sink-or-swim venture was barely treading water. It would have reassured me that MedAire was one among many startups that shared a common denominator — it can take a decade of struggle before a positive cash flow is realized. This was certainly true in my case, a slow climb and then a sudden, sharp liftoff into profitability. I charted our progress and was amazed to see how we turned the corner. Then, and only then, did I take a MedAire salary.

Today I often share these struggles with budding entrepreneurs to let them know they aren't alone, that patience is a positive, and that persistence does pay off. I also tell them that if they are not willing to hold the line and sacrifice sleep, salary, and their savings…then maybe they should reconsider a career as an entrepreneur. They have to be willing to pay the price. I certainly did while lifting MedAire off the ground, a Herculean effort.

Creating a prototype commercial aviation medical kit was exciting, even if I didn't necessarily agree with the mandated pharmaceuticals. The final mandates [51 FR 1218; January 9, 1986, effective August 1, 1986] set a minimum standard for kit contents requiring the following: a sphygmomanometer (blood pressure cuff), a stethoscope, three different sizes of oral airways (breathing tubes), syringes, needles, 50 percent dextrose injection for hypoglycemia or insulin shock, epinephrine for asthma or acute allergic reactions, diphenhydramine for allergic reactions, nitroglycerin tablets for cardiac-related chest pain, and basic instructions on the use of the drugs. The rule has been amended once, in October 1994 [59 FR 52640; October 18, 1994], to require protective gloves. By the way, the stethoscopes didn't have to be assembled. Seriously? Who has time during an

---

[16] Malcolm Gladwell. *Outliers: The Story of Success* (New York: Little, Brown and Company, 2008).

emergency to piece together equipment?

I felt the new FAA regulations were difficult to live with for other reasons as well. For instance, some of the mandated pharmaceutical content was very concerning, given the way it was packaged and made available. Any type of doctor or medical person might respond to an inflight emergency, experienced or not, which could be problematic. For instance, how many doctors have drawn the appropriate cc's from an ampule of adrenaline? A tiny amount is required for adults and a smaller amount for children, and the appropriate type of syringe might or might not be available for a medical volunteer to use. The mandate mentioned syringes but didn't specify size. It's very difficult to administer this drug in a medical setting, let alone on a plane, and mistakes could be lethal. This underscored, again, the necessity for good, solid protocols — and kits that exceeded the FAA mandates.

There were "Good Samaritan" laws[17] in effect not only in the United States but globally. Still, medical volunteers (mainly doctors) worried about their liability when stepping in to assist on commercial flights — another strong argument for protective legislation.

I consulted pharmacists about the mandated medications and ordered a large, black, plastic industrial-looking box with injection molding. A foam insert would hold the contents in place, with a snap closure that could be locked. The contents would be shrink-wrapped — assessment tools (blood pressure cuff and stethoscope) and supplies (drugs, one-way-flow pocket mask, and gloves). Then the entire kit would be checked for quality control, boxed up, and sent out — or would be once my customers materialized! I also thought ahead about how best to develop the accompanying reference guide to be included in the kits and went to sleep wondering how to provide adequate

---

[17] Pardun, John T. "Good Samaritan laws: a global perspective." Loy. LA Int'l & Comp. LJ 20 (1997): 591. See
https://digitalcommons.lmu.edu/cgi/viewcontent.cgi?referer=&httpsredir=1&arti cle=1449&context=ilr

guidance during any number of medical emergencies unique to air travel.

And what did I discover? My kits would cost $100 when lesser competing kits cost $50! Some of the price differences had to do with 1.) my lack of packaging know-how, and 2.) my lack of a fulfillment center, 3.) the fact that I had no employees or infrastructure in place. In other words, my competitors with packaging expertise could offer a much cheaper product.

Keep in mind that the commercial airlines were only required to meet the minimum equipment standards as required by the FAA regulations. They would update their kits and comply, of course, but would also seek to minimize the financial investment to do so. I could provide better thought out, supplied, and organized kits with assembled assessment tools that could be easily retrieved but sensed it wouldn't matter. Cost was the driver.

Much of this effort involved steadfast faith and a belief that the sales would come…before I went broke! My commercial kit sales were not going well. The name of my company caused some confusion, which didn't help.

"Mid-Air?" someone would inevitably ask.

"No, MedAire," I responded.

"Are you an air evac company? An air ambulance?" they asked next.

Then I'd launch into my 30-second elevator speech and get cut off. Click went the phone. I wanted nothing more than to be taken seriously in the aviation industry, and being as stubborn as my great-grandfather Timothy, it was difficult to make me go away.

It just so happened that Samaritan had an opening for an emergency room nurse, which I saw as an answer to a prayer. It relieved me of a sense of conflict concerning my full-time responsibilities as director of flight personnel. I resigned that position on excellent terms, no longer shouldering the responsibility of overseeing Air Evac's 144 flight nurses, paramedics, and respiratory therapists. I continued to fly part-time, however, because I needed the income. And as a 3-11 emergency department nurse (same key card, same employee number), I had more time to focus on MedAire, even when taking on part-time flight nurse shifts.

In the emergency department

I now leased an "executive suite" — an office within a suite of offices equipped with a phone and a receptionist who supported all tenants. As an interim solution, it doubled as an office and warehouse, and supplies were stacked floor to ceiling. I worked odd hours and weekend shifts at Samaritan and Air Evac so that I could cold call prospective customers during normal business hours. Yet, try as I might, my attempts to penetrate the commercial aviation market was frustratingly nonproductive.

That is, until I got a call from People Express (also known as PEOPLExpress) — our first commercial aviation customer! This boutique East Coast airline had the foresight to differentiate itself medically just prior to merging with Continental Airlines. Suddenly, MedAire had a $50,000 medical kit contract, huge at the time. I had to wrap my head around how to fulfill this order without having any employees at the time.

Aside from the People Express order, however, the commercial aviation market was largely a no-go. My cold calling was disillusioning and it felt like I was wasting my time. At moments like these, "internal dialogue" becomes extremely important. After all, we are what "we think we are." How I processed the hard times could affect my company's trajectory, and I pushed back against any "woe is me" angst. Instead, I affirmed (in my head) the value of positive thinking and trusted that I would get through it. Realistically, I needed some sort of "boost" to keep going and had faith that it would materialize.

Thankfully, Samaritan Health System had launched an "Intrepreneurial Program" in order to retain talent and support worthy startups. This was a chance to obtain proper funding and I applied with high hopes. Yet, there was a bit of some trepidation mixed in. Although I was a known quantity through my various roles as a Samaritan employee and my work in opposing Proposition 200 (which greatly benefited Samaritan), I was not fully steeped in the art and science of financial forecasting! This language scared the heck out of me, and I really sweated bullets as I put together the numbers.

Arnold Silver was financial counsel and assistant treasurer of Dynacor, Inc., the "for-profit" arm of Samaritan Health System, and formerly employed by Arthur Anderson. He helped me make sense of the daunting financial paperwork. Then he presented my ideas and a pro forma income statement and business plan to the Budget & Finance Committee at Samaritan:

> *The management of Samaritan Health Services is presenting for your consideration what we believe to be an attractive opportunity in the area in intrepreneurship. With that, management recommends to the Budget & Finance Committee that the program as outlined in this cover letter be accepted.*

How exciting! In a nutshell, Samaritan's initial reply was, "We'll own it, and if it doesn't work out, you can have your old job back."

My counter was, "No, I'll own it and pay you back. If it fails,

I don't want my old job back."

Fortunately, my terms were accepted, and I owe so much to Samaritan for formalizing this agreement, believing in MedAire, and supporting what I envisioned as our future services. What a relief to receive a much-needed $22,500 capital infusion and a line of credit (which would have to be paid back as well). The agreement required that I contribute $2,500 of my own money to show a good-faith effort. That might not sound like a lot of financial backing, but to me it meant onward and upward!

How fortunate for me that Arthur Silver was assigned as my business mentor and helped develop a Strength, Weakness, Opportunity, and Threat (SWOT) analysis. He also prepared me for rejection, and I'm forever grateful that he did. My commercial kits would face competition. Any new innovations I developed would face hurdles, and most inventions do. The bottom line was, could I withstand the storms? Could I build my business whatever the future might bring? My answer was a resounding "Yes!"

Chapter Twelve: And Then Came Frank

*When you realize you want to spend
the rest of your life with somebody,
you want the rest of your life to start as soon as possible.*
~ From the movie When Harry met Sally

The day I became "intrepreneurially" funded was the day I met Frank Garrett, my husband of 35 years, at the writing of this book. We ran into each other at a restaurant among friends. New to Arizona and a transplant from Tennessee, he was a never-married, baby-faced nuclear power and fire protection engineer, seven years my junior. We clicked despite his running joke that I didn't come with baggage... I came with *freight!* Yet, my two kids, two divorces, and three jobs (including a business with a large, pending People Express order) didn't phase him one bit.

I was leery at the time and didn't take him seriously. Yet, he was cautiously persistent and ultimately proved that three times is definitely the charm. We didn't really date much because I was busy. And I mean busy! In fact, I wasn't sure how to carve out time for Frank, other than we were both runners and could exercise together. He pitched in to help with the cabin on weekends (I thought it was an adorable place, but he described it as dilapidated), and with his engineering mind, set out to whip it into shape.

The cabin, by the way, served a lot of purposes. At times I rented it out or allowed my firefighter friends to stay in exchange for working around the place — odd jobs and whatever help Frank needed. There was so much traffic that I put a visitor book at the entrance to keep track of the comings and goings. One special day I flipped through the book and saw his handwriting. The message was, "Will you mary me?" — with "marry" misspelled. I thought it was an endearing way to propose, and at the cabin, no less. That put an end to our bachelor and bachelorette days and made both of us very happy.

"Twinning" in matching shirts

Frank at a Fifties party in the late 1980s

A close friend and me at the same Fifties party

Best of all, my sons liked Frank. This was significant because they were the priority, and knew it. If not for their blessing, there would be no Frank in our lives. Thankfully, for many wonderful reasons, he passed the acid test. He taught my boys to turn rotors on cars, change tires, wire things, and other practical skills. It has been so interesting "doing life" with an engineer, such a detail-oriented person who still finds solutions for any dilemma.

We exchanged vows in May of 1987 and chose a fun wedding venue on Lake Tahoe aboard a trimaran sailboat, the Windward. Unfortunately, there was only a brief honeymoon (a weekend) as I had to write the medical kit content card for use by People Express! I still had no employees and will never forget, believe it or not, that the boys and I would ultimately assemble one hundred People Express kits in Frank's townhouse — out the door and into the street — with Frank acting as quality control! The kits shipped, and I remember calling the Samaritan CEO and reporting, "We're officially in the commercial airline business!"

The four of us

Tying the knot aboard a trimaran sailboat

Our wedding celebration dinner

Busier than ever while trying to grow this unusual startup, I gave up my part-time flight nursing gig (with some nudging from Frank).

"I don't want to lose you," he said, concerned about helicopter crashes and the inherent danger of this line of work. As I mentioned, I had been considering this for some time, and Frank was right. Although flight nursing was so meaningful, I also had my own life to consider. Jumping out of helicopters was a definite risk, and I wasn't sure how long the odds would be in my favor. My death would leave my company rudderless — and worse, my kids without a mom and Frank without a partner.

Plus, I was already spread thin balancing MedAire, my emergency nursing job, and some semblance of family life. Still, it's hard to explain the flood of feelings that washed over me when I let that job go. It was like losing a limb, a part of myself, so profound was the flight nurse calling.

My efforts at selling commercial aviation kits were still less than stellar. What do you do in a situation like this? Well, you zig instead of zag. So while chipping away at the commercial airlines, I pivoted most of my attention to other opportunities in aviation. Luckily for me, Frank knew a group of engineers in a graduate program who were looking for a marketing project. They devised a survey aimed at the Fortune 500 industry to determine how business aircraft owners and crews handled medical emergencies. By business aircraft, I mean the corporate jets used as business tools often supporting smaller communities and utilizing smaller regional airports that were not serviced by the commercial airline industry.

All I can say is, "WOW!" This survey was a win/win — a great endeavor that provided invaluable insights as we strove to better understand the needs of this target market and expand our sales. The survey concluded that about 36% of these companies would be interested — an incredible response! The responding executives mentioned that they appreciated a solution to aviation-specific, inflight emergencies with kits and medical training. Compare this to Red Cross training, which was ground-based and involved contacting 911. This was not much help when flying six-plus miles up in the air. After all, there are no firefighters or EMS responders who can come to your aid in the clouds!

Better yet, the survey came back with names and contact information, a gold mine. But before I could reach out to this new, readymade market, I had to conquer two new ventures: 1.) kits designed for this sector and 2.) "Leg Two" of the three-legged stool — training!

First, I developed another prototype and had more "creative license," I guess you could say, regarding how I designed medical kits for the business aviation sector. I was aware that business jet owners had the means to afford top-of-the-line kits with all the extras I felt should be included.

I called a friend in the kit business, Dr. Frank Thomas in Salt Lake City, Utah, the Medical Director for Salt Lake City Life Flight. Air Evac utilized their "Thomas Bags" to house our equipment. We connected due to our mutual affiliation with the

Flight Nurse Association and air ambulances nationwide.

"I need a kit just like this," I said, and then snail-mailed him sketches of my prototype inspired by my own flight nurse medical kits (I had multiple bags for trauma, intubation, pediatric, etc. in the helicopter, each color-coded). My design for the MedAire kit included pouches of various colors, each with a see-through front to identify the contents rapidly, and a color-coded content card.

More research was involved, as well. My kits would have to meet (and exceed) international standards wherever a jet might fly globally, such as the Civil Aviation Administration of China (CAAC) and the Joint Aviation Authorities (JAA, Europe), among others. This was a proactive approach to doing things right, and if it sounds complex, I can assure you it was!

Meanwhile, Frank invented the "jig" for our bendable wire form ladder splints — in our garage, no less. Our ladder splints were made of rubberized metal to support broken bones and sprains encountered during turbulence, falls in aisles, or even for incidents on the ground. Later we added a soft padded splint for wrist injuries and pediatric cases. By jig, I mean the tool that allowed us to precisely bend these splints for insertion into our soft-sided medical kit bags. In other words, there was no guessing at dimensions or holding up the packing process because our assembly line workers used this folding template consistently. Then they slid the splint into the kit bag for a perfect perimeter fit (with the double benefit of stiffening the bag). This genius invention has stood the test of time, and MedAire still uses Frank's jig to this day. All of this is an example of how creative you can be when you don't have a huge marketing budget.

As the business kits were in development, I purchased mannequins and anatomical training dummies at $500 each so our customers could better understand how bodies reacted to illness and injury. I also developed, with the help of marketing contractors with medical expertise, our custom projector slides that may seem like no big deal today but were expensive. Each slide had to be placed precisely into a carousel. What an investment of time and money, and I worried because we were still not breaking even. Every cent was put back into the company. While our overall investment in equipment seemed astronomical, it was essential to train our customers properly.

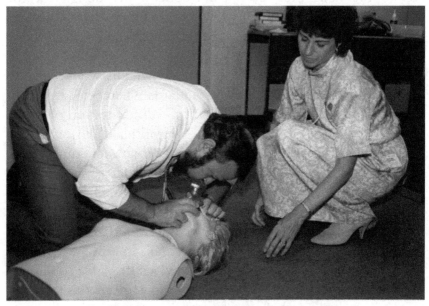

We taught our customers CPR and other lifesaving first aid skills.

The slides were carefully organized and stored in a binder so that we could quickly retrieve and pop them into the carousel without them appearing upside down or backward. That was considered spiffy technology back in the day, so outdated now that people don't even know what carousels are! I would eventually lug that carousel and slide binder all over the nation from New York to Los Angeles, airport to airport, and later to nearly every continent.

I, with the help of fellow flight nurses, wrote our training program titled "Management of Inflight Illness and Injury" — an enormous 11 X 17 padded manual with graphics and step-by-step contents. I was incredibly proud of the design, layout, and comprehensive information, and wish I had saved a copy just to show off the details! It focused on how to manage the effects of the gas laws with altitude physiology, cardiac events, food poisoning, and many other medical crises that required decision-making and proficiency. This was developed as a two-day course, eight hours a day. Of all the training flight crews have to undertake, this was one course they could take home with them and use personally as well.

International Multifoods in Minnetonka, Minnesota, became our first business aviation client and hired us to run an inflight emergency two-day training class Phoenix, which validated our survey of Fortune 500 companies and opened other doors. While there, we set up at a hotel for the two-day round of demonstrations, instruction, and Q&A. The only problem was the size of our gorgeous training manual.

"Where do we put it in the aircraft?" they asked, puzzled, as they held the behemoth manual. After all, they also had to stow a first aid kit and oxygen equipment. That's when I realized the manual size wasn't practical, despite the fact it was the most comprehensive resource on the market! You can imagine how I kicked myself because the cost was $50, which is what I charged each student for the course! Our new client was assured that we would deliver a 5X7 manual that fit in the cockpit, and we did.

What a valuable lesson, although it was a bit overwhelming to learn, listen, and allow customers to teach us. Entering a new industry meant responding to this input. Our customers knew what they needed operationally, and we knew what they needed medically. Customizing our products and services became our hallmark from then onward.

And now, thanks to the contacts gathered from the survey, things moved rapidly. How fortunate that I had worked with emergency flight nurses across the country who were interested in the MedAire training mission. I recruited them and now had a team that grasped and embraced this calling. Although I couldn't pay them much, they stepped up anyway. It gave them opportunities to travel and train and the extra bonus of developing expertise in all aspects of aviation beyond their professions.

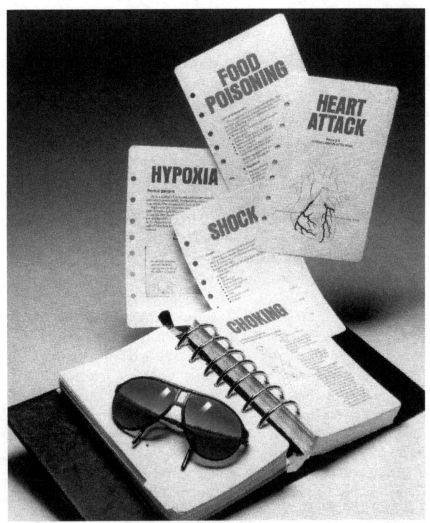

Our revised manual. Photo credit: MedAire

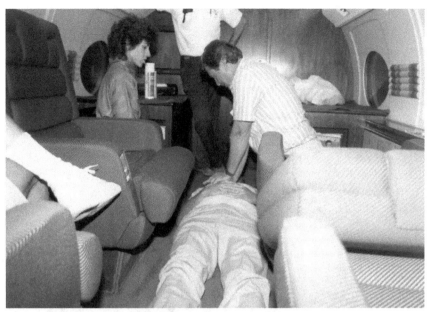

Advanced first aid training inside a business jet

My son Aaron posing with the team and displaying our kits

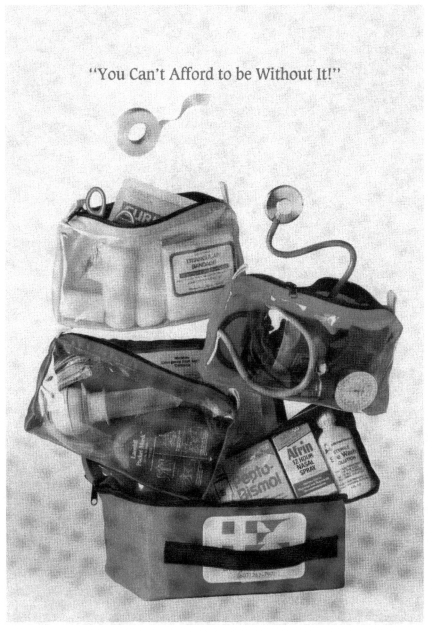

"You Can't Afford to be Without It!"

Organized, accessible, high-quality medical kits for the business aviation sector – Photo credit: MedAire

To make a sale, I visited hangars and climbed into aircraft with prospective clients. Then I asked to see their first aid kits, typically a metal or plastic box with a whole lot of bandages and dressings, nothing more. I showed them my kits designed specifically for the business aviation industry — soft-sided cordura nylon fabric with color-coded pouches and very organized. Each pouch covered most emergencies, along with our signature protective equipment. It was dust-proof, moisture-proof, burn-resistant, logically organized, and sealed with a security label. The quality of the kits complemented the quality of the aircraft. Owners wanted this kit for all the right reasons, and it was an easy transaction right off the bat!

"Done! Sold!" the new customer would say.

"Great. Now let's schedule a class so I can show you how to use everything in the kit," I responded. We became highly recommended by word of mouth endorsements, and these new customers propelled our marketing.

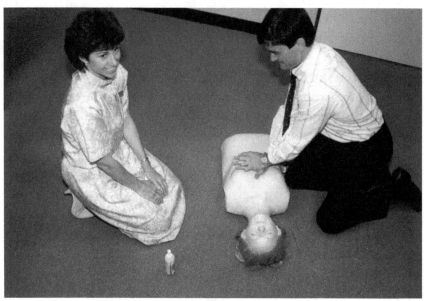

On the floor with a student and training dummy

We typically trained at aircraft hangars. Some had conference rooms, some did not, but regardless we ended up inside the aircraft for "if-then" scenarios. We reviewed the emergency equipment at the same time. This ensured that whatever happened, a plan was in place to address medical travel emergencies effectively.

Eventually, we held classes across the country and around the world as our business aviation customer base expanded. As for overnight accommodations during our far-flung training excursions, our nurses had travel budgets that included meals. I could only afford modest hotels for my staff and myself, nothing grand, although customers sometimes booked us into fancier accommodations, including meals.

That left an impression, being treated to meals, and I was truly impressed and grateful at this generosity. Years later when I was able to do the same, you bet I picked up the tab. I acquired this habit, which is ongoing today, because I look back and remember so well what it meant to be hungry — not just hungry for business, but hungry for something more nourishing than half a sandwich and chips.

We may never know how the kindness we extend to young, hardworking entrepreneurs affects their lives and outlook, but suffice it to say, it might just give them the inspiration to keep going, keep trying until they break into an industry.

It was interesting to train customers who might be competitive within the industry. This brought a confidentiality component to our services. Executives trusted us to safeguard proprietary information, and we did. Later, in some cases, we were aware of strategic activities and never once discussed these operations outside of the classroom setting. Discretion and integrity meant everything when it came to establishing trust and building our client base. It created word-of-mouth referrals and extended my marketing arm, very powerful and much appreciated. I loved training for this and many reasons and felt it was a privilege and a great business opportunity to gain insight into where MedAire needed to be in order to support the business activities of our customers.

I'll add an anecdote about ground personnel who requested training as well. I was invited to speak at a maintenance conference, got off the stage, walked into the audience, shook hands with the maintenance technicians, and observed if they had cracked, dry hands.

"You don't wear gloves, do you?" I asked. This sparked interest, and the maintenance techs asked if they could receive hazard training. The training course "Inflight Illness and Injury" was geared toward those who crewed the aircraft. I felt an obligation to provide a safety course for maintenance professionals as well.

Training the ground crew

Most of their existing training came from good and bad advice, passed down to new employees from older, long-term employees. To more fully understand their risks, I spent weeks at an aircraft assembly plant talking to aircraft maintenance specialists and engineers who designed the aircraft. I researched industrial hygiene as it related to the hangar environment. It became clear to me that some parts and systems aligned with the human body. Then, I contracted with an OSHA specialist and wrote a manual titled "Hangar Safety" that complied with OSHA's Hazard Materials, Haz Whopper standards, and others.

It was fun to train these professionals about hazards and prevention. I used the hydraulic system as an analogy for the arterial system in the human body as part of a two-day course covering CPR, First Aid, AEDs, reviews of new OSHA regulations, industrial hygiene, confined space safety issues, emergency equipment for the aircraft, and more.

It was easy to compare the fuel system with its many valves to the cardiovascular venous system and the backflow valves that keep blood moving back to the heart. Our muscles help in this endeavor; when you stand upright and blood flows upward to your heart, that's the muscles doing their work.

The hydraulic system is under high pressure, much like the body's arterial system moving blood away from the heart. For example, this system in the aircraft is responsible for moving the plane's wheels up during takeoffs or down for landings. Likewise, I analogized a plane's avionic system to our brain and electrical system and the skin of the aircraft to our own skin. Our skin, by the way, is a barrier that can be breached by chemicals such as methyl ethyl ketones (colorless, flammable) and other solvents — thus, the need for protective gloves.

The maintenance crews wore protective masks with cartridges filled with charcoal, which absorbs harmful aerosols and gases. However, if left on a counter in a work area, the mask continues to absorb harmful vapors. Workers put the masks back on and were exposed to the saturation, which went directly to the lungs. I advised them to store their masks in a locker away from the fumes and re-place the charcoal cartridges routinely.

In addition, workers were educated about teratogenic agents in industrial settings that could cause congenital disorders in future generations. The training was beneficial in helping workers protect themselves from various hazards, and the feedback we received was extremely positive.

Oxygen systems in the aircraft were complex and yet doubled for both emergency use (i.e., decompression) as well as for medical purposes. Learning how to extract the most from these safety solutions became my forte. MedAire helped by providing instruction and adjuncts for administering oxygen during a medical emergency.

Chapter Thirteen: Operation Warp Speed

To build a great company, which is a CEO's job,
sometimes you have to stand up against conventional wisdom.
~ Carly Fiorina, Hewlett-Packard

Perhaps MedAire's backstory is more unusual than most because I was not a Harvard-variety entrepreneur, not in the least. A lack of business training on my curriculum vitae attests to that fact. Many of my business contemporaries were "textbook trained" in standard university business models and time-honored methodologies of building and managing companies. My training was the opposite, derived from experience in the trenches and based on instinct, intuition, and a penchant for unconventional thinking.

And yes, in the back of my mind, I wondered if I should have carved out the time to complete a four-year degree. It's never too late to complete that goal, and perhaps I will. But in hindsight, a limited college-level background meant I had zero preconceived notions or boundaries in my thinking. I wasn't stifled or constrained when setting up a company with products and services that had never before existed. I could envision, maneuver, and invent — a distinct advantage for someone like me who excelled at jumping in, learning by doing, and figuring it out. In short, sometimes ignorance *is* bliss because then, as I often say, "impossible isn't a construct."

So now...*drumroll*... came what some, indeed, thought was impossible. I developed a way to connect flight crews, while aloft, with ground-based doctors by using communication channels such as high frequency radio, satellite, and teletype transmissions, for instance, Aeronautical Radio, Incorporated (ARINC, established in 1929), and its Aircraft Communications Addressing and Reporting System (ACARS, available in 1978). We subscribed to this teletype messaging service to allow communication with an airline's dispatch and cockpit when needed. The only other forms of communication in the 1980s were hospital systems that linked remote clinics to specialist consultations as well as some larger hospital systems providing base station support for the EMS community.

My own background as a flight nurse was an inspiration —the ability, on occasion, to radio an ER doctor from the field and obtain additional recommendations in order to improve the outcome for a patient. By the way, this is why I loved my flight nursing job. I was able to autonomously use my brain and training without waiting for an order from a physician, unlike my grandmother and those who worked in a traditional hospital setting.

I named "Leg Three" of our three-legged stool "MedLink," the missing link between inflight emergencies and board-certified emergency physicians. We offered a connection to the global communication systems in place among aircraft operators. I'm not sure why no one else had conceived this innovation. It was an untapped market and an earth-shaking development that would take us to new heights, quite literally. The fact was, the full-blown components — a triad of products and services offered by my startup — had never been attempted specific to the methodology and presentation to the aviation industry. Imagine wrapping your head around that notion! It meant stepping off a cliff and into a risky venture, somewhat frightening but also exhilarating.

MedLink would be the crown jewel of my vision and the opportunity of a lifetime. Samaritan, by the way, wanted MedLink wrapped into MedAire. I incorporated MedLink separately in 1987 and folded it in as service name. This telemedicine component would ultimately serve crews in the air (and later, crews at sea) as they faced situations beyond their skill level. How much better to connect them to emergency physicians and ensure the kits were used appropriately and for the right situations.

In the mid-1980s, however, telemedicine was virtually unknown. The telemedicine of today and the pioneering telemedicine of the 1980s and 1990s is vastly different. Many readers are familiar with "e-health" — a way to communicate with healthcare professionals over the internet (through websites, portals, Zoom, etc.) — especially with the advent of COVID-19.

Of course, these innovations were not available in the 1980s. Inbound calls to our communication specialists and physicians were usually routed through a third-party radio operator. We made due with the high frequency radio calls through Stockholm Radio in Sweden and Berna Radio in Switzerland, as well as the satellite and teletype messaging I mentioned previously. Only in the last two decades has the ease of satellite communications brought both clarity to the calls and now includes the capability of adding real-time video and transmission of vital signs, including EKGs from the air to ground. This advisory service is provided to specific commercial airlines, business aircraft, charter companies, luxury yachts, commercial shipping and remote land locations.

For a deeper dive into what telemedicine was in the 1980s I recommend the article "Telehealth and Telemedicine: A Research Anthology of Law and Policy Resources" by the CDC and the accompanying article footnotes.[18]

So what were the nuts and bolts of turning this particular vision into reality? Much of MedLink's success stemmed from where we set up headquarters — humble headquarters at first. When I became intrapreneurially funded, Samaritan Hospital had an unused office space across the street and offered it for one dollar per square foot — for a year! The condition of the building was a bit worn and tattered; however it was roomy, had phones,

---

[18] "Telehealth and Telemedicine: A Research Anthology of Law and Policy Resources," CDC.
See https://www.cdc.gov/phlp/publications/topic/anthologies/anthologies-telehealth.html

and was affordable. I was just thrilled to have a headquarters at all!

MedAire's first office

Standing: Flight nurse Janet Whalen, me, flight nurse Jeanie Herges, marketer Suzette Rogers, and my very first assistant, Lori (seated) – Photo credit: MedAire

Just starting out, a young CEO and her dream – Photo credit: MedAire

Samaritan also provided a room (the size of a closet) for the MedLink control center inside the hospital near the emergency department. We set it up operationally and technologically —

monitors, radio equipment, handsets, headsets, call assessment features, desks, chair, and staff.

I won't give away our proprietary innovations then or now, but can say I'm grateful for a wonderful team of volunteers (all professionals) and contractors who helped stretch our shoestring budget in those early days. We first laid the groundwork through product development. A commercial airline pilot, who happened to be a software coder and programmer in his sideline work, wanted to help. We needed to understand our customers' operations and build our capabilities to fit their needs, and thankfully he contributed his knowledge. Every airline had a route structure as well as an alternate route structure here and abroad. We sleuthed information about national and international airports and how they handled incoming emergencies — flights diverted or not, the types of medical events anticipated and experienced, the location of airports, ports of departure, hospitals, and many other specifics.

Our "database pilot" did a magnificent job and enabled us to extrapolate, chart, and graph worldwide facts and figures. We knew where the planes and ships were heading worldwide and could inform crews about the nearest appropriate airports, ports, hospitals, specialty care centers, and passenger accommodation sites. This incredible database became an asset that enabled us to support all parties from the airline dispatches to captains in the cockpits to the operational staff at the airports and their contractors.

I was continuously on the lookout for new state-of-the-art technology when it became available, thus permanently positioning MedAire as the bridge between hands-on emergencies and the remote support needed by responders. Suffice it to say, we were preparing to manage our customers globally wherever they flew (and undertook similar information-gathering for the maritime industry).

Overall, I call getting MedLink off the ground the "Original Operation Warp Speed" — the heady and urgent aggregation of information that became our operational and marketing platform.

Our first MedLink Space featuring my son Josh with a MedLink physician. Photo credit: MedAire

Second generation MedLink space – Photo credit: MedAire

Third generation MedLink space – Photo credit: MedAire

No matter where callers might be located, according to our business model, they would be able to radio our MedLink call center, speak with one of our MedLink emergency physicians (not yet hired), and receive instantaneous guidance during an inflight or onboard crisis. In addition to communication specialists, our doctors would be supported by our worldwide database of airports, hospitals, specialty care centers, ambulances and more.

In addition, while the international aviation language is English for flight crews, sometimes onboard volunteers spoke a different language. We had more than 100 foreign language interpreters available on the call within 30 seconds to a minute. That was the working premise — a one stop shop!

Thus, we launched a unique solution to the hit-or-miss intercom plea of "Is there a doctor on board?" In an era of medical specialization, a podiatrist or pathologist, for instance, is put in an untenable position when faced with cardiac, obstetrical, pediatric, or a plethora of other scenarios. With the advent of MedLink, our plan would connect a flight crew to emergency physicians in real-time — physicians trained in all aspects of illness and injury. Then our MedLink physicians would guide medical volunteers (those who step up to volunteer during an inflight medical event) in treating passengers, a groundbreaking feat.

Speaking of staff, we hired communication specialists for 24/7 coverage. Their role was help build the database and ultimately answer calls once we were operational. The business model was for them to gather details for each call and page the MedLink doctors who (again, once hired), would interact medically with our customers. By the way, finding these doctors is a story in itself, to follow. In the interim, there was more than enough work to keep the communication specialists busy "building the park."

And now… to find board-certified emergency physicians to assist MedLink customers.

Who would step up as MedLink's emergency physicians and bring this grand experiment — a 24-hour medical advisory service — to fruition? I had to recruit practicing board-certified emergency physicians experienced in all sorts of medical and traumatic emergencies as well as remote medicine and altitude physiology.

Luckily, three extraordinary Samaritan doctors initially signed on — Dr. Dave Streitwieser, Dr. Steve Murphy, and Dr. Bob Baron. They were already supporting Air Evac flight nurses and Samaritan's aviation medicine program, and there was no one better qualified to sit at the console and dispense medical guidance remotely. One day on my lunch break, I happened to find all three of these key people in a conference room. I strode in wearing my flight suit (most likely stained from the day's activities) and I pitched my MedLink concept, the biggest gamble of my life.

"No other company in the world provides all three elements of travel safety," I cajoled, explaining the importance of the three-legged stool and the emergency physician's place in the MedLink equation. "Will you serve as our doctors?" Then I glanced from face to face and tried to gage the reaction.

It was a tepid response. I'm sure this had something to do with my inability to pay them right away. I did, however, assure them their compensation would materialize once the company grew (and that became a six-figure truth for their practices many times over). They didn't say no, but weren't quite full-out believers at the time.

"We'll give it a try," they said with a bit of skepticism, "But the emergency department is our top priority."

Of course, MedLink calls were *my* priority, and so we coordinated flexible shifts with some pinch-hitting and backup to cover critical patients in between. In their training, I emphasized the importance of talking in plain English to non-medical flight and maritime crews, and not "Latin" as doctors are prone to do — and I had to practice that myself. However, the most important qualification to this position was (and is) customer service.

I also coordinated my three-to-eleven ER shift so that I could be available. And then, the first call came in from American Trans Air (no longer in business), an all-charter airline customer with passenger flights worldwide as well as military and commercial charter flights throughout the U.S. mainland, Hawaii, and San Juan, Puerto Rico. The Trans Air crew contacted MedLink at 11 p.m. from Stockholm Radio. A passenger on the flight was experiencing chest pain. When they referred the call to MedLink, our physicians diverted the flight into Shannon, Ireland, at that very moment.

Holy moly…it worked! The hypothesis was no longer a hypothesis. MedLink was official. I personally called the ICU unit of the hospital and spoke with the patient, John O'Brian, who gave me permission to use his name. He was so grateful for our intervention and was well on his way to recovery.

Dr. Dave Streitwieser in the early days – Photo credit: MedAire

Ultimately, two of our original three doctors stayed with MedLink for decades and became experts in the field of telemedicine. Two, among others, are still taking MedLink calls today. The number of MedLink emergency physicians has expanded exponentially — hundreds of who serve our customers worldwide. There isn't an emergency they haven't handled, and they know the aspects of aviation and maritime emergencies inside out, front to back.

During an emergency, the "on duty" ground-based emergency physicians guide caregivers (medical personnel volunteers or flight crews trained in basic first aid/life support and CPR) in the assessment and treatment of an ill or injured passenger or crew member. Benefits of this model include consistency in the level and accuracy of the advice, more informed decision making by the flight crew, and data-driven results impacting future training needs and risk management.

An indirect benefit of this level of expertise has demonstrated fewer unnecessary medical diversions among commercial airlines. Our MedLink service helps ensure that the recommended diversions typically end up with affected passengers receiving definitive medical care upon landing.

Some may not know what a diversion is. If, for example, a wide-body aircraft on an international flight decided to land mid-course due to an onboard emergency, this "diversion" could cost the carrier in excess of $100,000. That does not include the cost of landing at a non-station airport, passenger inconvenience, missing connecting flights, or possibly landing "heavy" and requiring maintenance after landing.

Yes, diversions have ripple effects. So who determines when a diversion occurs? The pilot makes that monumental decision after being notified of the status of the emergency. Is the passenger critical? Will the passenger be able to endure the entire flight? MedLink doctors, by interacting with the flight crew, the airline, or operator dispatch, relay all flight-related medical and safety aspects, including recommendations for diversions when a life hangs in the balance. This allows the pilot to weigh the decision to divert or not, and a diversion usually does happen under these circumstances.

The medical capabilities at the destination airport must also be considered. It would not benefit the passenger or the airline to divert to an airport without adequate medical facilities nearby. A good example is Seoul, Korea. While there are very good medical facilities in Seoul, it could take an hour by ambulance to access them. Depending on the criticality of the passenger, it might be better to continue on to a more suitable airport with good medical care nearby. All these factors must be considered when recommending a diversion, and based on our database, MedLink communication specialists can suggest appropriate destinations and facilities.

I caught up with Dr. Bob Baron as I wrote this chapter, and what a delight to talk about those early years. He was kind enough to contribute his bird's-eye view as follows:

> *Joan asked what our reaction was the day she approached us in her flight suit. She wondered how disheveled she looked and what we said when she left the room. I responded, 'Joan, we're guys. We didn't*

notice your flight suit. We did wonder how you would make your idea fly. Would customers pay for the service or would it be a flash in the pan?' Skeptical was an apt description as we pondered MedLink.

None of us doctors were entrepreneurial. However, we were (and are) excellent clinicians and already experienced in listening to chief complaints over radio and giving instructions to paramedics. Joan tapped us because we had been caring for individuals remotely, although it was different interacting with the airlines. Most of the time, the flight crew wasn't medically trained, and it was more difficult to try and figure out what the problem was. The crew usually asked if any medical person was on board, which was helpful in the event we needed to start an IV and talk about the medical aspects.

Joan did all the groundwork. She coordinated with Samaritan to set up a control room where we took calls, dark with only the monitors giving low light (which evolved over time). While we were on shift in the emergency department, a tone went off, and an overhead page stated: 'Doctor to MedLink.' Back then, at least two doctors were always present, five at most, and whoever could break free would excuse himself and walk across the hall. Then we'd push another button so the tone discontinued, and the doctors knew the MedLink call was being answered.

From our perspective, the technical aspects were somewhat mysterious — we didn't know how and why it worked and simply used the handset or headphones and receive transmissions from Stockholm radio or SATCOMS. A communications specialist had the airline dispatch and pilot on the radio, and handed over notes and partially filled out paperwork. The challenge here was that everything was relayed to the flight crew from the back. We listened, noted the primary chief complaint, discussed what was in the medical kit, put together a plan, and noted how long it would take to divert in case that was the outcome. The diversion rate was infrequent, about three to five percent. If the flight could continue, we discussed what else could be done to assist the patient.

By the way, the international flight and ground control language is English. Pilots, regardless of locale, are fluent, but Joan arranged 24/7 translation services when requested. For instance, in those days, some Brazilian airline pilots preferred to communicate in Portuguese. We'd pause for a moment and make a call to have a translator patched in.

Most of those early calls, in general, weren't that long. Two minutes, five minutes, and not that many during one shift until MedLink grew its customer base. I have photos of Joan's t-shirts for various steps along the way. One said "10,000 and Climbing" to celebrate 10,000 calls. In 2021, the numbers are closer to 20,000 to 30,000 calls, and the spectrum has evolved. MedLink had contracts with superyachts, drilling rigs offshore, and at one time, evaluated the medical kit and capabilities of Air Force 2. The expansion has been remarkable.

A young Dr. Bob Baron. Photo credit: MedAire

Dr. Steve Reinhart, another original MedAire emergency physician, provides a great overview of the evolution of the company and what it is like to be on the receiving end of

MedLink calls. Most importantly, he shares observations and some advice for air travelers, especially those with medical conditions, and a few "traveling animal stories" as well.

I've been with Joan since day one. When she told us about her concept and needed a group of physicians to back her up, we agreed. MedLink was quite an innovation. The first few days of calls were slow, and we waited in anticipation for the "MedLink doctor to the comm room" announcement. Today, the calls are nonstop, and we've handled some interesting cases.

Working as a MedLink physician is a lot like working in the hospital ER. Any kind of emergency can occur. And yet, it's an entirely different type of medicine — telemedicine. The person calling has to paint some sort of picture for the MedLink doctor. We know what questions to ask and try to determine if the patient is critically ill. Prior to 9/11, the flight attendant or a passenger (a doctor or nurse on board) could interact with MedLink from the pilot's phone in the cockpit. After 9/11, the procedures changed and became more complex. Everything is relayed second or thirdhand. The pilot talks to the flight attendant, the flight attendant talks to the medical volunteers, and they are patched through to us.

You never know what types of medical volunteers will come to the aid of patients — I've had lab assistants and veterinarians respond. However, at least in my experience, there was never a veterinarian available when a call involved an animal. Yes, every once in a while, MedLink is contacted for animal-related "emergencies" that are quite memorable.

For instance, I took a call about a salamander that had somehow boarded a plane. The crew was worried about it transmitting salmonella. Sometimes commonsense suggestions suffice, such as trapping the creature and using hand sanitizer. But other times, the situation isn't as cut and dry.

A doctor in Johannesburg received a call about a six-year-old Boston terrier with shortness of breath. We aren't animal specialists, and the doctor wasn't sure how to respond. How aggressive do you get in cases like this? Usually, if a plane is diverted (a decision made by the pilot — costly and involving logistics), an ambulance is on standby when the plane lands. This wouldn't be the case for the dog. The crew put the dog on oxygen and then called back. The dog was in full cardiac arrest, and they administered CPR and used a defibrillator. The poor thing expired despite their best efforts, and the situation highlights the unusual cases that can occur in flight.

I received a call about a large service dog that was ill. I explained that we aren't a veterinarian service but asked about the symptoms. This poor dog had a severe case of runny diarrhea and, unfortunately, sprayed passengers up and down the aisle. What do you do in a case like that? Suggest Imodium? Ultimately, they called back to inform us that the pilot diverted the flight, but not for the dog. The smell was just too overwhelming for the passengers and crew, and they had to land the plane.

A call came in about an allergic reaction. I asked what the patient was allergic to, and the answer was "cats." So I asked if there were cats on board, and sure enough, the answer was, "Yes, two cats are on the plane." They were stowed in crates, and apparently, their dander caused the patient to react. I suggested they administer epinephrine from the MedAire kit to help the patient endure the rest of the flight.

This brings up a good point. If you have an allergy, consider wearing an alert bracelet or have that information handy for the flight attendant. Keep your medicines close by. Some passengers pack prescriptions in their checked luggage where it can't be accessed. Instead, medicines should be kept in carry-on bags. It amazes me, the number of people who eat something on a plane that they are allergic to, which is very dangerous. Someone with a severe nut allergy might eat a cookie with nuts. Someone with a fish allergy may eat a meal with fish. The flight attendant will ask if they have their EpiPen with them and are sometimes told, "No, it's in my checked baggage."

For seizure disorders, it also makes sense to wear a medical alert tag. No one knows your history and whether this is a first-time seizure (which can be ominous) or if the seizure is related to epilepsy. The same goes for diabetics. If someone is unconscious, it helps to know if they are diabetic and the type of diabetes involved.

I remember one call when a young lady passed out, and a dentist responded. He asked what he could do to assist. Typically, when passengers pass out, they are laid down with their legs elevated and then are given a sweetened beverage to bring their blood sugar up. Since the dentist was involved, I asked if he'd make sure she'd brush her teeth afterward!

Communication specialists initially answer these incoming calls. They take down the information, including the airline, flight number, origination and destination, and how long it will take to arrive at the destination. Arrival time during an emergency can make a big difference — 20 minutes vs. 10 ½ hours — and we take this into consideration, especially with diversions. Sometimes the communication specialist has to notify a port authority if someone is coming in with an infection. There's a lot to think about and coordinate, including the nearest hospital that can appropriately treat the patient. It can be counterproductive to land a plane where state-of-the-art medical facilities are not available. They may have to fly into another country to access proper care.

Burns on board can occur from hot liquids, not an uncommon call. We received quite a few burn calls from one airline that served hot beverages out of a silver tea service, and the slightest bump or turbulence could cause a spill. Typically, burn gel and Tylenol for pain make the patient comfortable enough to reach their destination.

Passengers shouldn't fly if they have certain kinds of casts, especially new casts. One call involved a broken tibia that had been set in a cast the day before. The cast went all the way around the leg. Altitude plus sitting down caused swelling and loss of circulation to the foot. A cut down the side of cast allowed for expansion. Some procedures, too, should not be undergone before flying. I once received a call from a flight attendant concerned about a passenger sitting backwards in the seat shortly after takeoff. I asked for clarification and was told the passenger was on her knees with her chest against the seat. It turned out she had a Brazilian butt lift the day before and couldn't sit. Of course, the flight attendant was concerned for safety reasons but allowed the patient to sit in this unusual manner (or stand) until it was time to land.

Sometimes drug addicts misjudge the amount of time they can go without a "fix" and experience withdrawal symptoms on board. They usually "fess up" to a flight attendant, who calls MedLink. We have to determine how critical the situation is, how close to landing they are, and if supportive care will suffice. Alcoholics, too, can go into withdrawal. We ask for vital signs — MedAire kits have stethoscopes and blood pressure cuffs — although it's sometimes difficult to hear the heartbeat or get an accurate blood pressure reading with ambient noise on the plane. Some airlines, such as Qatar, carry MedAire's Tempus device that checks for blood pressure, oxygen saturation, and even acts as an EKG so that we can see a full picture of all vital signs — extremely helpful.

When COVID-19 first hit, the number of maritime calls increased. Some yacht owners and their families quarantined aboard their boats, meaning they spent more time than usual at sea. We had the typical calls (just more of them) regarding patients diving in the ocean and getting the bends, insect bites, food poisoning, symptoms of appendicitis, and more. Some yachts have helicopters and can get passengers to shore quickly, but more often it can take days. The maritime medical kits are comprehensive for this reason — something Joan envisioned for this industry.

Joan has revolutionized medical care for travelers. Thanks to her, tis remarkable advancement in remote care has been available since the late 1980s. We hear of telemedicine today, mostly due to COVID-

19. Joan, however, pioneered telemedicine more than 30 years ago, long before it came into vogue. Her work is nothing short of amazing.

There you have it, a day in the life of a MedLink physician. Many thanks to Steve for this behind-the-scenes view and kind words. MedAire has been blessed to have his caliber of medical expertise on standby — and our team of doctors has grown into worldwide team that services the travel industry 24/7/365.

A flight attendant stowing a MedAire kit – Photo credit: MedAire

Fast forward to 2006 when Dr. Paolo Alves, Global Director of Aviation Health, joined MedAire. He weighs in below about our data tracking capabilities.

I was a client before joining MedAire, a medical director for an airline. I knew Joan because she was my provider. As a MedAire customer, I developed a nice friendship and business relationship with Joan. I was hired by MedAire and amazed at the amount of data the company was collecting.

First as a client and now as an employee, I was a firsthand witness of MedAire's growth. MedLink initially operated out of a very small room with two or three workstations. Today, it's a huge center with strong teams at headquarters and multiple locations worldwide. Thus, MedAire is privileged to have an expansive window of observation of what is going on in the aviation sector.

As I look into medical events in flight, it's absolutely proportional to the amount of passengers and how long they fly. The best way to understand this is to look at air travel as a city in the sky. At any given moment, you have around a million people flying. If you can observe with medical eyes what's going on with the city of one million, you can track information, just like if you were sitting at the door of the ER in this city taking notes. That's the data gathering.

Things happen in this unique in-flight environment from many perspectives — a peculiar side of medicine not taught in medical school. Our database contains a massive amount of data points by events, operational (route, origination, destination, position of aircraft, etc.), and passenger demographics such as age and gender, but we do not collect names for privacy reasons.

These data points are a byproduct of our activities in providing medical advice, a public health matter across all demographics from the elderly vacationing with grandkids to tourism to business flights, all an excellent sample of the traveling population. The events are classified into medical categories by the doctors, according to their clinical impression. We extract information and use it to analyze, gather knowledge, and build intelligence to improve the whole system.

I've been invited to Joan's home in Arizona. Her very personal way of engaging with employees and clients is her key to success. It's all about relationships — she has proven that — and making others feel special. More than a businesswoman, she has always been devoted to her mission. Success was a consequence of her dedication.

I appreciate Dr. Alves very much. His "city in the sky" analogy describes how and why MedLink was (and is) able to gather data that benefits the FAA, the travel industry, and passengers around the globe today. We co-authored a paper in 2008 which was presented during the 26th Congress of the International Council of the Aeronautical Sciences titled "Aviation Telemedicine: Past, Present And Future."[19]

---

[19] J. S. Garrett and P. M. Alves. "Aviation Telemedicine: Past, Present and Future," *International Congress of the Aeronautical Sciences*, 2008. See https://www.icas.org/ICAS_ARCHIVE/ICAS2008/PAPERS/551.PDF.

Chapter Fourteen: Papers, Presentations and Persistence

*It usually takes me more than three weeks to prepare
a good impromptu speech.*
~ Mark Twain

I should talk about the in's and out's of marketing. We needed an extra marketing push early on and had access to Samaritan's marketing team and graphic designer. They loved working on MedAire products — so different than the usual hospital business. I owed them for it and ultimately paid them back two- and threefold. When we became self-sufficient, we found our own marketers and designers. I found creative ways to work around budget constraints with the help of people who supported our mission, and what a story our marketing became throughout the years!

Being a frugal executive, I was blessed to know Dale Verzaal of Burnt Toast, a graphic arts company well known from San Francisco to Dallas. Dale's children played soccer with my sons. He had an interesting studio, a converted garage with a glass door and the front end of an old Cadillac attached to the wall, as well as the butt end of a stuffed deer with a pencil sharpener under the tail. Years prior, I went to Miami for a deep-sea fishing trip, caught a dolphin fish, dropped it off with a taxidermist, and had it shipped to my home. I showed it to Dale, and we made a trade — the dolphin fish for two logos. It was a great barter.

Through a series of graphic designers and marketing interns, the incarnation of our air, land, and sea logos improved.

MedAire®, Inc.

The original MedAire logo – Photo credit: MedAire

MedAire®

Next-general MedAire logo – Photo credit: MedAire

Photo credit: MedAire

One marketer was promoted to vice president — savvy, book smart, and creative. She came up with the marketing strategy of offering cholesterol testing for pilots at our major business aviation conference and left after three years to raise her children, but what a huge difference she made in our media presence. Fortunately, my husband Frank recommended another marketing person who kept us on this trajectory.

I'll fast-forward here to Steve Holstein, a contractor in the early days who was hired as VP of MedAire's Marketing & Government Programs. He inherited our marketing assets and grew them to new heights from 2000 to 2006. Steve was — and is — a fantastically creative person who polished our image and impressed me to no end. I value his friendship and expertise today, a true support system well beyond our MedAire "in the trenches" days.

Let me tell you, it wasn't easy working 18-hour days and missing out on my sons' extracurricular activities through the years. They were accustomed to me working multiple shifts from the time I became a nurse. Still, I was a presence at home and not traveling from continent to continent in their formative years.

But suddenly, in their teen years, I was constantly on the road, marketing kits and training courses — and converting this exercise into MedLink sales.

For example, I remember a successful business aviation sale in the UK. As the class thoroughly examined the kit contents while simultaneously learning about anatomy and physiology, someone said, "I won't remember all of this."

My response was, "Our training manual will walk you through these medical emergencies. But if you need to talk to a doctor, our backup MedLink service will connect you from anywhere in the world in under a minute." Imagine the incredulity when I called MedLink from the class in real-time, a test patch that demonstrated how efficient and instantaneous the call was.

"So, you're taking the monkey off our back and putting it onto yours," the participant said as the classroom erupted in applause.

"Absolutely!" I agreed. "There is nothing better than talking to a board-certified emergency physician when you're up in the air and handling a medical event."

This concluded in a signed contract, a typical result when "showing" rather than "telling." These hands-on demonstrations were definitely the path to success, and I roamed the globe to make these conversions possible.

Once a large non-subscribing operator point-blank told me, "We never have any problems. I don't need you." I talked him into accepting one free MedLink call, just in case. Within 48 hours, we got a call from one of his pilots on a transatlantic flight. A passenger was experiencing a severe allergic reaction, and we told the crew how to manage the emergency. The following Monday, we had a new client.

As MedAire grew, I would eventually spend 280 days each year hopping my way across the globe and promoting the business. There were several ways to increase MedAire's presence, and one was to attend industry events — mingling within organizations, getting my company's name out there, and becoming one of the first female CEOs to enter the aviation marketplace. I also wrote abstracts galore (probably 60 in total) and tailored white papers to meet the subject matter sought by worldwide conferences every year. If my paper was accepted, I was invited to speak at the podium.

A booth at an international conference – Photo credit: MedAire

Before I flew, we mapped each continent, country, and city to coordinate my itinerary and conserve airfare costs, always budget-conscious. But I was also "motherhood-conscious" — always a concern in my heart. You bet I experienced heaping doses of working mother guilt — and then some. I'm sure those years were a bit of a blur to my sons as they finished high school and headed to college, and I also had to adjust to these absences myself. I missed my boys, and they missed me. I wondered how traveling fathers handled the absences. Did they pine for their children and worry from afar as I did? After all, it's pretty typical that fathers travel for a living. No one raises an eyebrow. But it's unusual for a mother to do so — a seemingly unnatural separation. And yet, lives, literally, hung in the balance. There was no other company that safeguarded the traveling public like MedAire — airline crews and maritime crews as well. And so, I followed my calling to bring MedAire's safety net to these sectors.

Fortunately, my sons' father cared for them in my absence. Frank, too, stepped up. My boys and I made the most of the time we had together when I was home — the cabin, for instance — and I'm so thankful that they worked alongside me and eventually became MedAire employees. One son, Josh, remains employed by MedAire today. Thankfully, I can say without a doubt that they grew into wonderful men, loving husbands, and the very best fathers. I'm not exaggerating — they really are well-grounded, sensible citizens and a lot of fun to be around. Most importantly, they value the time spent with their own children to an exceptional degree because they know what it's like to have a long-distance parent.

I'm relieved my sons have not taken the "constant traveling career path" and have employment arrangements that keep them closer to home than I ever was. It benefits their children (my beloved grandchildren). It also makes me realize what I, and they, sacrificed on behalf of millions of traveling strangers who are now safer, thanks to my understanding family.

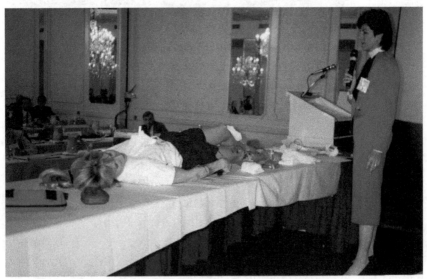

Emergency medical response demonstration – Photo credit: MedAire

Because I was on the road an enormous amount of time, you may wonder how I managed life with my husband, Frank. Well,

Frank had a wife who spent far more time aboard a plane than in our home. As a matter of fact, it was awful packing for each trip and leaving my husband, sons, and the beautiful weather in Phoenix, where life was so good. I had to bid Frank farewell and hop on a plane to "somewhere," most often another lengthy international trip. I was torn, but once on the plane, I shifted gears and forced myself into "work mode," knowing I had the support of both of my boys and Frank as well. Their love was so vitally important and kept me going when I was weary, jet-lagged, and homesick.

Frank weighs in below about our 35-year union — and he surprised me with his straight-from-the-heart observations.

I work for JoanCo. I'm the manager of the high maintenance department. It's a full-time job, and I "work for food." All kidding aside, I knew Joan was incredibly driven when I met her. I was busy as well, working on my MBA and overseeing nuclear industry projects during my own travels. I belonged to many organizations, sat on and chaired technical committees and boards, and was fully invested in my career. Between 1990 and about 1998, I built our first retirement home in Vernon, located down the street from the cabin Joan moved from the reservation. Most of my weekends and vacations were devoted to that project. We are now living in our second retirement home and have building plans for our third and last. Designing, building, and furnishing these homes was a significant piece of our life back then and provided great enjoyment and reward.

I guess you could say that Joan and I were both independent professionals who just happened to mesh. She was intriguing, a bit skeptical of me as a suitor, and I believe that was based on her past relationships. Somehow, I earned her trust and admiration. However, it did seem to take a long time. It was obvious that her startup was something incredible, truly one of a kind. I thought she was brilliant to fill a market need, and thus I became a true believer in MedAire myself.

During those first few years, our garage doubled as a warehouse and our dining room table was the accounting and financial center, something that I could help her manage. I put my engineering skills to use in helping with IT and infrastructure but was quietly supportive and comfortable in the background, watching as my wife blazed a trail around the world. I did sit on the MedAire board and attended conferences to watch Joan on stage. I've always been so very proud of this beautiful, gifted, multi-tasking woman who is as excellent a wife and mother as she is a business leader.

Not that I didn't worry. I worried about her flying aboard helicopters during search and rescues when there were a significant number of crashes in the aeromedical transport industry. I worried at the volume of international travel she routinely undertook, sometimes in less developed regions. I worried that she would exhaust herself. But I understood the mission.

Not to sound like an infomercial, but it astounds me that the company continues to innovate and apply leading technology. Today, MedAire is able to provide medical clearance for passengers before embarking if they appear to have symptoms of apparent infectious diseases such as mumps or measles. Airlines depend on MedAire nurses and physicians for crew support services as well — flight crews, traveling personnel, and business executives. If someone is ill and gets left behind on a continent, MedAire nurses talk to them daily and arrange for physicians to see them and pharmacies to dispense medications. The importance of what Joan brought to the world makes our personal sacrifices worth it. People are alive and well today because she made this tremendous effort.

We looked forward to being home at the same time, and those reunions were always great. It was surprising, actually, that we've always gotten along so well. We iron out our differences with mutual respect, and I think that's the key — respect and pulling on the same rope. And...absence makes the heart grow fonder.

I remember becoming an instant family — Joan and the boys and me. That was special too. I never tried to be a "substitute father." Instead, I felt my role was to show my stepsons how to be good husbands — supportive, loyal, invested, and "on-call." Indeed, they became great husbands and fathers themselves and have given Joan and me three exceptional grandchildren to dote on. There is nothing better at this stage in life than to watch them grow. When they travel, I know they are safer because their grandmother founded MedAire.

Reading Frank's words gives me an "Aw, shucks" moment. He's being very kind. It could not have been easy putting up with the feverish pace of my schedule, my absences, and my focus on the company. I've mentioned that MedAire was very much a family affair. I'm very grateful that he and my sons understood that this mission was larger than ourselves, something monumental and instrumental to the safety of millions of passengers and crews worldwide.

I've always been a "people person," happiest when interacting face-to-face and one-on-one. But guess what? The opposite was true on stage, and boy, I was on stage a lot. However, I was not a natural. I made myself a natural by sticking with it and improving over time. Practice does make perfect.

Here's another trip down memory lane. In 1987 I joined the National Business Aviation Association (NBAA) in Los Angeles. I walked the halls and visited safety booths to discuss MedAire. Some of the vendors told me MedAire was not a good idea and that I would never "make it." Nothing but negativity. But this inspired me to prove them wrong (and I did). MedAire set up booths too, the smallest at first due to affordability and then larger over the years. The largest annual exhibitions were at the NBAA and the Aerospace Medical Association. We had booths in Fort Lauderdale and other maritime yachting shows as well.

Our booth at a National Business Aviation Association (NBAA) conference – L-R: Gaye Johnson, my son Aaron, me, Vickee Altman, and Lee Patrick – Photo credit: MedAire

Another appearance at NBAA conference – Photo credit: MedAire

One of our premier annual events was the cholesterol screenings we offered at no charge during NBAA annual conferences, where we had an annual booth. We wanted to give back to the industry, noting that the greatest loss of pilot licensure is due to cardiovascular disease. Every year, MedAire nurses and doctors helped aviation professionals and other attendees get their cholesterol under control and enjoy healthier lives. This cholesterol testing turned out to be "marketing genius." An unintended benefit was the undivided attention we gave customers and business prospects who visited our booth. As they spent five, ten, or fifteen minutes in line and then in the testing chair, we talked about MedAire and MedLink. These customers and prospects also talked with our MedLink physicians — the personal touch MedAire has always been famous for.

Me with Dr. Jack Applefeld (critical care medicine), Dr. Dave Streitwieser (Medical Director), and Dr. Bob Baron (Co-Medical Director) at our MedAire offices – Photo credit: MedAire

Dr. Dave Streitwieser was instrumental at these NBAA events and even accompanied me on sales calls, enhancing the credibility of the company. Other talented MedLink physicians were instrumental in promoting the message, including Dr. Les Tukan, our Maritime Medical Director. Our maritime kits and training, by the way, were specialized due to the nature of ocean environments and had very different criteria than aviation. Dr. Tukan and I would eventually visit Antigua and conduct a training course there (in a cave, no less). I also spoke at an Amsterdam conference where I published a paper and presented it to yacht captains and yacht builders.

At the podium – Photo credit: MedAire

Our newer emergency physicians were able to experience the industry from a marketing angle as well. This was the case with Dr. Moneesh Bhow, so incredibly smart and talented, who provides an enjoyable rendition of his experiences below.

> *I joined MedAire early in my career because it blended my two passions — travel and medicine — into one. I was lucky to have learned from leading experts and follow in their footsteps, Dr. Les Tukan, Dr. Dave Streitwieser, and Dr. Bob Baron.*

> *I got to know Joan when Dave Streitwieser invited me to an NBAA*

Business Aviation Convention and Exhibition to meet clients and hold cholesterol screenings. I've been to at least a dozen screenings in a row and see people return year after year. 'Doc, the last time you told me to do this and that. Let's see how numbers look this year,' they say. One formerly overweight heavy smoker came by, and we didn't recognize him. He had lost weight, quit smoking, and thanked us for getting him on track.

When Joan attends these screenings, she's like a celebrity. People line up to talk to her. She remembers the little details — people's names, spouses, and their children. That's one of Joan's special qualities — she's observant. She gives them her complete one-on-one attention and makes them feel like they are the only people in the room. Even if an important executive is waiting in line to talk to her, she focuses on the person in front of her and makes them feel valued.

Once Joan took us to a fabulous dinner and spoke of how MedAire started on a shoestring budget. I never really knew the extent of the efforts she went through until this meal when her labor of love and the mission really became apparent.

She didn't have money to entertain clients but sometimes felt obligated to take them to dinner. If they ordered expensive bottles of wine and extravagant meals, she found an interesting way to settle the bill. She'd push the cork to the bottom of an empty wine bottle and say, 'I'll bet you the tab I can get that cork out.' The client said, 'No way!' and took her bet.

Joan had a clever way of folding a cloth napkin into the bottle, bouncing the cork around until it landed in the napkin, and pulling the cork out. People couldn't believe their eyes and everyone had a great laugh. Joan taught me the trick, and I'm not as fast as she is, but I did turn it into a free round of drinks and dessert after impressing a waiter.

One year in Kuala Lumpur, while sitting at an airport hotel bar, I overheard two crew members from Emirates airline say, 'It got a little scary up there. We had to call MedLink (he pronounced it 'Medi-link'). I leaned over and told them I was one of the MedLink docs. They were fascinated and expressed their thanks and the peace of mind knowing we were a resource they could trust. There's a sense of comfort when a doctor is available, especially on long flights over regions where pilots don't want to land. This might be for geopolitical reasons, lack of fuel availability, or knowing certain airports cannot accommodate the size of the aircraft.

When I'm flying, I introduce myself to flight attendants and say I'm with MedLink. Often, the captain or a flight crew member comes out to chat and thanks me for our air-to-ground services and usually shares a MedLink story. Everyone wants to know what our control room looks like. It used to be a small, dark room in the middle of the hospital with a lot of monitors, data, and advanced technology, kind of how I would imagine a CIA bunker.

Years ago, my wife and I were on a ski vacation in Telluride, Colorado. It was cold, and I was buttoned up and wearing a hat and scarf. You could probably only see my eyeballs. But out of the blue, I heard, 'Moneesh! Moneesh!' It was Joan! She just happened to be there the same weekend. How she recognized me all wrapped up, I'll never know. We went to the "Pink Party" that last weekend, a street fare-type of party, and had lots of fun.

Once I was wearing a Gulfstream hat, and the gentleman behind me asked, 'Do you fly?' I told him I worked for a telemedicine service… and before I could say the name, he said, 'Is it MedLink? Do you know Joan?' When I said yes, he raved about her. 'She's phenomenal. You should stick with her. She'll teach you and take you places.'

He was right. We've all learned from her business sense and people skills. The FAA and Congress have benefited from her testimony. Joan's telemedicine invention is genius, especially when you think about the 1980s and the lack of technology she faced initially. She used what was available, expanded on it, and now MedLink serves planes and ships throughout the world. When people told her it wouldn't work, she showed them it could. I call that tenacity. Every time I take a call, I think, If you're going to leave a legacy, this is the way to do it.

The passengers we help may not know the story behind it all, but we really are their safety net. So many owe their lives to Joan's foresight and sacrifice, as well as the MedLink doctors, nurses, and support staff.

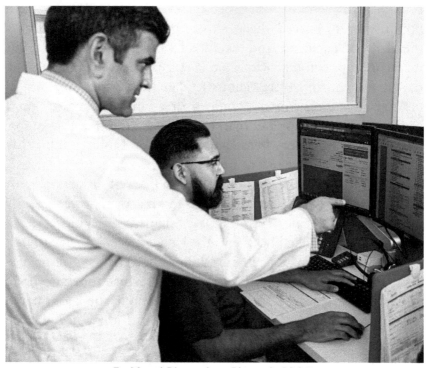

Dr. Moneesh Bhow on duty – Photo credit: MedAire

Well, Dr. Bhow's kind words have rendered me speechless. Honestly, I didn't anticipate the wonderful stories shared throughout this book. How great for readers to experience MedAire and MedLink through the lens of medical professionals on the frontline, much appreciated. I should mention that we always had fun. After taking down our booth, we all went to a festive place for dinner to decompress, laugh, and get silly.

Having a young and energetic team meant there was no end to the notion of "working hard and playing hard." Clients always wanted to hang out with the MedAire group. We looked at these relationships in a long-term sense and "invested today for tomorrow's activities."

I fondly look way, way back on one particular Flight Safety Foundation event in Williamsburg, Virginia in 1988, a great opportunity to spread the MedAire gospel. I was invited as a mingler, not a speaker, and assumed I would breeze through this marketing opportunity with ease. Yet this was a major function, the largest and most prestigious to date, and I had one shot at making an impression. I bought a dress in Los Angeles on a separate trip at an apparel market for next to nothing — a grey long-sleeved designer dress, half-length by Rabbit Rabbit. My goal was to look elegant but professional.

I'll never forget opening the doors to a sea of influential male aviation leaders... and freezing in place. It was nearly overwhelming seeing these industry titans, and I did a quick about-face and walked back into the hallway. I had to give myself a pep talk, feeling like such an oddity. There I was, a female of little renown, about to wade through the testosterone and hope to make an impression. Yet, nearly everyone in the room could benefit from my products and services, and I knew it. It fell on my shoulders to work the crowd and shake off this sudden shyness.

So, I took a deep breath. It was now or never. I reentered and immediately noticed the tallest person there — Don Short, a presidential pilot to President Lyndon B. Johnson and then Director and Chief Pilot of Corporate Air Transportation, Northrop Corporation. He smiled, and I made a beeline straight to him, recited my thirty-second elevator speech, and told him about myself. Very kindly, Don took me around the room and made introductions. He knew what I was up against, and over time helped me transition from the nursing mindset to the corporate world. I call this mentoring at its best, and I'll be forever indebted for his concern and kindness.

Don graciously shares his recollections below.

My first memory of meeting Joan was at a Flight Safety Foundation conference in Williamsburg, Virginia, and learning what she could do for the business aviation industry. What a gorgeous attention-getter, and equally impressive was her company MedAire, and what it offered. I introduced her to many associates of mine, former military pilots, and several civilian aviators. They did not see the merit to my disappointment — at least not at first. However, my personal experiences as a military pilot, especially piloting for President Johnson aboard Air Force One, gave me a different perspective. We had an onboard physician. On every flight, Admiral Buckley, personal physician to the President, was on the passenger list. All of my associates lacked that experience, which I viewed as another layer of safety. I wanted my associates to do better than we had by having a trained physician available — just a radio or phone call away. The chance that someone on board your company's jet could experience food poisoning, an allergy attack, or some other medical crisis is always a clear and present danger.

Joan got her points across and shared several innovations in the medical field as she worked the room. There was very little shared appreciation for in-flight medical services in the business aircraft community, nor did we realize the medical capabilities until Joan made that link available. She brought it all together for people in my category — pilots looking for a better "mousetrap" to enhance safety.

At one point in my military career, I was an intercept radio operator. A communicator. Which meant monitoring calls and becoming attuned to the various stations and services they provided. Later in my flying career, I had the opportunity to visit one of the most efficient and professional groups of operators from Bern, Switzerland. I had used them in-flight as our executives often needed to change flight plans through a direct and clear radio chat; that was Berna Radio's forte. No one did it better. As a subscriber to the MedLink services, I would, on occasion, initiate calls through Berna to Phoenix while in flight — sometimes over Europe or the Middle East — just to develop the protocols and gain experience at facilitating information exchange. I had heard various exchanges with other flights through the years, and during my occasional visits to Switzerland, shared this new business application with the station's management.

Another unsung part of Joan's startup came about when President Reagan shut down the USSR. Traveling the world with the "IRON CURTAIN" in place caused many circuitous routing and overflight restrictions. With that restriction lifted, the world became so much more accessible, with more medical facilities becoming available should an in-flight medical situation require a diversion. With a good communications station at our disposal and boundaries removed, MedLink had the potential of being a huge success, and countless people everywhere would benefit from that psychological feeling of survivability.

About this time, Joan was moving her business attention toward the airlines, and it was her impetus for the portable defibrillators we all know of today that broadened the industry's in-flight medical safety program.

Joan visited me in California, and I was glad to be a mentor early on. MedAire was something the industry needed, and she had already made some headway. For instance, she had spoken at a prior meeting before I met her and won over some clients. We happened to run into those clients during her visit.

I helped Joan make some comparisons. An example; how much was MedAire going to cost? In the late 1980s, membership was about $2,500 a year to train and make available MedAire's other assets that would support a flight wherever you may be in the world. I shared that a plane capable of international travel cared about 2,500 to 3,000 gallons of fuel, give or take, and the fuel was about $1.00 per gallon.

I told Joan, "My goodness, this should be such an easy sell for the price of one load of fuel — and many of us refuel two, three, or even four times a day. Moreover, catering bills on just one multi-day trip could easily cost the same." In context, the benefit was high for such a low cost, a drop in the bucket. With this knowledge, she could strengthen her sales pitch. And that's how it all got started, and MedAire took off.

I happened to be in the audience when Joan gave her very first presentation to an international group in Vancouver, BC, Canada. By then, she was well recognized and had earned an excellent reputation in flight safety circles. What a powerful story she has. We are all safer because Joan charted new territory in telemedicine and persevered.

By the way, I still carry a MedAire medical kit in my car from 25 years ago. I bet most of the equipment is original — an aviation folklore piece today.

What kind words! I'm so grateful to Don for his continued friendship and our affiliation with the Flight Safety Foundation — one of the first organizations that welcomed me into the aviation community. Years later, I presented a paper at the 48th annual International Air Safety Seminar in Alexandria, Virginia, titled "Physiological and Pharmacological Countermeasures to Fatigue."[20] In 1997, I received the Flight Safety Foundation's Business Aviation Meritorious Service Award — quite an honor![21]

---

[20] J.S. Garrett. "Physiological and Pharmacological Countermeasures to Fatigue." Proceedings of the Flight Safety Foundation 48th annual International Air Safety Seminar. Alexandria, Virginia, U.S.: Flight Safety Foundation, 1996. See also https://flightsafety.org/hf/hf_may-june96.pdf

[21] See https://flightsafety.org/foundation/aviation-awards/fsf-business-aviation-meritorious-service-award/

Flight Safety Foundation
Business Aviation Meritorious Award
to

Joan Sullivan Garrett
MedAire

For her dedication to the management of medical emergencies in flight and remote locations. She has affected for greater numbers of persons than would have been possible for her as a critical-care flight nurse with experience in emergency and trauma response.

Joan pioneered a worldwide health and emergency-medical-management organization that provides immediate professional assistance and response through electronic media around-the-clock.

Business aviation has expanded across the far reaches of the globe. Passengers aboard corporate aircraft fleets no longer feel anxious or isolated from emergency medical assistance while in route and out of reach of ground-based medical care.

Her singular mission of bringing peace of mind to those isolated from critical medical care as well as her additional missions of providing prevention strategies, on-site training and travel advisory services, has resulted in a significant advancement of safety in business and corporate aviation.

Flight Safety Foundation proudly recognizes Joan Sullivan Garrett for her contribution to business aviation and humanity.

April 30, 1997

CHAIRMAN, PRESIDENT and CEO
FLIGHT SAFETY FOUNDATION

CHAIRMAN, CORPORATE ADVISORY COMMITTEE

1997 Flight Safety Foundation's Business Aviation Meritorious Service Award

By now, my status as unpaid CEO had changed. It was obvious that MedAire — once an experiment and hypothesis — was a fully validated enterprise. I believed in my company, lived it, breathed it, and finally decided to take a MedAire salary in the mid-1990s. Now I could devote myself exclusively to our upward trajectory and reach our full potential. We were finally operating in the black with 30% growth per year, yet it was a difficult decision to give up my emergency nursing career at the hospital. Being a practicing nurse was fused into my core, and it was hard to let go. I did keep up with all of my nursing certifications and continuing education until 2018, knowing how valuable this skillset was in our R&D, instructional material, and training.

Speaking of R&D, MedAire's database grew with each call, each encounter. A 1996 report in the *Chicago Tribune*[22] reveals the lack of record keeping within the FAA; MedLink countered this lack of data, as always, through comprehensive tracking. In other words, our data became useful to the travel industry and, ultimately, the government when there was a question about the number and types of inflight emergencies.

It seemed that once we reached that magical year, 1997, we were unstoppable. MedAire set up offices in Europe. My son Aaron worked in business aviation sales and would gradually take greater roles, including managing director over international sales in Europe, the Middle East, and Africa (EMEA). Initially based out of Oslo, Norway, we moved to Farnborough Airport in England to better service our growing customer list.

I had the tremendous honor of spending time with Prince Faisal bin Hussein of Jordan, son of King Hussein and brother of King Abdullah II. This was in Amman, Jordan, during the 53rd Annual General Meeting of the International Air Transport Association (IATA). What a story that was! I was invited to speak and was at the podium in front of several hundred attendees and was scheduled just before the lunch break. Suddenly, Prince Faisal's armed security force filed in and lined the walls. Of course, I stopped speaking, and the room fell silent. Then a contingent carried in a red velour chair and placed it directly in

---

[22] John Crewdson. "How Many People Die On Airplanes?" *Chicago Tribune*, 1996. See https://www.chicagotribune.com/news/ct-xpm-1996-06-30-9606300406-story.html

front of me, after which the Prince was escorted into the room and seated.

Me with the Prince of Jordan – Photo credit: MedAire

"Please continue," Prince Faisal said, and I finished my presentation. Then he invited me to lunch (which was part of the conference), and I was seated opposite of him. What a delightful conversation! The Prince, a pilot, was curious about MedAire, who our clients were, the number of medical emergencies we encountered, and what we learned through our data. I greatly appreciated his interest in my company and that he took the time to meet me — one of my fondest memories. That evening, the entire assembly enjoyed a hosted dinner by the Dead Sea with great fanfare, and the Prince and his wife were in attendance. Wow!

Perhaps most notably, I went back to Washington D.C. in 1997, this time to testify before Congress. The U.S. House of Representatives, the Subcommittee on Aviation, and the Committee on Transportation and Infrastructure were, once again, reviewing the status of medical kits on commercial airlines.

Below is my testimony[23] that few have seen outside of the 1997 timeframe, yet it holds true today. An additional footnote takes you to my full statement.[24] The Honorable John J. Duncan, Jr., chairman of the subcommittee, presided.

> **Mr. DUNCAN.** *Our next witness is Ms. Joan Sullivan Garrett, who is president of MedAire, Incorporated of Phoenix, Arizona. Ms. Garrett?*

> **Ms. GARRETT.** *Thank you, Mr. Chairman and members of the committee. I'm Joan Sullivan Garrett, president of MedAire. Thank you for the opportunity to present information this morning, an analysis of managing in-flight medical emergencies on board commercial aircraft.*

> *MedAire represents more than ten years experience in dealing directly with more than three thousand in-flight medical incidents. Each and every one of them has been carefully managed and fully documented all the way through to the incident's final conclusion.*

> *With the power of knowing what medical situations are most likely to occur in flight, risk-informed decision-making can lead us to establishing medical preparedness standards in relation and proportion to their likelihood of taking place.*

> *Our experience base comes from our twenty-four-hour medical emergency hotline, MedLink. Any time a client has a medical situation on board their commercial aircraft, no matter where they*

---

[23] See http://commdocs.house.gov/committees/Trans/hpw105-23.000/hpw105-23_0f.htm. This transcript is a portion of the official hearing record before SubCommittee on Aviation of the Committee on Transportation and Infrastructure of the U.S. House of Representatives Concerning Medical Kits on Commercial Aircraft, May 21, 1997.

[24] See my full statement at https://www.google.com/books/edition/Medical_Kits_on_Commercial_Airlines/kr43MaVt8A4C?hl=en&gbpv=1&dq=joan+sullivan+garrett+%221997%22&pg=PA69&printsec=frontcover

are in the world, they can contact our MedLink communications center and talk directly and immediately with one of our sixteen board-certified emergency physicians. Our physicians are highly skilled in remote diagnosis and directing non-medically and medically trained people to collect data, provide aid, and stabilize situations.

They will offer advice and treatment recommendations so that pilots can make informed decisions as to whether or not they will divert their aircraft. In the event of a diversion, MedLink has an exclusive worldwide medical services database that is used to assist pilots in selecting a medically appropriate diversion site airport.

Additionally, through this database MedLink will notify and manage medical emergency response, transport, and hospital admission at the destination city.

Through our statistics, we are finding that eighty percent of all medical situations can be attributed to just one of five medical situations: 36 percent of our calls are neurological in nature such as stroke or seizures; nineteen percent are cardiac-related, however, that number is steadily climbing and is at twenty-three percent so far this year; eleven percent are respiratory in nature such as asthma and allergic reactions; ten percent are gastrointestinal; and 4 percent are primarily diabetic-related issues.

Our emergency physicians suggest that, in dealing with the top five medical situations that make up eighty percent of their calls, most would be well-managed if there was an overall greater focus on first aid basics.

As an example, in the area of CPR and first aid training, they believe more emphasis should be placed on skills such as early recognition, gathering vital signs, emergency airway management, and greater knowledge on risk from blood-borne pathogens and the utilization of personal protective equipment.

For medical kits, our physicians see a reoccurring need for airway management tools, IV equipment, and emergency drugs such as injectable Epinephrine and injectable Atropine; however, this would require monitors and qualified medical professionals on board.

In the area of first aid kits, our emergency physicians see continual needs for items such as self-injectable syringes of Epinephrine for severe life-threatening allergic reactions and no medical volunteers on board; Albuterol metered dose inhalers for quick relief during asthma attack; and they believe automatic external defibrillators, or AEDs, should be considered, in essence, a part of the first aid kit.

The American Heart Association says more than one thousand people die in the U.S. every day from cardiac arrest. It is not unreasonable to expect that some of these people might be on board an aircraft in any given day.

In the event of sudden cardiac death, also known as ventricular fibrillation, the definitive treatment is rapid defibrillation.

If the shock comes within three to four minutes of fibrillation, a patient's chance of survival can range from fifty to as high as ninety percent. If the shock comes after ten minutes in the case of ventricular fibrillation their chances are virtually zero.

Additionally, cardiopulmonary resuscitation by itself in such situations has a success rate of less than five percent.

Today's defibrillators can be used by non-medical personnel who have training in their use. Training ranges from three to six hours, and from then on can be easily incorporated into ongoing CPR course completion.

These devices are much easier to learn and administer than the process of CPR. They are designed so that it is impossible for the AED or the caregiver to do harm to the patient, only good.

In closing, I would like to offer an observation that could soon develop into a disturbing trend. Our MedLink physicians tell us that medical professionals are becoming fearful, even refusing to get involved in offering medical help for fear of legal liability.

The legal liability to volunteers, airlines, and flight crews is staggering. Today we are finding that in nearly eighty percent of our calls a medical professional has volunteered their services; however, in 1996 we found that physicians volunteered in less than fifty percent of those cases. I predict in the future this willingness will decline. I would argue that, unless action is taken to limit liability in these situations, there is little value in worrying about medical equipment or training when everyone is fearful of being sued for using what they know.

Mr. Chairman and committee, this concludes my testimony. I do have a short, thirty-second video that will explain the process of our operation, and then I would be happy to answer any questions you or the committee members may have. Thank you.

Mr. DUNCAN. *That's fine. Thank you very much for your testimony. You may go ahead and show the video at this time.*

[Videotape presentation — Communications Patch Between MedLink Emergency Physician, Commercial Pilot, and On Board Medical Volunteer]

The following is the transcription of an audio tape created following a life saving incident in May, 1996. The communication specialist who handled the call narrates the tape.

BACKGROUND

MAY, 1996
Passenger, female — 6 to 7 month pregnant.
Journey began in Cairo, Egypt. Ultimate destination, Los Angeles.
Incident occurs over Omaha.
A doctor is on board.

Communication Specialist

I got a call from an airline. They had a pregnant female on board. She was bleeding.

Pilot

We're enroute to Los Angeles and we're over Omaha. And we have a patient...lady...38 years old...female. She's conscious. She's 6 months pregnant. She's traveling from Cairo. She's had what she considers to be a contraction...and lost quite a bit of blood.

Communication Specialist

They did have a doctor on board, that felt they could continue on to California which was their destination.

Onboard Doctor

She's been fine today in her flight from Cairo and has been feeling the baby all day along until about an hour ago...right after they ate.

She got up and she just had a large amount of bleeding which she felt to be something like a half liter...and when I came in and evaluated her, her blood pressure looked fine...running about 170...her pulse was about 70.

We have her laying down, giving her a little oxygen for the baby. The main issue is...number one...she says that when we try and sit her up a little bit she feels like she's having more bleeding. And number two...I couldn't really hear any heart tones on the baby.

She's not feeling any fetal movement at at this point...and when I try and just elicit some movement from the baby by palpitations, she doesn't really feel anything.

If anything she get a little pressure or pain when we press on the baby. But I wouldn't say any kind of major pain.

So...it seems to me she was probably stable to get from here to Los

Angeles.

Communication Specialist

And...I got my [MedLink] doctor on the line and he asked... "Well ,what about the baby?" The (onboard) doctor says, "Well, it's a good sized baby...she's about 7 months. There's no fetal movement since the bleeding started.

At that time, my [MedLink] doctor made the decision, that we recommended the diversion of the aircraft.

MedLink ER Physician

The concern is that if she is really quote-unquote six months pregnant — this child is still potentially deliverable at this age.

It seems to me from the information you're giving me that we need to have her get medical attention as soon as possible — this could be an early abruption.

Give the control back to the pilot, and we're going to...and we'll have our dispatcher talk to them about diverting to closest city.

Communication Specialist

And the captain said, okay great. We took them down into Kansas City.

Airline Dispatch

Okay....you've been released to destination Kansas City..IIFR...you're going to be KNB 16-50...go ahead.

Passenger

When I became very sick...at the time...all I knew was that the plane was diverted to Kansas City, Missouri. And I was taken to a hospital.

Communication Specialist

I called the hospital and talked to the charge nurse of the ER. I told her this is the situation…

We have got a lady seven months pregnant, she's bleeding. I said she has lost about a liter and a half on the aircraft already…every time they stand her she loses even more.

And I said there has been no fetal movement.

And so she said…Well, I'll call in my team.

Within an hour of the aircraft being on the ground, they had performed a C-section, and the baby was in ICU and so was mom in ICU.

Passenger

They have saved my life, as well as my baby's life. My husband and I would like to thank them…to thank MedLink very, very much for that.

…Everything turned out well, and my baby is here beside me in the hospital. Yes… he's beautiful you know!

What a rewarding experience to play a part in saving a mother and premature newborn. Sharing this case in front of legislators (who actually listened) meant a lot to me as MedAire's CEO, but even more so as a medical professional. There was no doubt about it — delivering this baby was possible because the MedLink emergency physician overruled the onboard doctor and recommended that the plane divert.

Chapter Fifteen: At Sea

There are more "firsts" to chronicle, namely in maritime. In fact, our maritime products and services deserve a complete chapter based on the anomalies inherent in ocean travel — diseases, accidents, and complications that crews face aboard vessels.

Beyond our remote medical care programs for business aviation, air charter companies, aircraft manufacturers, 150 airlines, and 75% of Fortune 100 companies, we ultimately came to service half of the world's superyachts and the commercial shipping sector as well. These numbers seem incredible in hindsight, astounding accomplishments all based on a dream, tremendous hard work, and top-notch employees.

As MedAire grew and diversified, our maritime customers were — and are — vital to our customer base and have much different needs than the aviation sector. Maritime telemedicine can be as adventuresome as the ocean itself, as covered in a *Professional Mariner* piece that I recommend to those interested in this particular type of remote medicine.[25]

In it, an overview of MedAire's "at sea" services is detailed with future innovations in the pipeline. We developed maritime medical kits, training, and telemedicine with a vast ocean environment in mind, fraught with dangers that don't exist

---

[25] Rich Miller. "Telemedicine advances hold promise of savings in lives and money," *Professional Mariner, Journal of the Maritime Industry*, May 19, 2009. See https://www.professionalmariner.com/telemedicine-advances-hold-promise-of-savings-in-lives-and-money/

elsewhere. Back in the day, what I called the "Maritime Bible" was a big orange book, quite outdated. It was supposed to guide ocean-going vessels in safety practices, including medical emergencies. With this woefully lacking manual as a base, we developed our own standards and created kits and assessment tools to replace the tackle boxes often used to store medicine and bandages — and I'm not exaggerating when I say tackle boxes.

Once during a marketing trip to the Chelsea yacht harbor in New York, I talked to a boat owner and asked to see his kit. I knew this "Show me your kit, and I'll show you mine" demonstration would be eye-opening. The prospect was a bit skeptical but lugged his enormous fishing tackle box to the deck and allowed me to compare it to a MedAire medical kit.

"How do you know what's expired?" I asked about his medicines. "What equipment do you use to address broken bones, deep cuts, and near-drownings?"

As you can imagine, our product line impressed him, and he bought the medical kit and training courses. From then on, we knew to walk the docks, attend boat shows around the world, and explain "up close and personal" what we were offering and why. It's a fun industry in which to work, less formal yet lavish and filled with yacht owners who want to do the right thing aboard their vessels. By the way, many yacht owners had private jets, which helped in the crossover market. It felt good to be appreciated by these customers.

Maritime kits took into account a different set of parameters, namely, that it could take days to reach shore. Our four kit levels were designed for the customized needs of yachts and tenders or dinghies (small boats that take owners and guests to and from the shore). You'll see below the types of seaborne illness and injuries that can occur, and you may wonder how we prepared for these emergencies. After all, not only did we create medical kits for our maritime customers, but demonstrated how to treat a person on board for days at a time before the ship could make shore.

Among others, we relied heavily on Paul S. Auerbach, MD's book, *A Medical Guide to Hazardous Marine Life*, to identify potential threats and create a practical manual for our customers. A basic first aid kit addressed minor injuries such as a cut from stepping on a shell, sunburn, and seasickness (disinfectants, bandages, gel, ointments, antihistamine). The next-level responder kit was the same size as an aviation kit for more serious first-on-the-scene emergencies (airway, trauma, bleeding, assessment tools, and over-the-counter meds).

A third maritime kit addressed elevated trauma, for instance, if someone stepped on a scorpionfish, was poisoned by exotic dining on an pufferfish or became infected with the dreaded neurotoxin ciguatera. It presents as a nasty form of seafood poisoning caused by plankton that accumulates in fish, in some cases grouper, tuna, eel, sea bass, mackerel, barracuda, and more. Potentially, it can make passengers very sick with gastrointestinal and even neurological issues.

Scombroid poisoning is also a concern. It presents much like an allergic reason and is caused by people eating fish contaminated with a high level of histamines. Intestinal issues, rash, sweating, stomach pain, swelling of the mouth, trouble swallowing, vomiting, headache, and flushing of the face, neck, arms, and torso can result. Tuna, mackerel, mahi-mahi, bluefish, and marlin are often the culprits.

Or, say, someone was attacked by a shark or run over by a Ski-Doo (not uncommon). We included diagnostic tools, EpiPens, intravenous solutions, catheters, wound care supplies, suturing equipment, splints, and injectable and oral medicines. A fourth kit, a massive pharmacy kit, was kept under lock and key in the belly of the boat and accessible only by the Captain. It contained replenishment supplies (due to long voyages), and narcotics such as codeine and morphine.

In our very first maritime sale, MedLink gained a customer and a consultant all in one. Bill Mahaffy was both a paramedic and a ship captain aboard the yacht TIME. He heard about us, made contact, and we invited him to our operation center in

Maritime kits, color-coded for quick identification and use – Photo credit: MedAire

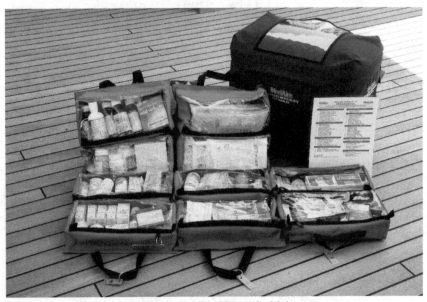

Maritime kit interior – Photo credit: MedAire

Arizona. And thus began an incredible opportunity as we met and exceeded the needs of ocean-going vessels, thanks in large part to Bill's insights. We later hired him, and he best describes those exciting early times with stories about his handiwork and our first business maritime and commercial maritime sales.

My client, Seth Atwood, was an industrialist and financier who already had a plane and wanted a yacht. His 38.5 m motor yacht TIME was custom-built in Sturgeon Bay, Wisconsin — a new product offering by Palmer Johnson. His daughter, Diane Atwood, helped design the interior. The idea was that he would voyage to various parts of the world and attend boat shows, thus drawing attention to the newest yacht in the Palmer Johnson manufacturing line.

A view of the yacht TIME – Photo credit: Bill Mahaffy

Mr. Atwood needed a qualified crew member for his new yacht with a unique skill set. He placed an advertisement in an emergency medical journal, essentially searching for a nationally registered paramedic who was an open ocean diver and a nonsmoker with yacht experience. My boss noticed the ad and hid it in her desk, hoping I wouldn't see it. My medic partner found the ad, and sure enough, I fit the description. It sounded almost too good to be true.

I responded to the ad and said, "This can't be a real job." The reply was, "Yes, it's a real job. We'll fly you to a boat show in Fort Lauderdale for an interview." Of course, I said, "Deal!"

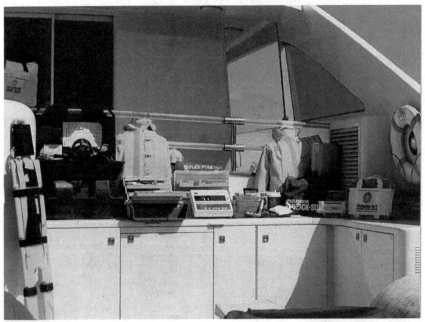

Medical safety equipment aboard the yacht TIME – *Photo credit: Bill Mahaffy*

Candidates from all over the country showed up to compete for the position. I asked a lot of questions about "medical control" requirements. Because of Mr. Atwood's interest in aviation, he already knew of MedLink. "Don't worry, we have MedLink — that's our medical control," I was told. I got the job and was flown to Phoenix for a week to interact with the MedLink staff, in awe of their communication center at Samaritan.

It was great spending time with the team and Dr. David Streitwieser (who today is the Medical Director of MedLink's Global Response Center). Maritime regulations in the 1980s were rudimentary and lacked effective medications; some were so dated they were no longer manufactured. We put together an inventory and customized a MedAire maritime medical kit according to my input, including at-or-below sea level' conditions and any contingencies that could occur on an extended voyage. It was a collaborative effort to help design this particular type of kit that had never existed before.

The yacht TIME *in all its glory – Photo credit: Bill Mahaffy*

I recall the yacht captain asking, "So, what do you think this job is going to be like?" I said, "This job is going to be 90% polishing stainless steel and swabbing decks and 10% percent medicine." But the point was to be prepared regardless. Out at sea, it can take days to reach the shore, and you may have to treat injuries and accidents over a prolonged period of time. In fact, a couple of medical issues did occur, and then the MedLink system followed me on all the boats I captained subsequent to that. In the interim, I became a licensed surgical physician assistant and later a vascular surgery P.A.

After I had worked for six years in the field of cardiothoracic surgery, MedAire recruited me as their Director of Maritime Programs. I worked full-time for MedAire seven days a week and had seven days "off," in which I worked as a hospitalist. It kept me clinically active, and it's hard to describe how meaningful this was to me personally and professionally. I was privileged to be a part of it all and witness Joan's passion.

Captain Bill Mahaffy spotting for hazards – Photo credit: Bill Mahaffy

We advertised in a lot of upper echelon yachting magazines, including Yachting Matters *published by Colin Squire in the UK. He invited me to contribute articles, and I began writing for other publications as well. We had two or three competitors, but nothing close to what MedAire offered. We undertook a huge R&D push and studied what the United Kingdom and the MCA (the British version of the U.S. Coast Guard) had in place. Our kits were upgraded above the 2000 international commercial standards — something no one else had done. Eventually, international regulations shifted to parallel MedAire's standards.*

We were the medical advisory provider for the Military Sealift Command, and I enjoyed spending time with the liaison and Medical Administrator, Shelley Croyle, in Washington, D.C. As a company, we kept up with all the various genres within maritime — commercial shipping, cruise ships, and luxury yachts in different sized categories such as below 50 meters, above 80, etc. that determined what program we recommended for each customer. Toward 2005, yachts weren't just traveling to Fort Lauderdale, the Caribbean, or the Mediterranean. We saw transits in remote regions of high latitude in the arctic and antarctic and offered gear specific to these environments.

Some boats were enormous. I traveled to Germany to train the crew aboard the late Microsoft co-founder Paul Allen's boat, which had a helicopter, submarine, and decompression chamber. I spent a week at Duke University doing a hyperbaric medicine course. Joan was good at keeping me focused on our superyacht clients, including attending industry events and boat shows, giving presentations, and sitting on safety-at-sea panels.

Here's a funny story. One Sunday afternoon, I was calling bingo as a volunteer in my local Pennsylvania fire department engine bay for 25 elderly ladies. On Tuesday, I was on the French Riviera (Cannes) giving a presentation to a room of attendees worth $100 billion. These experiences were a foundational part of my entire life and forged expertise in marketing and sales. I learned to relate to *any type of audience and forged contacts and friendships worldwide who were great at spreading MedLink's benefits.*

If I called a brokerage, they had at least heard of the boats we serviced. Crews were eager to sign up for our curriculum and onboard training. It was great word-of-mouth marketing for MedAire. While training in a marina or shipyard, it was not uncommon that someone found out we were in the vicinity. They'd come aboard and ask us to look at their boats or even respond to a medical issue — even if they weren't customers. Of course, we assisted, and often these people became our next sign-ups.

At the end of my time at MedAire, we designed an equipment system that allowed vessels to seamlessly refurbish their medical stores and meet a lot of regulatory requirements. They could turn in an old kit, and we gave them a new kit, and companies still use this service today. I'm proud to have been a part of MedAire's maritime services and provide health and safety protocols. It's great that Joan has delved into the importance of remote medicine at sea in this book.

I appreciate Bill's excellent insights. He graciously put me back in touch with Shelley Croyle, former Civil Service Medical Administrator of the Military Sealift Command.[26] Shelley shares fascinating details below for those not familiar with the amazing work carried out by the MSC.

I worked at Headquarters in Washington, DC, from 1998 to 2013. The Military Sealift Command (MSC) is the primary logistics pipeline for military forces with ships, presently and at one time or another, in almost all oceans worldwide. Nearly all noncombatant types of ships/craft are represented under the MSC umbrella — support, logistics, transport. MSC owned the ships and

---

[26] See https://www.msc.usff.navy.mil/, the official website for Military Sealift Command, the transportation provider for the Department of Defense with the responsibility of providing strategic sealift and ocean transportation for all military forces overseas.

the contracted crews, or fully contracted the ships and crew.

Ships in the maritime industry are operated by small, extremely proficient, and highly technically trained crews. However, there is no extra backup personnel if someone is injured or falls sick. Medical evacuations and rapid deployment of a replacement crew member is dangerous at sea, costly, and results in critical delays. It's not feasible to put physicians on hundreds of small crew vessels that essentially stay at sea and make deliveries (like UPS) worldwide.

Medical care aboard shipping is governed by multiple regulations worldwide — the U.S. Coast Guard, Admiralty Law, and Civil Service regulations, with MSC having oversight of merging requirements for the safety of the crews. As such, MSC employs Medical Service Officers, Independent Duty Corpsmen on active duty crewed ships, or a lesser trained collateral duty Medical Department Representative on ships (of course, only one per ship).

The Navy and the military have fabulous worldwide medical treatment capabilities and treatment centers. However, this is geared primarily towards the active-duty populations and their beneficiaries worldwide. The integration of civil service crews and civilian crews is tenuous at best, trying to integrate them into this military system. MSC has/had only three physicians and a small staff to respond to questions and issues for patients aboard our ships. I researched the industry to find how other organizations and industries managed the 24/7 worldwide access to advanced physician coverage and reached out to MedAire in the early 2000s.

MedAire not only provided us with 24/7 medical advisory support but was able to facilitate medical evacuations out of ports with limited capabilities due to proximity or political issues. The nearest port for medical treatment or evacuation may not be common to the military evacuation system's coverage nor politically friendly. Critical delays and confusion were common. Military personnel in critical organizational positions get trained in the integration of civilian crews, then transfer every few years.

MedAire, being a civilian corporate company with a worldwide network, was able to circumvent these kinds of issues and facilitate evacuations quickly with little fuss. They were able to bridge issues that the military system "stuttered" at. When MedAire was asked to provide physician guidance and support or medical evacuation, they didn't stutter. Simply — 'How can we help and how soon do you need it?' was the response.

Many thanks to Shelley for this rare glimpse into the Military Sealift Command, something many have heard of for the very first time. It was such an honor to work with a person of his caliber and earn the trust of the MSC.

By the way, Maersk was one our earliest customers, and this relationship reminds me of a story. One of our commercial maritime customers — a huge vessel — hit a bad storm which threw people all over the decks. There were numerous broken legs and arms, as well as head injuries. You can imagine the panic and chaos, yet MedLink was there to manage those patient cases and any other complexities specific to oceanic travel.

We heard great feedback from ship captains. Once, the Black Molly, a yacht, had just picked up their medical kits in the Mediterranean before heading to the Cape Verde Islands. A storm erupted off the coast of Africa and damaged the mast, which hit the first mate and caused a severe head injury. The crew was able to suture the head wound with the help of the manual included in the medical kit. While tenuous and difficult, MedLink provided guidance through the teletype messaging service, ARINC. MedLink arranged for the patient to be admitted to a cat scan facility on Cape Verde Island and helped manage the case over a period of days.

I'll never forget a MedLink call from a yacht in the Caribbean — not a client, but someone who called on behalf of a jet skier. The propeller went right across his back and caused massive injuries. We heard screaming on the other end of the line, and then it disconnected. There was no way to trace the call by radio, and we never heard back. It always haunted me, not being able to help and not knowing the outcome, and my staff felt the same.

Here's an anecdote about my own close call on water. No, it wasn't at sea but rather on Lake Powell in Arizona. Lake Powell sits on the Utah and Arizona border and boasts a 2000 mile shoreline with many inlets and bays. Frank and I bought a used intercoastal motor yacht that had been manufactured in Wisconsin and somehow made its way to Lake Powell. We fondly called it the Siobhan houseboat, a wonderful, roomy vessel with two decks and a galley below.

Our family houseboat, Siobhan

During our maiden voyage, the boat was filled with family — my sons, their spouses, friends, and our seven-month-old grandson, the only grandchild born at this time. From our beds (including hide-away beds), the water lulled us to sleep that evening. I was awakened at 5:15 a.m. by our grandson, who was cooing in his crib in our bedroom. I wrapped him in my arms, headed downstairs, and turned to take another set of stairs to the galley. My right foot slipped on the thick carpet, and then both legs went out from underneath me. *Whoosh!* All I could do was twist my body midair so that I'd land on my back and *not* on the baby.

I hit the edge of a stair with a thud and heard a pop. As my little grandson screamed, my son Aaron arrived on the scene. The baby was fine, thank God — but I was not! That "pop" I heard was my lung. With every breath, I felt pain and subsequent pressure in my chest. The fall caused an opening inside my lung that let air escape into the pleural space surrounding my lung. With each breath, more air entered the space, thereby collapsing my lung — a pneumothorax.

We were in a remote area, 21 miles up the main channel, and there was no place for an emergency helicopter to land. We had a MedAire medical kit on board, and I could have performed a needle thoracotomy on myself (14 gauge needle, second intercostal space, mid-clavicular line on top of the rib) to correct my collapsed lung, but I felt we could make it to the marina in time. I called a MedLink doctor en route, told him I had a traumatic pneumothorax, and asked him to notify the hospital in Page, Arizona, that I was on my way.

Aaron loaded me onto a speedboat, and I hoped the water wouldn't be too choppy. "Go fast but avoid the bumps," I told him. Normal respiration is 12 to 24 per minute, and I took mine down to 7 to 8 per minute by putting myself into a trance-like state to control my breathing. *If I die, I couldn't be in a better place,* I thought. That may sound morbid, but honestly, the water was beautiful in the serene early morning setting, and I was at peace despite the pain.

Thankfully, the water was calm, and we managed to get to the local hospital. Since there were no significant exterior wounds, the hospital put me in a holding pattern. My son was having none of that and insisted that I be seen right away.

"Jesus!" exclaimed the x-ray technician. I had a 70% lung collapse, and a surgeon was called in to place a tube into the left side of my chest. I had to be transported to the Good Samaritan Hospital Trauma Center and, of course, insisted on an Air Evac fixed-wing aircraft (knowing the proficiency of Air Evac teams after having been an Air Evac employee myself).

It was strange being a patient. I was used to being on the other side of the equation! The hospital staff took care of me for five days, and I fully recovered after about a month at home. What a dramatic episode, and believe me, we replaced the carpet on those steps with skid-proof material!

One last personal anecdote, this one tying MedAire's maritime component to my grandmother. If you recall, she told me about the "nurse in the air," Ellen Church, but also told me about a "nurse at sea," Violet Jessop (1887–1971).[27] Grandmother Mary had grown up hearing about this remarkable ocean-liner stewardess, mostly because the sinking of the Titanic was such huge news around the world. Violet Jessop was notable because she survived not one but three ship disasters — the Olympic in 1911, the Titanic in 1912, and the Britannic in 1916. Thus, she was dubbed "Miss Unsinkable" and "Queen of sinking ships,"[28] and I call her "the luckiest nurse in the world" as well for dodging death and beating the odds!

One thing my grandmother didn't mention, however, was that Violet Jessop held an abandoned baby in her arms as the Titanic went down. I stumbled across a transcript years later that detailed this experience as she sat aboard a lifeboat and awaited rescue by the Carpathia.[29] Can you imagine?

As we built kits, trained, and offered MedLink services to the maritime industry, I often thought about my grandmother's stories. She had a seemingly prescient ability to name-drop remarkable nurses from bygone eras that seemed, somehow, to mesh with my professional journey, both air and sea. It never ceases to amaze and inspire me and fills me with happiness that

---

[27] "The daughter of Irish immigrants who survived the Titanic, Britannic, and Olympic disasters: The amazing stories of Violet Jessop and her multiple brushes with near-death while at sea." *Irish Central*, April 22, 2021. See https://www.irishcentral.com/roots/history/violet-jessop-disasters

[28] "Violet Jessop, Miss. Unsinkable." *History of the Titanic*, July 15, 2020. See https://historyoftitanic.com/violet-jessop-miss-unsinkable/

[29] John Shepler. "Violet Jessop, Survivor of the Titanic, Olympic and Britannic Shipwrecks." See https://www.johnshepler.com/articles/violet.html

she remains a special part of our corporate lore.

By the way, and perhaps most important to my grandmother, was that fact that Violet Jessop was Irish Catholic. I find it fascinating that her Irish immigrant parents landed in Argentina, where she was born, and that I had spent time there too in my training escapades (and dining on those delicious steaks). For this reason, her service was legendary within the Irish community as well. It is always a source of pride when Irish heroes, and especially Celtic women, made their mark in service to others. I definitely share this sentiment with my grandmother.

Chapter Sixteen: The Corporate Lens

It was an extra joy that my family witnessed "the firsts" as MedAire evolved from a startup into the expansive entity we are today. I've mentioned People Express as our first commercial aviation customer and American Trans Air as our first MedLink call. below I share a "look back" at an original equipment manufacturer (OEM) signup that was an important launching pads and shaped MedAire's reputation.

Gulfstream Aerospace was our first OEM to include medical kits with automated external defibrillators, training, and MedLink as a value-added bundle with every aircraft sold. It brings back a vivid memory of a Flight Safety Foundation conference in Detroit, Michigan. The Director of Flight Operations, Ted Mendenhall for Gulfstream, was in the audience when I gave my presentation. He invited me to present at their "Breakfast meeting" in Savannah, Georgia. This was a huge and wonderful opportunity for MedAire.

I wore a business suit, looking every bit an executive, and brought in a flight nurse in full flight gear to demonstrate. She added a certain credibility as someone from the trenches and brought our first aid kit to life, tangible and hands-on. It's so much more impactful to show rather than just tell because our kits and training were truly were incredible to behold.

Gulfstream signing with Robert Cooper in 1989 – Photo credit: MedAire

*Presenting Gulfstream CEO Brian Moss with a Kachina doll from MedAire for our ten year partnership –
Photo credit: MedAire*

*Allen Paulson, founder and CEO of Gulfstream Aerospace, receiving cholesterol testing with Robert Cooper
and others – Photo credit: MedAire*

Following that meeting, Robert Cooper, Vice President of Marketing, said, "We need this for our customers." And so, the relationship began and has remained strong from 1989 through today. Allen Paulson, founder and CEO of Gulfstream, was such an amazing corporate leader. I admired him very much, especially his participation in industry events. He stopped by our booth for one of our early cholesterol screenings — much appreciated — and I noticed how he kindly drew attention to MedAire in various conversations. His interest and support were invaluable, and he is dearly missed by many more than two decades after his passing.

This collaboration with Gulfstream kicked MedAire into high gear, followed by other OEMs — Boeing Business Jets, Bombardier, Dassault (kits), Embraer Executive Jets, and Textron Aviation (Cessna, Beechcraft), and Pilatus (EU). In 1998, we extended our services to Europe. Those OEMs became our champions, and they remain our champions. MedAire has the majority of the world's fractional and aircraft management companies as customers today.

In 2000, I met Barbara Barrett, who so kindly wrote the foreword of this book. Today, most know her as the 25th United States Secretary of the Air Force comprising the U.S. Air Force and U.S. Space Force. But back then, she was a pilot, lawyer, entrepreneur, and diplomat whom I admired very much.

I had just written an article for the Air Medical Journal titled "Twelve Thousand Inflight Medical Emergencies: What have we learned?" and was a finalist for the Ernst & Young's Entrepreneur of the Year Award. I was excited to be a candidate. After all, the award "celebrates the audacious entrepreneurs who test the limits of the possible and catapult us to what's next and beyond" — and I seemed to fit that description!

Barbara was a judge in the Ernst & Young award process. To give you an idea of her notability, I'll mention just a few of her achievements from a very long list (which blew my socks off).

She sat on the boards of Raytheon Company and Exponenet, Inc., a science and engineering firm. She was legal counsel for The Greyhound Corporation. Prior to that, she served as Vice Chairman of the U.S. Civil Aeronautics Board and negotiated agreements with Great Britain, China, Poland, Ireland, Peru, the Philippines, Jamaica, and other countries. Then she became the first female deputy administrator of the Federal Aviation Administration (FAA) and managed 47,000 employees worldwide with a $6 billion annual budget. Both posts required U.S. Senate confirmation and top-secret clearances.

As if all that wasn't impressive enough, Barbara served on the President's Advisory Committee on Trade Negotiations and for seven years, was Chairman of the Arizona District Export Council and also civilian advisor to Secretary of Defense Dick Cheney and General Colin Powell during the Persian Gulf War. She ran as a Republican candidate for Governor of Arizona in 1994 and was a trustee of Thunderbird, the American Graduate School of International Management, where I had taken some coursework. Wow! I could go on and on, but suffice it to say she was eminently qualified to serve on a panel of judges.

MedAire was in its fifteenth year of operations, and my achievements were nowhere near Barbara's (not even close). Yet, she listened with interest as I filled her in on the adventures of building my business, literally, out of my garage. I noticed she was a wonderful interviewer, so sharp and attentive. What a total honor that she and the other judges felt I was deserving of the award of which I became the recipient in 2001.

As mentioned previously, I was a huge proponent of defibrillators. MedAire was ahead of the curve and began offering automated external defibrillators in the early '90s for both business aviation and private maritime customers. We had discussions with Tore Laerdal, an innovator I admire very much, and partnered with Laerdal Medical in Norway to make these portable AEDs available to customers. Since MedAire had a significant presence in the aviation and growing maritime industries, we entered a marketing sales agreement to promote the Laerdal AEDs.

Me as an Ernst & Young Entrepreneur of the Year Award recipient – Photo credit: MedAire

Tore invested significantly, our sales were impressive, and I'm forever grateful that we had such a productive relationship and a longstanding friendship. I'll point you to a YouTube video featuring Tore at a TEDx Talk.[30] How interesting that the video begins with references to "Annie." This is the same mannequin we used in our training (more on that later). Tore has devoted his life to lifesaving technology, and I'm extremely proud and indebted to the impact he's made on my life and many other lives.

I was very fortunate to travel and operate in Norway. We utilized our Norwegian nurses to do the training for us in Europe. They were committed, loved working for MedAire, and became very good lifelong friends. Jannicke Mellin-Olsen, MD, DPH, and past president of the World Federation of Societies of Anaesthesiologists became my dearest friend. She was MedAire's medical director for Europe, the Middle East, and Africa for ten years and her partner, Jorma Salmela of Finland, worked as a surgeon for the International Committee of the Red Cross in several war-torn countries for many years.

Another very dear friend, Tove Groneng, is a special nurse among many nurses who trained as MedAire instructors and taught our program throughout Europe. They were committed, loved working for MedAire, and became such amazing contributors to the company's success in Europe. I feel so fortunate to have spent time with them over the years, and it underscores how universal MedAire was and is.

As always, there were naysayers to the defibrillator movement. I was gobsmacked every time I heard someone push back against this lifesaving device. My counter was making sure our customers realized the chance of survival decreased by ten percent every minute that elapsed during a cardiac arrest without a defibrillator being used. Whether at sea or in flight, it takes time to divert a flight or voyage. By the time a captain makes land, the passenger could very well die. What really matters during a heart attack is an immediate emergency response with a defibrillator.

After we demonstrated the user-friendliness, the sale was usually clinched and defibrillators became a win/win for MedAire

---

[30] "Helping save lives through innovative partnerships: Tore Laerdal at TEDxStavanger." See https://www.youtube.com/watch?v=d9bYTgUcsP8

and our customers. It bothered me, however, that these devices were not mandated on U.S. commercial airlines —a monumental concern and a glaring oversight. I felt it was up to me to do something about it. As always, I spread the message through the media.[31, 32]

At one conference, I spoke as an advanced cardiac care provider — a commonsense nurse who happened to become the subject-matter expert. I recall being sandwiched between two airline medical directors employed by the commercial aviation industry. They opposed onboard defibrillators, which was ridiculous. I explained it was not a matter of *if*, but *when*, defibrillators would be placed aboard commercial airlines. One of the medical directors said to the gathering, "Over my dead body will we put defibrillators on our aircraft." This clearly demonstrates the level of resistance I encountered.

The failure to restore a normal heartbeat or correct an arrhythmia could possibly result in preventable deaths. Once the heart stops beating, with every passing minute, there is a decrease in survivability. After uttering these simple facts, you could have heard a pin drop — the legal ramifications were alarming, and I'm not sure why it wasn't obvious to everyone involved in this debate.

Onward to Capitol Hill. It was a great honor to consult with the U.S. Federal Aviation Administration and provide congressional testimony in favor of this lifesaving technology in 2001. I presented MedLink's hard data regarding cardiac events and resulting diversions. Our statistics provided hundreds of thousands of inflight medical events and prompted the United States Congress to require AEDs on all commercial craft over 2400 pounds in 2004, a victory for travelers far and wide.

---

[31] "Enhanced Emergency Medical Kits Increase In-flight Care Options," *Flight Safety Foundation, Cabin Crew Safety*, November-December 2000. See https://flightsafety.org/ccs/ccs_nov-dec01.pdf

[32] "Many Flight Attendants Learn to Use Automated External Defibrillators," *Flight Safety Foundation, Cabin Crew Safety*, November-December 2000. See https://flightsafety.org/ccs/ccs_nov_dec00.pdf

One of my official headshots – You've probably noticed many incarnations of hairstyles (and this was my favorite.) Photo credit: MedAire

I should add that in advance of this final ruling, MedAire was chosen over the Red Cross to train 22,000 United Airlines flight attendants at their global bases in CPR and the use of defibrillators — a great honor that had us traveling like never before!

It just so happened that pilots were in the news as well, with controversy surrounding their forced retirement at the age of 60. This led to a hearing regarding "S. 361, A Bill to Establish Age Limitations for Airmen" led by John McCain in the Committee on Commerce, Science, and Transportation in March 2001. Trent Lott, Kay Bailey Hutchison, John D. Rockefeller, Barbara Boxer, John Edwards, and others were committee members.[33]

I was not a proponent of the FAA's Age 60 Commercial Pilot Rule rule, nor were the pilots themselves, nor the organizations that represented them. In my opinion, pilots who were health-screened and tested for flying aptitude were very capable of flying at age 60, although I was not called to testify. However, I served on the Flight Safety Foundation's Corporate Advisory Committee, the Fatigue Countermeasures Committee, and the Oxygen Committee (and would ultimately be named vice chairman of the Flight Safety Foundation Board of Governors in 2004.)[34] Thus, I was referenced in the testimony of others through a *USA Today* article, "Do Passengers Get Enough Oxygen? Experts Examine a Threat That Affects Everyone Who Flies."[35]

My quote was directed toward the causes and effects of

---

[33] One Hundred Seventh Congress, First Session. "Hearing Before The Committee On Commerce, Science, And Transportation, United States Senate," March 13, 2001. See https://www.govinfo.gov/content/pkg/CHRG-107shrg87970/pdf/CHRG-107shrg87970.pdf

[34] Angela Gonzales. "MedAire Exec to Chair Board," *Phoenix Business Journal*, December 19, 2004. See https://www.bizjournals.com/phoenix/stories/2004/12/20/newscolumn2.html

[35] Robert Davis. "Do Passengers Get Enough Oxygen? Experts Examine a Threat That Affects Everyone Who Flies," *USA Today*, March 6, 2001.

hypoxia, mainly concerning those who are older and have health problems before ever stepping on a plane. It wasn't until years later that pilots were able to fly up to the age of 65 — with stipulations.[36] And I should mention that I would eventually provide expertise and interviews to the *Wall Street Journal*, *Financial Times*, the *BBC*, the *Discovery Channel* as just a start on many travel safety issues.

What a leap from the 1980's when no one, especially Congress, would listen to a word I said. Now they were including my interviews in testimony. You know without a doubt that you have become a trusted voice and go-to authority when this occurs, and it was gratifying and validating all at the same time.

From a corporate lens, but also a personal lens, I could write a whole series of heartwarming stories that accumulated over the years, and this seems to be a good place to savor those moments. I quite enjoyed visiting hangars and corporate offices to demonstrate how and why an injury or illness was treated. I also enjoyed traveling to yachts for training too, wearing shorts and going barefoot on the beautiful teak decks. I extended invitations to our customers to visit us in Phoenix and loved hosting dinners, once bussing 280 guests to my home. They enjoyed barbecue, dishes made by a chef, and a guitar strummer. *Mi casa, su casa.* It demonstrated that our customers really were part of the MedAire family. It was part of our corporate philosophy, for the personal touch is what draws customers. As far as I was concerned, the MedAire handshake was a hug.

Once flying back home from Europe aboard British Airways during the holidays, I asked the crew what they planned to do over Christmas. They were stuck in the U.S. for two days, and I felt sorry for them. I offered to give them a tour of the MedAire office and instead surprised them with Christmas dinner at my house. The crew stayed until 3 a.m. and had a great time! No doubt, they relayed this experience to British Airways.

---

[36] "How Old Can Pilots Be?" Airline Pilot Central, January 7, 2019. See https://www.airlinepilotcentral.com/articles/news/how-old-can-pilots-be.html

As Dr. Bob Baron mentioned, we often received satellite radio transmissions from overseas — Copenhagen, Denmark, Berna Radio in Switzerland, and Stockholm Radio in Sweden. One day, our emergency physician and a communication specialist took a high-frequency radio call from Stockholm, relaying a message that a Middle Eastern airline was experiencing an onboard emergency.

The pilot described a pregnant female in her twenties traveling to a Middle Eastern destination with her three children, all under five years of age. The young mother was hemorrhaging, and the flight attendants were unable to control the bleeding. The MedLink physician gave them incredibly detailed instructions on stopping the flow to try to save the pregnant mother's life. He recommended the pilot divert the aircraft so she could receive urgent medical care.

The flight landed in a military base in Turkey. MedLink arranged for intake at a local medical facility and had the young mother transported. Remarkably, the pilot, in agreement with the passengers, waited three hours on the tarmac while she was treated for miscarriage. The flight attendants looked after her three children until her return.

MedLink was a new service at the time, and the Middle Eastern airline was not a customer. However, Stockholm Radio knew we could help, and we did. This set the threshold for our services as we grew, ensuring that passengers were medically safeguarded on air, land, and sea no matter where in the world they traveled.

Several times, business aviation pilots commented that the training helped them personally. They began adding it on their resumes as a professional credit, but also became better stewards of their own health. One pilot had been in denial about a pain in his left arm and chest, but thanks to the training, went in for an examination. He reported back that the MedAire training saved his life.

You may recall that in Chapter Twelve, MedAire wrote the "Management of Inflight Illness and Injury" training manual and designed coursework so that pilots could take the information home and use it. It warmed my heart to receive this affirming feedback.

Chapter Seventeen: The Lighter Side

Everyone wants to live on top of the mountain,
but all the happiness and growth occurs while you're climbing
it.

~ Andy Rooney, Journalist

I titled this chapter "The Lighter Side" because the MedAire team enjoyed not only heartwarming moments but a lot of funny escapades too. These are the personal experiences we encountered across the globe, many never before told.

Patty Campbell, a nurse practitioner with a master's degree, was there from the start and worked with MedAire for two decades. Our relationship was unusual. As director of flight personnel, I hired Patty as a flight nurse and director of education at Air Evac. When I resigned as director of flight personnel, she was promoted to that position. I went to Samaritan as an emergency room nurse but worked as a flight nurse part-time and therefore reported to her. Then she joined the MedAire team and reported to me once again. She knows me so well and is a lifelong friend.

Patty did a lot of training, especially maritime training, and taught our customers things we'd never dream of teaching in aviation, such as suturing, starting IV's, and needling a chest for a pneumothorax (collapsed lung). I credit Patty as a talented medical author and editor as well, instrumental in writing, updating, and revising our training manuals. It's a source of pride that I relied on the best and brightest to assist in compiling all of our proprietary materials. She weighs in below with some behind-the-scenes escapades and a sprinkle of humor.

When Joan and I were flight nurses at Air Evac, she walked into the office one day and said, 'Look at this newspaper article. The FAA is going to require medical kits onboard. I'm going to start a company and make these kits.' Oh yeah, right, I thought. A month later, there were floor-to-ceiling medical kits in her office, and she was on her way to creating MedAire. But she soon realized that the users of the kits would need training and recruited flight nurses to train her clients.

Once she had her clients trained on the medical kits, she began to conceptualize MedLink. 'As flight nurses, we call and talk to doctors about further care during flight. Why can't flight attendants do that?' she mentioned. And MedLink was born. Joan is an amazing visionary!

I worked directly with the MedLink doctors and my boss was the director of the ER. When Joan asked, 'Can you go to China for a month?' My boss was very supportive of my job at MedAire and I was able to get time off in the ER for my travels and return to my ER position.

The first time I taught for MedAire, Joan gave me her curriculum for a maritime assignment in Bonaire, in the Caribbean. I flew from Phoenix to Florida for a stay-over in Miami at a large two-story hotel, all open-air with no internal corridors. I ordered room service, washed my hair, and put it in curlers so I'd be ready for the flight the next day. It was sweltering hot, and I put on my babydoll pajamas and then started going through the curriculum and enjoying my room service meal.

When I was finished with my meal, I put the food tray outside the door and then entered the outside walkway to move it further down so I wouldn't step on it on my way out in the morning. Unfortunately, the door locked behind me. There I was in babydoll pajamas with curlers in my hair, barefoot no less, with no other option than to make my way to the front desk for help, darting behind palm trees, hiding in bushes, and hoping no one would see me as I made my way to the front desk.

When I finally got to the lobby, it was filled with businessmen waiting to register. They took one look at me, and all were wondering what in the heck I was up to. I cut in line, terribly self-conscious, and the receptionist stared at me like I was crazy. I explained my dilemma and she asked, "Do you have an ID? I can give you a key if you have an ID." You can imagine my reaction. "DO I LOOK LIKE I HAVE AN ID?!" I responded and finally convinced security to meet me at my room. I promised to show them my ID once my door was unlocked.

Despite that rocky start, it turned out to be a great training trip aboard a yacht in the Caribbean. The training was extensive — not just the emergency component, but how to care for a patient over the course of days out at sea until they reached shore. We had to train these crews to be nurses and provide ongoing care to the victims.

I never knew what assignment Joan would ask me to do next. Once I flew to Los Angeles to meet Steve Jobs in his Gulfstream and tell him about our services and provide him with some training. Next, I might be sent to the Caribbean Islands, Hawaii, Thailand, South America, etc. So there was a cultural component to our travels as we learned about other cultures and medical care. In Thailand, we always wore long dresses and kept our shoulders covered when we were visiting a temple or out in public. We quickly learned that we couldn't wear our shoes in a temple. We just figured it out, complied with the custom, and everyone was happy... except for the time we touched someone's head during CPR training. That was a huge no-no, as it turned out.

Now, what's the first thing you say when you check on someone who might be ill or injured? You ask, 'Are you OK?' Although all CPR mannequins are named "Annie," we altered it to "Annie Annie Are You OK?" Annie Annie was involved in some hijinks during our travels. When Joan and I were flying from Argentina through Chile to Texas, Joan bought some Argentinian wine. We opened up Annie's chest and stuffed her with the bottles, which — whoops! — had to go through the x-ray machine at customs. As Annie Annie went through the scanner at three in the morning, we realized they might take the wine away. So we struck up a conversation with the agents, who seemed more interested in us than the contents of our large cases, and off we went on our merry way.

MedAire won a contract with United Airlines after competing with the Red Cross for the bid. We trained 22,000 flight attendants worldwide at all of their bases. Joan, Caleb, a nurse anesthetist, and I flew to Bangkok, Thailand, for one of these training sessions. Joan arranged a dinner event but at the last minute couldn't attend because she wasn't feeling well and wanted to stay back and rest. When I returned to the hotel room, Joan was very ill on the bathroom floor, feverish and semi-conscious with vomiting and diarrhea. Obviously, a severe case of food poisoning.

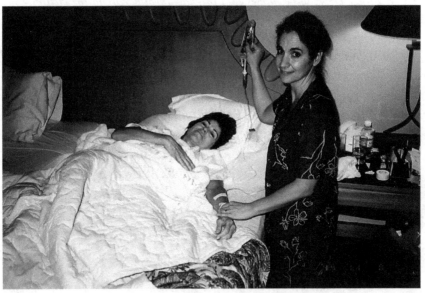

Patty attending to a very sick Joan – Photo credit: Patty Campbell

Joan was very dehydrated, and we knew we had to give her fluids and anti-nausea medications. I called for Caleb next door to come and help. I'll never forget when he ran into our room wearing pink fluffy slippers he had found in his hotel closet and carrying a CPR mask! I emphatically said, 'Put that CPR mask away... she's not that bad!!' We had just completed a maritime class in Phuket and had extra IV fluids left over, so I took a picture off the wall over Joan's bed, started the IV, and hung the IV fluids from the nail. Caleb went to the nearest hospital, talked to the ER doctor, and return with anti-nausea medications, which we promptly gave to Joan. We stabilized Joan, and she was fine the next day and ready to travel.

Here's another interesting close call. We once taught President George Bush's Air Force One crew and the 89th Air Wing during a week in January 2006 in Washington D.C. The crew lady in charge expected military precision in everything we did. We had our usual locked cases shipped directly to the hangar and got up early to prepare for class with everything well in hand. Except, we forgot something essential. 'Did you bring keys?' I asked Joan. 'No, did you?' she replied. There we were, staring at each other in disbelief after having gone through an extensive background check to land this prestigious assignment. So, we had a flight attendant bring us a paperclip (which didn't work) and a screw driver. Because time was of the essence, and in a panic, we broke the locks with the screwdriver just as the lady in charge came through the door. She looked at us, down on our knees, and asked, 'Is there a problem?' Joan and I looked at each other and then quickly assured her, 'No, everything is fine!' just in the knick of time.

And if you wonder about the 'land' component in MedAire's 'Air, Land and Sea' logo, Joan had several clients at ranches and lodges in very remote locations who hired MedAire for custom medical kits and training. For instance, Alaska has many large private resorts in the wilderness which are enjoyed by congressmen and other VIPs. These lodges provide many outdoor activities, such as hunting, fishing, watersports, etc., which can result in a variety of injuries. Medical care is quite a distance away, requiring transportation by boat or plane. We provided training for handling emergencies in these remote locations. We set up real-life safety scenarios — not just how to handle emergencies but critical thinking skills that incorporated survival skills as well.

Our land-based training was intensive and built survival skills. Photo credit: Patty Campbell

If a grizzly bear attacked the person you were hiking with, what would you do? How would you take care of this person? What equipment do you need? If you can't move them and the nearest lodge is three miles away, what are you going to do? And most importantly, where is the bear and what are you going to do to keep the victim

238

and yourself safe?

This specialized training was the secret sauce of MedAire and set MedAire apart from its competitors. Whether it was an archery-related accident, a mountain lion attack, or an incident at the shooting range — our job was to prepare people to react appropriately and safely.

Training to treat an archery lesson gone wrong (note the arrow in the chest.) Photo credit: Patty Campbell

We discussed the unique needs and concerns with clients to ensure the curriculum and training addressed their particular situation. We once taught a crew at a private lodge and dude ranch for the owners of a construction and remodeling business in a remote wilderness area in Arizona. They were refurbishing cabins and buildings and had many encounters with rattlesnakes. We thoroughly covered snake training and emergency care after a bite along with our usual land-based training. It was this type of custom training that was the success of MedAire.

And speaking of cabins, Joan had a darling cabin that was originally on the Indian Reservation. When the land leases were canceled, she bought the cabin and moved it to the current location outside of Vernon, Arizona. She sold it many years ago when she and Frank built a beautiful mountain home down the road.

It just so happened that Joan, our friend Karen Maier, and I were horseback riding in the mountains one day and noticed the 'for sale sign' at her old cabin — it was back on the market! 'I love that cabin,' I said and brought my husband back a few weeks later to make the purchase. At Joan's insistence, we bought the adjacent lots as well, three acres backing up to the national forest. My family still enjoys that cabin today.

Joan always made our excursions fun and full of wonderful memories. Karen, Joan, and I would jump in her old Datsun and head for the forest to go sledding, skiing, or snowshoeing. Once we were sledding in really deep snow, and afterward, she pulled out her crystal flutes and a bottle of champagne to enjoy in the snow! Joan was always the best hostess. That's what made MedAire so amazing. Our clients loved her because she went the extra mile. She had the gift of really listening to their needs and making them feel special.

The most memorable experience is when Joan took me to the Alaskan Iditarod. She was invited every year, and one time brought me along. It was the most amazing experience. We stayed in a beautiful lodge on the Iditarod trail so that we could mingle with the mushers, dogs, and veterinarians. It was a great time among many great times, always fun and exciting.

The Iditarod's mandatory 4th check point – Photo credit: Patty Campbell

What a thrill to visit the outback in Alaska!

Working with MedAire for over 20 years was a very rewarding part of my career. I authored, edited, and updated the aviation and maritime training manuals and published several books about inflight and maritime emergencies, some still in use today. Our publishers were Kendall Hunt Publishing Co. and Dorling Kindersley of London. I visited the UK to work with the medical director of British Airways to co-author the "Manual of Inflight Medical Emergencies." We had to write two similar but different versions due to the differences in emergency care between the U.S. and the UK. I authored the Maritime First Responder Guide for emergencies at sea.

Joan and MedAire provided so many wonderful opportunities for me during those years. But the best part has been our lifelong friendship.

I really appreciate that Patty opened this time capsule which exemplifies the extensive global traveling we did nonstop, some just for fun. It also brings to mind the highest levels of governments throughout the world that were our customers. We literally wrote the rules for aviation and maritime telemedicine worldwide.

And they're off and running! Photo credit: Patty Campbell

And yes, the Iditarod Trail Sled Dog Race[37] is a wonderful event that I've always enjoyed. I was invited several years in a row, and with life moving at such a fast pace, it was nice to step off the hamster wheel and fly to Alaska with great aviation friends. I would be remiss not to mention the wonderful host for this experience, Ron Duncan. Ron, his pilot Hon, and a very amazing executive team rolled out the red carpet for those of us from the "lower 48" to experience this extraordinary event. I thank Ron for this incredible experience.

The dogs were amazing, mostly Siberian huskies with lineages from Russia, so eager and excited to pull long-distance. Interestingly, this breed, smaller than the native Alaskan malamute, played a saving role during a diphtheria outbreak in 1925. Teams of Siberian huskies traveled 674 miles in six days during a lifesaving "Nome Serum Run" — a trip that would typically take the postal service (that also used dogs) 25 days, according to an article in the BBC.[38]

The fun started at the ceremonial start in Anchorage (to great fanfare), after which we flew by helicopter to a big glacier field and had a cocktail hour. The race's official restart begins in Willow and ends in Nome after a mandatory break and rest points. It can take more than a week to reach the finish line.

As Patty mentioned, we visited with veterinarians along the trail and learned about the extensive care given to these athletic dogs, mostly Alaskan huskies. This amazing breed is born to race through sub-zero temperatures, blizzards, and strong winds across the tundra, rivers, and mountain passes. Mushers are the rock stars, many local but some from other states and countries. It was a joy building relationships with them as well, including four-time Iditarod champion Lance Mackey. Most of all, I loved witnessing the partnership between the mushers and the dogs.

---

[37] "Iditarod: The Last Great Race." See https://iditarod.com/

[38] Louise Crane. "In 1925, a remote town was saved from lethal disease by dogs," *BBC*, October 17, 2016. See http://www.bbc.com/earth/story/20161014-in-1925-a-remote-town-was-saved-from-lethal-disease-by-dogs

The exciting start of the Iditarod – Photo credit: Patty Campbell

It was such a pleasure to get to know musher Lance Mackey. Photo credit: Patty Campbell

The vast Alaskan wilderness reminded me of the training we offered in remote areas in parts of the mainland and Alaska. Patty described some of the medical and traumatic emergencies faced in those regions, and I looked forward to this "rugged" outdoor type of wilderness training with its own set of challenges and protocols.

Another view of a wilderness training course — Photo credit: Patty Campbell

So many good memories have come flooding back and I wish I could share a thousand anecdotes — but that could fill another book. So I'll settle for a few additional choice moments that are etched in time. For instance, Patty often wore curlers, the heated kind. Once she forgot the difference in voltage from one country to the next and wrapped her hair in a curling iron. Suddenly, the handle melted away from the rod, and a flame shot out! We removed the fried section of her hair with scissors.

While training United Airlines flight attendants in Santiago, Chile, we had weekends off and roamed the city. The first weekend I found an intriguing gaucho saddle made of leather and sheepskin. I thought, *If I ever have time to ride Rosie again, this would be sensational!* So I sat on the saddle to size it up and confidently exclaimed, "Yes, I'll buy it." It wasn't expensive, but the shipping sure was! I couldn't wait to put it on Rosie... and after all that effort, no, it didn't fit! So I gave away this exquisite Chilean saddle and promised myself that I would stick with the local saddle shop for all of Rosie's tack.

The second weekend (after training all week) we decided to fly to Buenos Aires, the "Paris of South America," and meet an aviation attorney friend. Her client was the Sheraton Hotel, and when I asked her for a hotel recommendation, she said, "I'll take care of it for you." We checked in to a large suite... but didn't realize it included a complimentary butler until just before checking out. Darn! We could have been waited on hand and foot, which would have been a rare treat! While there, we went out to a nightclub and sat near the dancers who performed the most beautiful tango. I was inspired to learn how to tango, and many years later tried ballroom dance lessons but "failed" because I kept trying to lead Frank!

After checking out of the hotel in Buenos Aires, I said to Patty, "Let's go have lunch." We had a several-hour wait before going back to Santiago to finish our last week of training for United Airlines and found a little restaurant in a mall connected to the hotel. It was so pleasant to end our stay in this quaint spot, and the waiter bought us a bottle of wine to enjoy with our lunch. Patty, being a vegetarian, ordered a salad. I ordered one of those famous Argentinian steaks. It was divine. I ooh'd and ahh'd until she finally said, "Okay, can I have a small bite?" She has not been a vegetarian since!

Patty and me at the beautiful Sheraton Hotel in Buenos Aires (with hotel staff) – Photo credit: Patty Campbell

Patty also jogged my memory with her "cultural tale" in Thailand (the head touching), which reminds me of a trip to Abu Dhabi. I wore shorts, the modest knee-length kind made of silk. Apparently, even though these were the equivalent of granny shorts, they inadvertently drew attention to me. I was wolf-whistled right in front of my son, who was traveling with me. Awkward, to say the least, which is why I recommend the book *Kiss, Bow, Or Shake Hands: The Bestselling Guide to Doing Business in More Than 60 Countries.*[39] I read it when it debuted in 2006. By then, we were well-versed in most cultural norms, but I still found it helpful.

There must be a gazillion Annie Annie stories — yes, the same Annie CPR mannequin referenced in Tore Laerdal's YouTube

---

[39] Terri Morrison. *Kiss, Bow, Or Shake Hands: The Bestselling Guide to Doing Business in More Than 60 Countries* (Massachusetts: Adams Media, 2006).

video. The most famous tale of all involved a questionable "Irish cheese" scenario when I traveled home from training the Irish Air Corps one year. I decided to buy my family several samples from the Grafton Street cheese shop. It would have been delicious if only the cheese had survived the trip. I had no room in my luggage and stuffed the cheese, nicely wrapped, inside my trusty CPR mannequin. It must have gotten warm in the belly of the plane because it came off the turn style wrapped in a big orange belt. I was not allowed to retrieve it! Instead, I was ushered to the customs agent, who nearly keeled over when the case was presented. He pointed at the exit, indicating "Get out now!"

All I could say is, "I'm sorry for the stinky cheese!"

There was no way to get the smell out of plastic, and we had to replace poor Annie Annie to the tune of $500 — ouch!

And by the way, Annie Annie wasn't our only training mannequin. "Patty Parts" was about the size of a doll and smaller than our CPR mannequins. And no, she wasn't named after Patty Campbell. She had anatomically correct features and removable organs — brain, liver, lungs, heart, etc. — thus the name. What a great teaching aid and Patty Parts traveled with us around the globe. I once hurried through the Chicago terminal without properly securing Patty or her parts. Suddenly, and unbeknownst to me, a larynx, a kidney, intestines, eyeballs, and half a cerebellum spilled onto the walkway. The nurse who was with me scooped up this trail of organs to the surprise of those walking behind us!

It wasn't unusual to meet high-profile people along the way. I trained August Bush III and met CEO John Hunt in Utah and many others in both private and commercial markets. And here's a bit of trivia — I once trained Harrison Ford who operated a Gulfstream. We met at his New York hangar, and I was struck by his humility and the excellent questions he asked over the two-day course. Early the second morning he had a commitment and asked if I'd wait, and I did. He returned, finished the course, and tested.

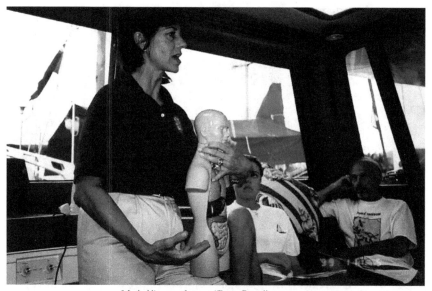

Me holding our famous "Patty Parts" mannequin

Last but not least, our medical kits were aboard Disney planes as well. It was fun training the Disney flight crew at "The happiest place on earth" in CPR, emergency first aid, and the use of defibrillators. I'll always treasure Michael Eisner's gracious thank you note following an executive training session in Florida. What an impressive piece of Disney memorabilia and a favorite keepsake.

Welcome! ★
Emergency Preparedness

THIS AFTERNOON'S SCHEDULE:

Introduction (Promenade Ballroom)
Joan Sullivan Garrett
President, MedAire, Inc.

Overview of Automated External Defibrillators
Vickee Altman, RN, BSN MEd
Vice President Education
and Standards, MedAire, Inc.

BREAK
(Time to head for your first Breakout Session)

1st Session

TRAVEL HEALTHY
(Promenade Ballroom – Stay right where you are!)

BREAK

2nd Session – CPR/AED
(Marvin Gardens B)

BREAK

3rd Session – Emergency First Aid
(St. James B)

The schedule for our Disney training class – Photo credit: MedAire

June 5, 1998

Joan:

Thanks for traveling to Orlando
last week to participate in our
corporate retreat. The
presentations were informative
and enlightening.

Please thank your staff on my
behalf.

MDE:bh

MICHAEL D. EISNER

An autographed "thank you" from Michael Eisner – Photo credit: MedAire

Chapter Eighteen: Global Impact, Global Problems

In the midst of chaos, there is also opportunity.
~ Sun Tzu

We had grown from a 4,000 square foot office to 8,000, with an opportunity to expand to 13,000 (the entire sixth floor). That was an incredibly risky move, but we couldn't function efficiently in our old space, and it made sense to step out in faith. The space had incredible potential, and I wondered how best to harness that potential. It seemed an open area would be ideal, an environment where everyone worked together as a team. That's when I learned about feng shui,[40] a "natural science" philosophy that had been around for centuries and was trending (somewhat) in the late 1980s. I was interested in its tenets — that it promotes harmony in homes and workspaces (a wind-water concept drawing from the natural world).

Why not give it a try? I thought. After all, critical thinking and emotional intelligence often intersect outside the box — away from preconceptions and labels that discourage exploration. And so, I called a feng shui master.

He reviewed the whole office plan and suggested we arrange the CFO's desk away from his office door to prevent money from "flowing out the door." We hung mirrors in the workstations so people could see behind and catch views out the office windows. My office received extra carpet padding to promote an additional layer of comfort to visitors and highlight the "importance" of my office. Oh — and we hung crystals in the common work area as well, meant to make people cognizant of their universe.

---

[40] Ernest John Eitel. *Feng-shui: or, The Rudiments of Natural Science in China* (Lane, Crawford & Company, 1878).

These concepts were strange, yes, but they also made sense. The whole goal was to improve work habits, mood, and a sense of serenity even in the busyness of our work. It turned out to be a good investment… and then what happened? The Twin Towers were attacked in New York City, and 9/11 became our national nightmare. The entire industry was grounded, not flying at all, and created an uncertain future. Even when the skies opened back up, people were afraid to book flights and travel.[41]

During frightening times, leaders get up every morning, go to their offices with heads held high, greet employees at the door, and thank them for showing up despite the uncertainty. "We are going to get through this," I said time and again and meant it. My people needed to see and hear it. And we did pull through.

Then came the Enron scandal in 2001, resulting in a widely publicized FBI investigation, bankruptcy, and the utter betrayal of Enron employees and shareholders. This debacle flooded television screens for months and led to the Sarbanes-Oxley Act of 2002 (SOX or SARBOX) to protect investors and make corporate disclosures more transparent.

The federal government was in no mood to see shareholders tricked into inflated stock prices or the public subjected to any other kind of fraud. Honestly, for Enron to implode in the first place told me that new regulations were needed. What I didn't expect was the laser-like attention the Securities and Exchange Commission (SEC) had toward private companies that were not listed on the stock exchange. MedAire, incorporated in Nevada with headquarters in Arizona, was a privately held company, and yet we were certainly affected by the fallout along with other private corporations across the U.S.

For instance, we were held to the same whistleblower and corporate governance standards as publicly traded companies.

---

[41] Gabi Logan. "The Effects of 9/11 on the Airline Industry," *USA Today*, April 24, 2018. See https://traveltips.usatoday.com/effects-911-airline-industry-63890.html

The legislation is footnoted[42] and entire books have been written about the Act. Students of economics and regulatory history might benefit from reading about the hoops that CEOs jumped through during this storm and ever after, it seemed. I recommend two articles that help put these requirements into perspective, one from *The Economist*[43] and one from the *Wall Street Journal*.[44] It's also a timely reminder for entrepreneurs today — know the law and operate within its framework, or else!

Believe me, I'm very much an advocate of crossing all T's and dotting all I's and relied on my CFO of five years to shepherd us through the copious filing requirements and regulations under which we now had to operate. It was no small undertaking for our legal and financial staff, especially since MedAire was exploring global expansion amid the new regulations.

You may wonder why we entertained this notion of expansion overseas during a regulatory crackdown. The answer could be written as a case study with in-depth analysis to examine, interpret, and generalize the findings. It's tempting to write such a case study, and I've been encouraged to do so for this and other MedAire ventures. Yet, I don't want to lose the narrative — the very human responses, emotional nuances, dramatic miss-steps, and the agonizing external factors in play that created the "perfect storm." It's best told as a story, and what a story it is, playing out like a John Grisham novel full of intrigue, court battles, and ultimately a satisfying conclusion (although it didn't feel like it at

---

[42] 107th Congress (2001-2002). "H.R.3763 - Sarbanes-Oxley Act of 2002," Congress.gov. See https://www.congress.gov/bill/107th-congress/house-bill/3763

[43] "A price worth paying? America's response to Enron and other scandals was the Sarbanes-Oxley law. It is costing plenty—but is it working?" *The Economist*, May 19, 2005. See https://www.economist.com/special-report/2005/05/19/a-price-worth-paying

[44] Deborah Solomon. "Crackdown Puts Corporations, Executives in New Legal Peril: More Than Ever, Businesses Face Risk of Prosecution; Post-Enron, a Changed View," *Wall Street Journal*, June 20, 2005. See https://www.wsj.com/articles/SB111922792995963697

the time). I label it a learning experience and a shake-up that reverberated throughout the company.

Around 2001, some of our U.S. corporate customers asked MedAire to support them beyond their flight department in developing countries, specifically China. Of course, we wanted to assist these customers. Basically, we were already handling calls from Cargill, Intel, and Motorola aviation departments, but to fully support them, we would need to set up operations in-country. And that's how we began to explore the Asian market, as requested.

Indeed, to support our customers, we were segueing into the assistance market. It didn't go unnoticed. We received a letter in March of 2001 from our largest competitor, International SOS (ISOS), suggesting a strategic partnership. We met in Singapore to discuss ideas to leverage MedAire's customer base and the sales network of ISOS and pool our aviation customers. I declined because my board of directors was hesitant, and I didn't want to hand over the "recipe" to my business.

If only I had a crystal ball with which to prognosticate the future. Knowing what I know now, I would have taken ISOS up on its offer, starting slowly and determining if this partnership would benefit both companies. Honestly, it would have saved a lot of time and effort since MedAire eventually became a subsidiary of ISOS a few years later anyway. At that moment, however, I was cautious and wanted to keep my options open.

The decision to venture overseas and our rationale for doing so included increasing our upward trajectory. MedAire was soaring, and honestly, international expansion sounded intriguing. In 2002, we were approached by a company in Australia and basically asked, "Do you want to enter China? We have medical clinics in eight provinces in China, and more in Malaysia, Thailand, and Indonesia." In short, we had an opportunity to acquire various western-style medical clinics across Asia called "Global Doctor." And so I asked myself, *Should we dip in our toe?* I didn't get a good ping. Intuition has always been my North Star, so to speak, and I wasn't totally convinced this was the right path for MedAire.

I decided to send my MedAire CFO and a newly hired president to Perth, Australia, for some deep digging and due diligence and awaited their feedback. Let's just say that turned out to be my first mistake. Going against your intuition, by the way, is almost *always* a mistake.

My CFO and president returned from abroad with "good news." According to them, Global Doctor was as clean as a whistle and worth acquiring. The acquisition made perfect sense in order to access and deliver urgent medical care to expatriates and travelers in countries where corporations were establishing business operations, .i.e., Intel and Cargill. The strategic locations and offerings of these clinics provided the western-style quality of healthcare familiar to the employees of these corporations. Digital x-rays were interpreted by physicians in Australia, and delivery of care was by physicians trained in Europe, Australia, or the United States, predominately. Staff members were bilingual and of the resident country, for the most part.

MedAire's intent for these clinics was to standardize the offering and ensure consistency of care, regardless of where they were located. What was impressive about these clinics was the staff. They were excited at the prospect of being a part of the MedAire family and welcomed our vision of western-style medical care and treatment.

It seemed to be a great way to go toe-to-toe with our competitors, generate revenue, and take MedAire to the next level. However, I still had reservations. I felt we didn't have the resources and in-house capability to move forward and would need the backing of Samaritan Health System. Samaritan was still providing hospital space for MedLink operations and supported our various expansions (as they do today). The plan was to augment the clinics' expertise by offering telemedicine services through our Samaritan relationship for pediatrics, internal medicine, toxicology, and other specialties.

In short, we needed Samaritan to pull this off. I spoke to Samaritan's CFO about Global Doctor, and he was vehemently against it. If we took this step, it meant MedAire would become a publicly traded entity on the Australian Stock Exchange and bring a whole new set of rules and regulations into the dynamic, not to mention a considerable financial investment.

Also, as a U.S. company acquiring a foreign company, we would have to follow a complex international reverse approach governed by the SEC — very onerous and very serious. I had to justify our acquisition of Global Doctor clinics and defend my strategy to Samaritan…without being 100% convinced this was the right move. In other words, I had to act immediately and decided to move forward *if* I could get Samaritan to agree. A meeting was organized with Samaritan's CEO, CFO, Risk Manager and members of my executive team and board representation.

Before that occurred, however, there's a backstory. If you recall, I utilized feng shui to design MedAire's interior space when we located to a larger office. Although unconventional, I appreciated the feng shui philosophy and felt it benefitted my staff. Would feng shui help in this situation too? What would the feng shui master advise regarding a "meeting of minds" at this crucial junction?

With so much on the line, I figured there was nothing to lose and everything to gain by revisiting this method (and I encourage those interested to read John Molenda's book *Rethinking Feng Shui*.)[45] This time, the feng shui master gave me special instructions to address my plight — not for architectural layout, but the specifics of generating a desired personal and professional outcome. It sounded a bit odd yet interesting, and I was up for anything to achieve a resolution that would enable us to move forward with Samaritan's support.

---

[45] John Molenda. "Rethinking Feng Shui." In *Historical Archaeologies of Capitalism* (Springer, Cham, 2015) pp. 181-199.

On the day before the meeting, I was in total prep mode. I'll give you the CliffsNotes version since it was such a long and convoluted process, and some of the specifics have faded with time. That morning, the feng shui master brought me a paper bag containing red powder and told me to boil three eggs, peel 13 oranges concentrically without breaking a peel, and lay five-foot red cloths inside and outside my front and back door. A timeline and specifics for each action was attached to these tasks. Once he explained every nuance, the feng shui master left. Off to the store I went to buy eggs, two dozen oranges (in case I broke a peel and had to start over), and the red cloth.

I boiled the eggs — no shells could be broken — and put them into the paper bag full of red powder. Then, according to my instructions, I walked 180 feet (perhaps it was 280 feet) toward the desert with this bag, at an elevation higher than my kitchen. I chanted words I no longer remember and hoped no hiker would come down the path and catch me in the act because I surely looked ridiculous. Once at my destination, I peeled the eggs inside the bag, mindful that no shells fell outside the bag, or I would have to start over. I held the eggs in one hand, and with the other hand, threw the bag of shells and powder as far as I could into the desert (biodegradable, I should add), chanting all the while. I ate the hardboiled eggs as I headed back to my house.

Then I had to wait until 5 p.m. to peel the oranges. I sat in my family room with a paring knife, carefully carving concentric, unbroken circles of orange peels into a bowl. Then I was to tear them into small pieces and toss them into every room, including closets in my house, and open the doors and windows (it was summer and hot outside). As a final step, I placed the red cloths evenly outside and inside my front and back door, and promptly at 8 p.m., stepped across my threshold and did a final chant.

Mind you, it was dark, and my home bordered the desert. A coyote, javelina, or rattlesnake could have moseyed right in! Frank was traveling on business, and I was on my own if a nocturnal intruder decided to pay a visit. Honestly, Frank's absence was a good thing because he would have called the white coats if he saw this commotion!

Finally, I closed the doors and windows and proceeded to gather up all of the orange peels I had strewn about my home. Let me tell you, it took hours to clean up every room and closet, and my instructions were not even completed yet. The feng shui master told me to arrive at the conference room early the next day, sit with my back against the wall facing the doorway, and position my team (the MedAire CFO and president included) to my left. The Samaritan CFO and risk manager were positioned to the right, and the Samaritan CEO sat by the open door opposite me. After the presentation, Samaritan's CEO agreed to stand by MedAire for at least another year. Apparently, the feng shui worked. The CFO's objections were shot down. He pushed away from the table and walked out of the room, just livid.

I didn't really blame the CFO for his reaction. Despite all the feng shui rigmarole, my inner voice was still cautioning against the acquisition. The SARS (severe acute respiratory syndrome) outbreak, originating in China, had hit the aviation industry hard,[46] and I wondered how it would impact Global Doctor.

The clinics appeared to be equipped and strategically positioned to handle the outbreak. I should have hired international accountants and other regional resources to paint a clearer picture. I made a trip myself and visited three clinics — Beijing, Bangkok, and Indonesia. They stood out as having "invested" practitioners and excellent relationships with businesses in their locale. Their locations were strategic, and medical practices were good. Training and certification of the medical staff had begun for American Heart Association certification in Basic Life support and Advanced Life Support for Adults and Children. The professionalism and commitment demonstrated at each clinic were very reassuring despite the concerns for structure and backend legal footing.

My team, overall, was excited about this opportunity,

---

[46] "SARS 'devastating' for airlines," *CNN*, May 21, 2003. See
https://edition.cnn.com/2003/BUSINESS/05/21/asia.sars.airlines.biz/index.html

including the majority of my board of directors. It appeared to be a sound business move. Global Doctor was delisted on the exchange and replaced with MedAire, stock symbol MDE.

The Australian Stock Exchange provided access to growth capital, and this prompted me to think about going public in the U.S. at some time in the future. However, under the Sarbanes-Oxley Act, a company the size of MedAire might spend more than $1 million in fees to ensure compliance when issuing an initial public offering (IPO). We already had our hands full just managing our corporate governance and the operational, legal, and HR mandates under which to function in each foreign country. I was determined to do this right. We were an ISO-certified company, meaning we met or exceeded international standards for quality management and best practices.

Almost immediately, however, it was clear that we had acquired a hornet's nest. If I were to step into a time machine and go back to the days of due diligence, I would have been more involved. I would have hired skilled legal and accounting firms, set clear objectives, and monitored the progress rather than delegating this responsibility to my team members (and myself) who were not experienced in mergers and acquisitions. Audits on a country-by-country basis should have been performed. This is one of those areas that we couldn't afford to skip but also couldn't afford to undertake.

After the merger, some deficiencies were uncovered country by country. Clinic business structures, as well as the financials and operational platforms, were not what they appeared to be on the surface in these cases. An audit was performed, highlighting employment requirements that fell short. Those clinics not meeting our expectations were shuttered. Again, we were beholden to the Sarbanes-Oxley Act, something U.S.-initiated and perhaps unfamiliar to Global Doctor and its shareholders (which were now our shareholders). Undoubtedly, these restrictions and regulations added fuel to the fire. I did not have my thumb on the pulse of the Global Doctor shareholders. I should have met with them upfront.

What became abundantly clear was there must have been a level of dissatisfaction among these shareholders before we ever acquired Global Doctor. They expected to see immediate progress and profitability in what this MedAire entity was now. MedAire, unjustly, was viewed as their "white knight," and expectations for liquidity were misplaced. There is no doubt in my mind that given time and oversight by qualified management, MedAire would have turned these clinics around, and Global Doctor would have become the strategic asset we had envisioned.

However, the stock price dipped. Our shareholders were complaining, and our competitors were circling. Time was against us, hence, an opportunity for others to "step in" and leverage the situation. Control hung in the balance.

Needless to say, there were changes to my C suite. I turned to my board members for advice — a steadfast group with incredible savvy and experience. It's times like these that the "fight or flight" instinct really kicks in. The hair on the back of your neck raises, pupils dilate, adrenaline flows, and you either run away or face your adversaries. *We can fight this battle,* I decided, especially with the board's support and my Irish moxie in play. I hired a new female CFO and attended investor meetings — my first taste of what it was like to head a publicly traded company.

By the way, MedAire had a company softball team in Arizona and was involved in a league, lots of fun. Just before flying to attend my first investor meeting, I slid into third base and severely sprained my ankle. This meant I was about to venture forth on a roadshow… on crutches! Electrotherapy helped, as well as hot and cold compresses and Arnica (a gel to increase circulation). The upside was that we could board the plane quickly on a wheelchair, and the downside was that I was physically uncomfortable while traveling, giving presentations, and meeting the Global Doctor staff and shareholders.

I remember those shareholder meetings as somewhat stifling, meaning that I could no longer interact as I did when MedAire was privately held. No more "hug as a handshake." No more "diverse team thinking" and brainstorming out loud. My role had changed, and so did the way I was able to interact with people. Being governed by both the SEC of Australia and the U.S., I couldn't wear my marketing hat, so to speak, or bring to the table the visions I had for future growth. There was no "Just trust me — you can believe in my track record." It was more a telling of what would happen and statements of fact rather than my usual conversational approach. I felt very much like a fish out of water… or rather, a human stranded in water with the sharks circling!

My entire predicament is summed up in one illustration

The shareholders were also unhappy with my second major expansion move, which was to launch Security Solutions. This suite of crisis management and client-specific risk assessment services included security alerts, incident response plans, onsite security audits, and other services designed to assist flight crews in preparing for and resolving potential security risks abroad. My rationale was that safety and security were a natural fit — not mutually exclusive, but in the same family — and to this day, MedAire offers this valuable security service.

Security Solutions was a bone of contention as well. Our shareholders did not seem to appreciate this new venture at all. Nor were our competitors pleased. They competed at vastly discounted rates and began taking clients from us and vice versa.

This is where the story gets interesting.

Chapter Nineteen: A Twist of Fate

Show me someone who has done something worthwhile
and I'll show you someone who has overcome adversity.
~ Lou Holtz

It turned out that International SOS became our parent company. I have had many people tell me that this acquisition, merger, takeover (or whatever it was) will also be taught in classrooms someday — not as a "how-to," but as a precautionary tale with a happy ending. Yes, it had a very satisfying conclusion that benefited both MedAire and International SOS, but not without some back and forth as is typical in these types of negotiations.

I'm sharing the saga here a bit differently than I did in front of cameras and news reporters in 2004. It was reported (erroneously) that I was stepping down as MedAire CEO at that time. No, I stepped down in 2008 and was the architect of my exit. My job was to protect my employees, customers, and myself... and it wasn't easy. This backstory is a retrospective of those teachable moments that might help someone navigate a similar minefield one day — without losing a limb.   I didn't have a definite exit strategy in place. It's one thing to be without an exit strategy when you are "all in" and building an enterprise. It's quite another when you are *acquiring* an enterprise such as Global Doctor. I looked at and began talking to AXA in 2004, another travel assistance company, as an entity with which to possibly do business or partner. I felt AXA was a good fit, very close in culture and vision. Other companies were interested in MedAire as well. The news was out that Global Doctor was underperforming and affecting our bottom line. The truth is, we had tens of millions of dollars in which to absorb our loses. Given time, I had no doubt that our stellar reputation, solid industry experience, and utter determination would overcome this temporary setback. Yet, I underestimated the interest and intent of our competitors.

Our competitors saw MedAire as the golden standard. Some tried to replicate our service but failed. Customers who were drawn away complained that our competitors' service level was nowhere near what MedAire offered. They missed our corporate culture, our level of genuine care, and our years of expertise. There was simply no substitute for what MedAire and MedLink offered — we had our service offerings down to a science, and our business was rock solid.

In 2004, our revenues were about $24+ million but rose to $28+ million in 2005 and $30+ million in 2006, climbing, even with Global Doctor's negative impact on our bottom line. Still, due to the intense buying up of shares from competitors and others, we were in a quandary and ripe for the picking. Our opponents saw and exploited an opportunity, Business 101, and in an odd way, it was somewhat flattering that we were drawing such interest from rival companies. We may have been making a splash for all the wrong reasons, but a splash nevertheless.

As I mentioned, we faced a steady drumbeat of shareholder complaints. A dissident group, who did not trust a word I said, decided to make changes in management, meaning me. They wanted me gone. It was disorienting, going from beloved CEO in the aviation and maritime market to a perceived ogre who was supposedly destroying the very startup I had founded from scratch and nurtured into a large and profitable corporation. Again, we felt we could turn the clinics around or sell them, but MedAire's market worth continued to drop in the meantime. Yet we had a pronounced presence in the travel industry. Who wouldn't want to sweep in and take us over? From a purely logical business angle, it made perfect sense that our opponents would make an effort.

Over time, 90% of my energy and attention was spent managing shareholder issues. One Australian shareholder, in particular, caused a lot of tension. Try as I might, I could not bridge the gap in communication or inspire goodwill. I could not make the dissident shareholders understand the prohibitions of the Sarbanes-Oxley regulations under which I had to operate. I could not convince them to hang tight and allow MedAire to work its magic.

There was a tremendous amount of energy expended on this back and forth, not just from our opponents. I pushed back against particularly egregious actions. No, I could not look the other way when a clinic was out of compliance. No, shareholders could not fly to my Phoenix office and ransack our books. No, there would be no insider information or trading. And by the way, don't call me again at three in the morning!

Oh, and one more NO. A representative of the opposition showed up at our Phoenix office and demanded we turn over the keys. *Excuse me?!* I was at an investment meeting in Dallas when I got the call from my assistant. I told her to send the intruder on his merry way, and we turned the matter over to legal counsel. I was past being shellshocked, yet it was hot under that microscope, let me tell you.

Place me in the middle of a medical emergency, say a gunshot wound to the chest or a heart attack, and I'm in my element. Put me in the middle of feuding international shareholders and contentious stakeholders, and I'm not in my element at all. Those early days were a complete dust-up — truly a story for the textbooks — and I'm honest about what it did to my overall health. My anxiety was accompanied by weight gain and high blood pressure. I told my husband, "This is killing me!" To say I was miserable is an understatement.

Following is a brief synopsis of how this situation played out, keeping in mind it had the best possible result (even if it didn't feel like it in the moment). As Kenny Rogers sang, "You gotta know when to hold 'em, know when to fold 'em..."

A group of MedAire shareholders believed they had 50% of our shares, enough to assemble a new board and not renew my employment contract. However, they did not comply with MedAire bylaws, follow important notice and information requirements, and provide enough votes "of record" by registered MedAire shareholders. In reality, they had barely 25%. MedAire, being incorporated in Nevada, fell under Nevada's requirements of having a two-thirds shareholders' vote to replace a board, so the dissident shareholders failed in that respect as well. I should mention that MedAire supporters were also buying shares and that I owned a percentage of shares but was constrained in buying more due to SARBOX regulations and other factors.

Once again, my Irish roots came into play. When my company is under fire…handle with care. We filed a complaint in the U.S. District Court for the District of Arizona, which upheld MedAire's temporary restraining order. We learned that International SOS was buying up shares. International SOS issued a consent resolution, and we noticed the recommendation that four out of six new board members would be ISOS employees or employees of its subsidiaries. A consent resolution, by the way, is a vehicle shareholders can use (in this case, under the Australian Stock Exchange) to remove board members and executives. We also knew this had everything to do with competition in the assistance markets.

If I had to turn MedAire over to another company, it would be on the best possible terms. And that's precisely what happened. We rejected the consent resolution. And then, after a lot of soul searching and dissecting the situation, and contrary to the advice of my board members, my decision was to call a meeting and open the door to negotiations. Why hemorrhage money and jeopardize my health, not to mention subject my board members and concerned customers to this drama, when, perhaps, a win/win could be struck. Thus, I accepted an invitation to a meeting in London with Laurent Sabourin, Group Managing Director, as well as the CEO of ISOS.

Laurent's presence in the room was beneficial. We did, ultimately, strike a deal and put a lid on the dissident shareholder action. In the end, ISOS acknowledged my company shouldn't be absorbed or restructured but rather remain independent. Indeed, ISOS augmented our position and vice versa. And to think…if only I had agreed to the overtures of ISOS in 2001, we all would have been spared the entire ordeal. Hindsight is 20/20.

I was relieved and ready for this change and accepted the position of chairman of the board with a five-year buyout. Below, Laurent gives his perspective from the other side of the negotiating table. It really is remarkable that he took the time to contribute to this book, much appreciated. It brings balance to those heady days — another learning opportunity for anyone in our shoes.

MedAire and ISOS have had great success for two main reasons. 1.) We have built on Joan's foundation. She created a unique business model that cannot be easily duplicated. As the consequence, the MedAire Brand is equally unique and cannot be easily replaced. 2.) ISOS has been able to bring good administrative management and financial support to MedAire. We leave the medical and innovative side to them so they can do what they do best. MedAire has a broader global outreach as part of ISOS, and I'm not sure it would have been able to penetrate international markets if it had stood alone. That's another key success factor today.

I would not call our agreement with MedAire a "takeover." Nor was it a merger because we didn't merge. From our perspective, a merger or takeover would involve a grand plan with investment advisors — the type of acquisition situation you might read about in newspapers. That was not the case at all. Joan listed on the Australian Exchange and had many shareholders from Indonesia, Southeast Asia and Australia. They were not happy with MedAire's performance and came to see us. We sent them away — we are not management for hire. But it attracted our attention. We knew of Joan, had occasional contact, and were driven to a discussion.

Of course, we looked at public information and the financials. It appeared MedAire needed to raise money. The best way to accomplish that is for investors to buy shares. This is how we became involved, first as an observer and then, bit by bit, as a shareholder. Eventually, there was a point, I think, that we became the largest single shareholder.

At one stage, I recall we were described as a "white knight" by the Australians. That's another factor in this whole complicated story, for Joan did not perceive us as such. By then, we believed that collectively, with other shareholders, we had 50% of the shares. At a shareholder meeting, a decision was made to vote Joan out. Subsequently, Joan came back as she is quite a negotiator. A phrase comes to mind — warm and cold. She often took our side of the table by surprise with her negotiating style. Sometimes we didn't know where we stood. But we did know that MedAire was a good fit for ISOS and vice versa. And so we persisted until, finally, an agreement was reached.

The outcome was the right outcome for her and us. As chairperson, she continues to have influence and makes an imprint as an industry contact. That is one of the reasons why MedAire does so well — the company's culture has not been destroyed. That's unusual, for most businesses in this situation lose originality. It's hard to scale up a business and keep the original spirit intact.

It concluded positively in the end, and we are very happy. I believe Joan is happy too. Frankly, there should be some interest in this book not only from like-minded entrepreneurs today but senior executives and corporate leaders. Lessons can be learned regarding how to build a business so excellent that it survives a merger, acquisition, takeover, or whatever the situation and retains its corporate structure and culture. ISOS had the foresight not to convert MedAire into Intl SOS, an unusual approach that has worked well. Had we converted it to the Intl SOS brand, it could not be the success story it is today.

What great lessons! Former adversaries can become partners and collaborators. Corporations can make mistakes and survive. Not every takeover has to be hostile in the end. Things often work out as they should. And yes, negotiating style has a lot to do with it, in my case, the tactical "warm and cold" Laurent referenced above. There's a lot to be said for strategy.

We survived the storm and found balance. I knew MedAire was in good hands with International SOS, a natural segue that encapsulated the best of both companies, and we became a privately held corporation once again. Today MedAire's reach is phenomenal, and our services remain unparalleled. I was very glad to become chairman of the board, especially in the very beginning when we became an ISOS subsidiary. It ensured I could keep an eye on the ball as I let go of the reins and enabled me to weigh in on the iterations of my replacement as CEO.

My first successor did not know enough about the corporate culture of MedAire to operate it efficiently, in my opinion. He ran it as an assistance company without understanding the depth and reach of our products and services in the aviation and maritime markets. My second successor did understand our culture and was committed to the company. Thus, I felt MedAire was in good hands and feel this way today under the leadership of CEO Bill Dolny.

I think it's important to share the perspective of Roy Herberger as well, a MedAire board member with a bird's-eye view of this saga. What an accomplished person, an academic with thought processes I admired then and now. He understood the magnitude of the decision-making, stood alongside me, and weighs in below about this slice of MedAire's history.

I would say MedAire's ordeal stemmed from the unpolished actions of dissident shareholders who envisioned taking over MedAire. For example, the records show that some were holding shares under multiple names. For this and other reasons, Joan had defensible legal footing. We didn't want to be taken advantage of, and we may never know the subset of issues driving this group of disgruntled people. But the truth is, it became awkward for the board and our loyal shareholders. Joan could have fought this thing for a long time. We would have stood by her to the end. But I think Joan, always practical, viewed this as a hostile commingling of objectives. Her mission was to preserve and safeguard the company financially and culturally, along with her employees and customers. Rather than engage in a bloody coup, she agreed to a bloodless coup. She took the high road and was masterful in her exit strategy.

The acquisition of Global Doctor was a pivotal event. We saw it as a development opportunity and listed publicly in Australia due to the cost savings. Doing so in the U.S. would have been exorbitant. I think Global Doctor would have become a good asset. However, we had a limited amount of time in which to turn it around. In the meantime, Global Doctor's impact on the income statement stood out as a serious watch item. This concern gave an anchor to the dissident shareholders' dissatisfaction.

I've been part of several hostile takeovers, and it's never fun if you are the one being taken over. Personalities matter and I congratulate Laurent for recognizing that Joan's relationship with her people was of critical value. MedAire's history shows just how important these corporate culture issues would be to the future of this ISOS relationship. It would be fair to say that the transaction was a big alligator to swallow. The combination ultimately, however, made sense and it has worked out well over time.

As Roy says, it was, indeed, a "big alligator to swallow." Yet, I crafted the outcome, protected my key employees and customers, honored the management agreements in place, and ensured the business would hold the same quality standards into the future while continuing to innovate. In other words, as I often stated, "You don't change for the sake of change. You keep your core values and adapt to the market."

As dramatic as it was in real time, this journey led to where we are now. My decision to step down as CEO in 2008 was right for me personally and professionally. I admit I was tired after more than 20 years at the helm. My husband reminded me that my travels during this decade had not slowed down. If anything, it escalated. I don't want your eyes to glaze over, so I'll mention just the international travel: France, United Kingdom, Australia, China, Spain, Singapore, Belgium, The Netherlands, Finland, Denmark, Sweden, Norway, Antigua, British Virgin Islands,

Puerto Rico, Panama, Costa Rica, Hong Kong, South Africa, Indonesia, Thailand, Canada, Ireland, United Arab Emirates, Oman, Switzerland, South Korea, Mongolia, New Zealand, Argentina, Brazil, Chile, and Russia — over and over again. Multiply this by three for travel within the United States and exponentially for business meetings, industry events, and media interviews.

Whew! I was ready to relax a bit. Many happy moments and significant events occurred despite the challenges, an unforgettable decade that forever changed — and improved — MedAire and myself. I share some of the take-aways in the following chapter. All CEOs worth their salt have accumulated a treasure trove of wisdom, and perhaps something will resonate as you read through my musings ahead.

Chapter Twenty: Paying It Forward

What is the essence of life? To serve others and to do good.
~ Aristotle

I suppose quite a few autobiographies have an "advice" element — lessons learned and shared, fumbles and fallout, serendipitous moments, and best practices. Mine is no different. I've certainly made my own management mistakes, and the best possible result is to stay open to changing behaviors and thought processes. What makes mistakes valuable is their teachable quality.

Many lessons were forged as I walked through the fire, and perhaps I experienced them so I could learn, evolve, and share the lessons with others. Why in the world would anyone want to hoard their knowledge? It's much better to tell the stories and "pay it forward." It costs nothing but can mean everything, and so here are my insights, a mix of hard-earned advice, heartfelt suggestions, and a few strong opinions.

As dire as the Global Doctor situation was, it turned out that our presence in Asia enabled us to be among the first medical rescue teams on the ground when the 2004 tsunami hit Phuket, Thailand. Our ability to respond was much timelier and more appropriate due to foresight that might not have been possible without the Global Doctor acquisition. This disaster took 230,000 lives in a few short hours areawide (India, Indonesia, and Thailand), just horrible. We were able to airlift medical supplies into the devastated areas of Aceh, Indonesia and continued to support the region.

Another success story in Asia was MedAire's capability to evacuate a potential SARS patient (a physician) at the request of a U.S. government agency. Our Global Response Center coordinated the transport from Hong Kong to a hospital in Georgia, an 18-hour flight with the complexities of this rapid-onset illness.

Isn't it ironic that an unfortunate business decision put us in the right place at the right time to assist others? I remember thanking God that we were able to help.

The *Wall Street Journal Transcript* interviewed me in 2004,[47] quite an honor, in which I talked about MedAire services but also, in part, about my job. The gist was that when I went to bed at night, or when I just stopped and reflected, I thought about my unusual job. Very few jobs impact so many lives in environments that never before had a solution. I credited my staff in this article, handpicked for their brilliance, who believed in the mission and vision and were passionate about their own jobs.

That's an important takeaway throughout these last chapters — thanking your employees, contractors, volunteers, and supporters and having a sense of gratitude for those who make it happen behind the scenes. No CEO alive has ever attained success without good people in his or her corner.

What a ray of sunshine for MedAire to receive Arizona State University's W.P. Carey School of Business 2005 Spirit of Enterprise Award. Arizona Governor Doug Ducey was then the CEO of Cold Stone Creamery, also in competition for the award. MedAire was one of five companies to receive award recognition during ceremonies held at the Arizona Biltmore on September 27th. I remember saying, "We are honored that one of the largest business schools in the United States would take a look at our business and give us this type of recognition." I also commented, "We are in business because of the peace of mind that comes from meeting our clients' needs 100% of the time." To meet a customer's expectations 100% of the time is a lofty goal, but to target a 50% satisfaction rate is equivalent to "Why bother at all?"

---

[47] "CEO Interview, Joan Sullivan Garrett," *The Wall Street Transcript,* January 12, 2004. See https://www.twst.com/interview/joan-garrett-MedAire-inc-medrf

We set the bar high!

The world is at your fingertips. Photo credit: MedAire

And speaking of mantras, I personally try to follow some of the most basic: "Treat people like you want to be treated," "Never ask someone to do something you aren't willing do yourself," "Be humble," "We can all be servant leaders," and most importantly, "Where there is no vision, the people perish." (Proverbs 29:18).

There's the "vision" reference again. I cherish that verse because it goes right to the heart of what matters most to me — as always, saving lives. In some small way on this great, big planet, I was blessed with a vision that has kept many from physically perishing. That has been worth every sacrifice, every minute spent away from my loved ones and all the heartburn that comes with running a business.

How extremely satisfying to visit MedAire's headquarters and bask in what the company has accomplished! Photo credit: MedAire

I don't recall all of the articles in which I mentioned "vision," but I stumbled across an interview in *Chief Executive* magazine, the December 2006 issue, regarding top challenges CEOs would face that year.[48] Yes, indeed, my parting remarks touched on the topic again — it was my responsibility to "be the visionary" for my company. You have to step up to the plate and look to the future, and that takes vision.

Oh — and another good motto to live by is: "The buck stops here." This old classic was inspired by the sign on Harry Truman's desk. Apparently, I've referenced it a lot in interviews, including the tail end of a 2006 article in AIN online.[49] No matter who falls short, no matter who drops the ball, the buck really does stop at the CEO's door. Yet as CEOs, it behooves us to develop our people so that they can, indeed, venture forth and represent our companies independently. We must give them some autonomy — a lesson learned over time after grappling with the temptation to do everything myself.

What happens when we fail to delegate? Everything constantly rolls up to us. In my case, I was kept too busy with reports, problems, and escalations that could be handled by my staff… if they had the freedom to do so. It was incumbent on me to equip my team to make decisions and deliver on our promise — without involving me.

I shared the "secret sauce" to ensure they could operate with very few parameters, including financial parameters. They took care of our customers under three caveats: 1.) Is it in the best interest of the customer? 2.) Is it in the best interest of MedAire? 3.) Is it legal to the best of their knowledge?

I had close relationships with these employees, again, very much like a family, and felt a huge responsibility and sense of obligation toward them and their own families. I owed them this empowerment. We can assume that all managers likewise care about their employees and customers, but does it show? Make

---

[48] "Making the World Safer to Fly," *Chief Executive*, December 2006. See https://www.twst.com/interview/joan-garrett-MedAire-inc-medrf

[49] Kirby J. Harrison. "'MedAire expanding beyond medical expertise for travelers," *AIN Online*, November 6, 2006. See *https://www.ainonline.com/aviation-news/aviation-international-news/2006-11-06/MedAire-expanding-beyond-medical-expertise-travelers*

sure it shows. Employees will follow a leader who cares. Customers will sign on with a company that demonstrates its commitment to service and going above and beyond.

Speaking of customers, this brings to mind my dear friend Michael Quiello, Vice President of Avelo Airlines, Chair of the Board of Trustees of the National Aviation Hall of Fame, and former Vice President of United Airlines. He exemplifies the "customer turned friend" that is so important to me.

Michael has relied on MedAire through United Airlines and Avelo Airlines. When I was nominated for the National Aviation Hall of Fame, he was the person who broke the wonderful news that I would be inducted into the Class of 2020. The organization's motto, "Honoring Aerospace Legends to Inspire Future Leaders," truly captures my role in engaging young people and attracting them to careers in science, technology, engineering, and mathematics (STEM) within the aviation industry. I am forever grateful to be recognized for my contributions to flight safety with this prestigious honor.

Michael and I spoke recently, and I shared details about my difficult childhood, something I don't bring up often. We discussed how my journey could have gone either way —down the destructive road or down the road of self-determination. I chose self-determination.

"What advice would you give your fifteen-year-old self?" he asked, rather profoundly.

Good question. I had to get back to him on that, but came up with: *Joan, get your pilot's license.* Let me tell you, I gained enough flying experience to land a small plane if I absolutely had to, but never followed through. In all honesty, the real reason I denied myself this opportunity is because my ex-husband (the surgeon) wanted me to. Isn't that silly? I would have greatly enjoyed piloting a Cessna, but out of obstinacy, bit off my nose to spite my face. Another regret is that I didn't take up golf, which would have been a nifty lifelong sport. The good news is that I still can.

What interesting conversations I've had with Michael. I explained that I couldn't really give my 15-year-old self the typical advice because I already knew to value a dollar, work hard, overcome, rise above, escape to something better, and open myself to destiny. He took note of my unusual path and made a comment about the "three I's" — Identify, Influence, and Implement. Without the hard lessons and challenges, I wouldn't have been able to do all three as a future CEO. Maybe one, maybe two, but not the trifecta. He noted that I was able to take a calculated leap of faith and pioneer telemedicine because of the challenges I faced and the choices I made. It's all about choices.

Again, profound.

I felt pretty darn good after these talks. Michael told me, "I know it's been a long time since you've been in the day-to-day 'walking the halls' mode, but when someone mentions your name, they are all smiles. They miss you." How wonderful to hear that kind of feedback, and it's because I cared so deeply about my people (and still do).

I hired the best possible team members, invested in them, encouraged them to succeed, and had high expectations. However, mistakes are unavoidable. It's what you do and how you react that can make all the difference. That's why it's important to create a learning culture. We conducted root cause analyses on each and every complaint, changed practices to ensure mistakes were corrected and retrained when necessary. In addition, being ISO certified ensured there was a process for handling any arising issues. We always followed up with the customers involved and made every attempt to satisfy their concerns.

We've all experienced bad management and poor leadership as consumers and employees. We've witnessed the "Peter Principle" effect when people are promoted beyond their level of competence. A wise manager works with employees to empower and equip and also recognizes when someone is ill-suited in their position. Perhaps that's one of the most difficult decisions of all, to redirect someone's career in a work environment that feels very much like family. Yet if we procrastinate on personnel decisions, the problem snowballs. Don't procrastinate, especially when dealing with a challenging employee or workplace problems. To *not* act hurts everyone. In other words, pay now or pay dearly later. My husband Frank's analogy is you can get an oil change now, or pay for a new engine later.

Here's an analogy that I'm sure parents worldwide have encountered. If you've ever gone grocery shopping with a young child, perhaps you are familiar with the "I want a toy" or "I want candy" situation, to which you said NO. There were times as a young mom when I simply didn't have an extra dime to spend on junk. Or, it seemed senseless to waste money on things my kids already had. Plus, I wanted them to understand the value of a dollar and that money didn't grow on trees.

If my boys threw a tantrum in the aisle, insisting on their goodies (to the disapproving stares of other shoppers), I could either cave in to avoid the embarrassment, or hold my ground. If I caved, my children would expect treats each and every time I stepped foot in a store. If I stood firm, despite the tears and wailing, my kids would learn that "no means no."

I endured the momentary discomfort and nipped the bad behavior in the bud. The same applies in the workplace. If an employee cannot follow rules, undermines the mission, and makes life miserable for others despite coaching and training… then goodbye and best wishes. Tolerating this behavior only ensures it continues. There it is again — the "pay now or pay dearly later" paradigm. It fell to me to make decisions that were well thought out and fair to all across the board. No favorites!

It's difficult for workaholics to carve out work-life balance. Believe me, I know. Think of it in terms of setting an example. As a manager, executive, or CEO (rank doesn't matter in this scenario), model the healthy behavior you wish others to emulate. Show up with a positive attitude, work hard, take walks around the building at lunch, and go home at a decent hour (in this instance, I wasn't the best example). Take your vacation days.

Take breaks. Walk your dogs and share pictures at work. Show your employees that they are more than a cog in the wheel. Encourage them to relax, rest, refresh, and reinvigorate.

Catching dinner and decompressing

The dynamic duo

Encourage feedback. If no one's opinion matters but your own, why have employees at all? Your staff — and contractors too — will feel more productive and more likely to innovate within this type of positive working environment. It reflects directly as a "positive" on your leadership.

The notion of relaxation may sound counterintuitive. After all, many entrepreneurs thrive on an all-consuming fast pace and live in "overdrive." However, not everyone is wired to be an entrepreneur. Not everyone has the same over-the-top compulsion. In fact, you can expect burnout and turnover when cracking the whip and expecting your employees to be "just like you." Their calling may simply be to support your calling — absolutely vital. We could not accomplish the mission otherwise. It's important to acknowledge that.

Have you reached your full potential? Are you everything you wish to be? If not, close the gaps. Pursue your formal education, whether you're retired or not, just as I did at Thunderbird School of Global Management and through other educational opportunities. I've seen many online courses that qualify for continuing education while simultaneously counting as college credit. Encourage mentorship and volunteerism — something outside the daily grind. For instance, employees (and you too) can attend symposiums, join organizations, assist with Meals on Wheels, and bolster whatever skills that may lack through the expertise of others. Think of ways to elevate your "game" and take advantage of these outreach activities, and encourage others to do the same.

Identify mentors and model yourself after those who have blazed trails and overcome adversity. If they have gained admiration for their effective leadership, then you can learn something from them, even if it's an alternative way of exploring an opportunity. What famous business leader do you most identify with, and why? Who do you wish to emulate? Consider personality testing to determine your strengths and augment your weaknesses. Perhaps perform a SWOT analysis on yourself!

In a nutshell, if you follow your gut, decide and move on, make no exceptions, and tackle difficult situations without avoidance, then you are on a great leadership trajectory.

Chapter Twenty-One: Rewards Along the Way

Well, I'm back to gardening. A few years ago, I asked my grandchildren where certain food items come from. The reply was, "From the grocery store!" I received a similar reply from my granddaughter, four at the time, when I asked where money came from. "From the bank!" was her reply.

My goodness, what an opportunity to teach some timeless principles! I explained to these precious, curious children that we are far too addicted to convenience and don't have to *totally* depend on the stores for our existence. Food comes from the good earth. Money comes from hard work. To demonstrate, I got them involved in feeding the steer (unnamed!), digging potatoes, picking tomatoes off the vine and eating them, weeding, and watering the "starts." I wanted them to appreciate the ranchers and farmers and the richness of our country's history. I wanted them to learn to be self-sufficient.

"You reap what you sow" is one of the purest axioms, along with "What goes around, comes around" — not so much in the karmic sense, but in the sense of bounty. There is something to be said for feeling the soil and watching the garden mature. It's a break from all the "noise" in the electronic world. Really hard physical labor, such as lifting heavy bags of mulch, digging with a spade, and fertilizing the soil is good for the soul.

And then we harvest.

My specialty is growing about 13 varieties of garlic. I love to cook using the spices and vegetables from my garden. Many times I "pick" an entire dinner. The season, however, is short-lived. Soon it's time to plant in the fall in order to harvest, once again, in the summer. It never ends — and that's a lesson too.

I love this outdoor growing center where my grandchildren grow and harvest our bounty.

Another view of the garden with the grandkids' play area in the back.

Renewal is eternal as long as the effort is eternal. It's not a chore but a cycle of purpose and meaning.

I wish I could take readers along for a walk outside the garden and into the forest to breathe the scented air, woodsy and aromatic. It's indescribable, really, to be shielded under canopies of branches, with the bluest skies peeping above and a filter of sunlight warming my shoulders. It has to be experienced to be truly understood, this majestic and pristine slice of ecological heaven. A forager could live off the land if he or she knew the food sources. Picking the edible versions of wild mushrooms, for instance, and knowing they'll end up on the supper table makes these treks more of a treasure hunt. Our ancestors knew where other treasures grew, the medicinal plants that saved lives in a distant past. The nurse in me wants to understand these remedies too, and now I have the rest of my life to explore Mother Nature's mysterious, inexplicable capacity to heal.

Me and Rosie enjoying an afternoon ride

These "rewards along the way" are the simplest pleasures and don't have to cost a lot. My definition of luxury is "fresh flowers and clean sheets." Well, maybe also a nice glass of wine. You are as young as you feel, and I'm thankful for that. Proactivity is a requirement that comes with it, an investment in exercise, healthy eating, and yes, good wine. You can't put it off, at least not for long, and it's become a part of my lifestyle. Since my husband Frank is a younger man and a bit of a challenge to keep up with, I put in the extra effort from my end. He'll tell you, though, that he has to keep up with me!

Me and Frank enjoying some holiday downtime

Ah, the incredible joy of playing and having fun. Life is too short (I know this so well). With semi-retirement comes the luxury of pursuing hobbies, spending time with family and friends, and checking items off the bucket list. Actually, Frank and I are still compiling our bucket list because we finally have time to think about it! Maybe we'll take the Orient Express one day or visit the Blue Train in South Africa. The biggest "box" on the list, however, has already been checked — the luxury of finally spending more time together and just "hanging out." That's something we've worked toward our entire married life, an end goal of togetherness. Now it's a reality. There's a lot to be said for the domestic bliss of "terra firma" as opposed to the constant shuttling around in the clouds. I'm more grounded physically and spiritually, and we've hit a nice, comfortable gait.

It's also wonderful to mentor younger generations, aside from my grandchildren, and help them understand the free enterprise system of our great nation. History repeats its mistakes if we allow it. We can never emphasize enough that we inhabit an utterly amazing country. Nowhere else on earth could a nurse like me build a global company like MedAire.

Carl Schramm, author of *The Entrepreneurial Imperative: How America's Economic Miracle Will Reshape the World (and Change Your Life)*, believes in our "unparalleled skills as entrepreneurs" to impact "how our government, corporations, and nonprofits operate, but also our day-to-day lives as working Americans."[50] What an amazing book! I read it when it was first available in 2006 and completely agree that one of the rewards of living in America is the ability to apply our skills, ingenuity, and passion as entrepreneurs. We have the freedom to build, and build we have!

When I hear politicians downplay the entrepreneurial impact on our nation, I remember the long nights I laid awake, praying that I could meet payroll and wondering how to fund the next round of innovations — innovations that would improve the safety and security of millions of travelers. Many small businesses become large businesses because company leaders put in the sweat equity. No one should discount the immense effort it takes to invent and create, provide jobs and benefits, and (especially) make the world a better place through vital products and services. Yes, entrepreneurs have always been the builders. Free enterprise has always been the path to opportunity and invention.

I consider my time at the ballot box a sacred duty for this

---

[50] Carl J. Schramm PhD. *The Entrepreneurial Imperative: How America's Economic Miracle Will Reshape the World (and Change Your Life)* (New York: Harper Business, 2006).

reason. When high profile people announce that they will leave this country if their candidate of choice doesn't win, I know they haven't spent time in a socialist or communist country. I have. I can assure you that people in those countries do not have the freedoms we enjoy. Those oppressed citizens are monitored, rationed, and yearn to be in our shoes, here in the United States, where there are opportunities to improve the lives of our families and ourselves. If the oppressed citizens build a business, it can be taken over by the government. If they dissent, they can be thrown into a gulag. Traveling abroad opened my eyes to the blessings of the "Land of the free and the home of the brave." I wanted to kiss the tarmac every time I returned home.

It is so very, very important that my children and grandchildren have the same opportunities in life that I did. I want them to reap the rewards of their American heritage — the freedom to worship, assemble, vote, start businesses, and live as free human beings with inalienable rights and Constitutional protections. What intellectually honest person wouldn't want that for their loved ones rather than the destruction of motivation we see going on today?

Shouldn't we be teaching children to work hard and live on a budget? Shouldn't we expect the same from our government officials? These questions lay on my heart, yet I truly believe our nation will rally. I know we are headed toward better (and saner) days. America will pull out of this cycle and come to her senses, claiming the exceptionalism we inherited in 1776. And with that, my soapbox moment concludes, although I'd wager a bet that these opinions are shared by the majority of voters from coast to coast.

Most people who really know me will tell you I'm a down-to-earth person with a sense of humor. However, that may or may not be the "first glance" impression, and there have been times when I had to step back, remove all traces of a corporate persona, and re-introduce myself to those I love — especially new members of my family. I think my daughters-in-law were a bit intimidated before we were well-acquainted, and that was something I had experienced myself as a newlywed. I've been in their shoes. And since I absolutely adore these women, such perfect partners for my sons, I thought long and hard about how to welcome them. It turned out that time spent together forged a bond. I took them on a trip to Europe, the three of us, and got to know them on a personal level just as they got to know me. What fun we had shopping, dining, and listening to each other's stories. It was such a delight to be accepted into their worlds, and to this day I enjoy their company very much.

Likewise, it is truly humbling that my dear peers and colleagues continue to recognize me as a medical response pioneer in the realms of aviation and entrepreneurship today. Over the decades, they became more than colleagues, more than associates, and I count them as friends. Their endorsements and nominations for industry awards have been a wonderful way to usher in semi-retirement. It seems I can finally rest on my laurels a bit.

For instance, the year 2017 was heartwarming and full of surprises— the NBAA Meritorious Service to Aviation Award, the International Aviation Womens Association Woman of Excellence Award, and a Hall of Fame induction during the 50th anniversary of my alma mater, Mesa Community College.

As mentioned earlier, it was incredibly meaningful to be inducted into the National Aviation Hall of Fame and enshrined in 2020 (thank you again, Michael Quiello and President and CEO, Amy Spowart). My company and I received the David M. Clark Award as well, established by the Aerospace Medical Association to recognize corporate members who make significant contributions to the advancement of aerospace medicine.

Preceding this was an induction into the International Air & Space Hall of Fame in 2019. What an event that was! Jeff Bezos, founder of Amazon and the Blue Origin space company, was among the inductees. I spoke just before he did and felt uplifted to be among this caliber of aviation and aerospace innovators, a who's-who of visionaries.[51]

Speaking publicly on behalf of MedAire is one thing, but speaking personally as an award recipient is quite another. Sometimes words fail me because the recognition is so deeply meaningful. As always, I'm indebted to my team, especially those with me from the beginning, mentors who encouraged me along the way, and forever my family. It is a phenomenal feeling that MedAire has provided groundbreaking and life-saving services for people of all cultures and continents, the true reward. I hope very much that it sparks an idea or innovation in other fields, a ripple effect across diverse industries in the quest to improve our lives, health, and security.

Me and Ed Bolen at the Meritorious Service to Aviation Award ceremony – Photo credit: MedAire

---

[51] Ken Stone. "Richest Man Jeff Bezos Due in San Diego as Air & Space Museum Honoree," *Times of San Diego*,

August 7, 2019. See https://timesofsandiego.com/tech/2019/08/07/richest-man-jeff-bezos-due-in-san-diego-as-air-space-museum-honoree/

Celebrating my induction into the Mesa Community College Hall of Fame – Photo credit: MedAire

At the International Aviation Womens Association Woman of Excellence Award ceremony – Photo credit: MedAire

At my induction into the International Air & Space Hall of Fame with friends from the International Aviation Womens Association (IAWA) Photo credit: MedAire

Me and Frank at the International Aviation Hall of Fame Awards ceremony – Photo credit: MedAire

It seems appropriate to wrap up this book with applause for the entrepreneurs who tried and failed and tried again. I suppose failure is something that some business leaders avoid talking about at all as if it's a bad or shameful occurrence. But I disagree. Failure is proof you tried. Failure tells the world that you cared enough about a product or service to give it your all, hell or high water.

You have to admire those who learn from mistakes and rally back, rising from the flames to do better. The trail we blaze is never perfectly straight. The road to success often zigs and zags and leaves remnants of failure in its wake. Those remnants have a function. They become steppingstones for future leaders who can then avoid our mistakes... and make their own. And so, the cycle continues, an entrepreneurial quest for the best possible outcome.

I hope you'll read an article in the *Epoch Times* titled "2 Historic Business Flops by Legendary Entrepreneurs Reveal a Poignant Truth About Failure."[52] In it, motivational speaker Dennis Waitley is quoted as saying:

> *Failure should be our teacher, not our undertaker.*
> *Failure is delay, not defeat.*
> *It is a temporary detour, not a dead end.*
> *Failure is something we can avoid only by*
> *saying nothing, doing nothing, and being nothing.*

Amazing and embraceable words, for sure. The article also quotes President Teddy Roosevelt's "Man in the Arena" speech, perhaps the most brilliant philosophical rendering of wisdom that I have ever read. Anyone who has ever stepped into the entrepreneurial arena can surely relate. To all the naysayers in the world, to those who take joy in Monday morning quarterbacking,

---

[52] Lawrence W. Reed. "2 Historic Business Flops by Legendary Entrepreneurs Reveal a Poignant Truth About Failure," *Epoch Times*, May 11, 2021. See https://www.theepochtimes.com/2-historic-business-flops-by-legendary-entrepreneurs-reveal-a-poignant-truth-about-failure_3806624.html

and to those who are quick to say, "I told you so," I leave you with Teddy Roosevelt's words:

> *It is not the critic who counts; not the man who points out how the strong man stumbles, or where the doer of deeds could have done them better. The credit belongs to the man who is actually in the arena, whose face is marred by dust and sweat and blood; who strives valiantly; who errs, who comes short again and again, because there is no effort without error and shortcoming; but who does actually strive to do the deeds; who knows great enthusiasms, the great devotions; who spends himself in a worthy cause; who at the best knows in the end the triumph of high achievement, and who at the worst, if he fails, at least fails while daring greatly, so that his place shall never be with those cold and timid souls who neither know victory nor defeat.*

Theodore Roosevelt
26th President of the United States
Speech at the Sorbonne[53]
Paris, April 23, 1910

---

[53] Christen Duxbury. "It Is Not the Critic Who Counts," Theodore Roosevelt Conservation Partnership, January 19, 2011. See
https://www.trcp.org/2011/01/18/it-is-not-the-critic-who-counts/

ABOUT THE AUTHOR

Joan Sullivan Garrett
MedAire Founder and CEO 1985–2008
Chairman of the Board 2008–Present

As flight nurse early in her medical career, Joan Sullivan Garrett envisioned a worldwide solution for travel safety on air, land and sea, anywhere in the world, after losing a young patient in the remote Arizona mountains.

She founded MedAire in 1985 and pioneered global telemedicine through radio, teletype, and satellite communications — something never before attempted. MedAire began to support inflight and onboard medical emergencies in 1987 through its service company, MedLink, connecting aviation and maritime crews to ground-based board-certified emergency doctors in real time, whether 36,000 feet in the air or in the middle of an ocean.

Joan is the prolific author of industry white papers, a well-known speaker, and a subject-matter expert in the realm of inflight physiology, critical care, cardiac care, and remote medical services. She captures the story of her entrepreneurial journey and MedAire's phenomenal success in her autobiography, *One Life Lost, Millions Gained.*

Awards and Honors

1997
Flight Safety Foundation Business Aviation Meritorious Service Award

2001
Ernst & Young's Entrepreneur of the Year Award

2005
Arizona State University Spirit of Enterprise Award

2017
NBAA Meritorious Service to Aviation Award
International Aviation Womens Association Woman of Excellence Award
Hall of Fame induction during the 50th anniversary of Mesa Community College (alma mater)

2019
International Air & Space Hall of Fame

2020
National Aviation Hall of Fame
David M. Clark Award

CPSIA information can be obtained
at www.ICGtesting.com
Printed in the USA
BVHW012016081121
621124BV00003B/117